Evidence
for Paralegals

ASPEN PUBLISHERS

Evidence for Paralegals

Fourth Edition

Joelyn D. Marlowe
Prosecuting Attorney

Suzanne Cummins
University of Arizona

Wolters Kluwer
Law & Business

AUSTIN   BOSTON   CHICAGO   NEW YORK   THE NETHERLANDS

Aspen Publishers
Attn: Permissions Department
76 Ninth Avenue, 7th Floor
New York, NY 10011-5201

To contact Customer Care, e-mail customer.care@aspenpublishers.com, call 1-800-234-1660, fax 1-800-901-9075, or mail correspondence to:

Aspen Publishers
Attn: Order Department
PO Box 990
Frederick, MD 21705

Printed in the United States of America.

1 2 3 4 5 6 7 8 9 0

ISBN 978-0-7355-5852-6

Library of Congress Cataloging-in-Publication Data

Marlowe, Joelyn D.
  Evidence for paralegals / Joelyn D. Marlowe, Suzanne Cummins.—
4th ed.
    p. cm.
  Includes index.
  ISBN 978-0-7355-5852-6
  1. Evidence (Law)—United States. 2. Evidence (Law)—United States—Problems, exercises, etc. I. Cummins, Suzanne. II. Title.

KF8539.Z9M35 2008
347.73'6—dc22   2007036938

About Wolters Kluwer Law & Business

Wolters Kluwer Law & Business is a leading provider of research information and work-flow solutions in key specialty areas. The strengths of the individual brands of Aspen Publishers, CCH, Kluwer Law International and Loislaw are aligned within Wolters Kluwer Law & Business to provide comprehensive, in-depth solutions and expert-authored content for the legal, professional and education markets.

CCH was founded in 1913 and has served more than four generations of business professionals and their clients. The CCH products in the Wolters Kluwer Law & Business group are highly regarded electronic and print resources for legal, securities, antitrust and trade regulation, government contracting, banking, pension, payroll, employment and labor, and healthcare reimbursement and compliance professionals.

Aspen Publishers is a leading information provider for attorneys, business professionals and law students. Written by preeminent authorities, Aspen products offer analytical and practical information in a range of specialty practice areas from securities law and intellectual property to mergers and acquisitions and pension/benefits. Aspen's trusted legal education resources provide professors and students with high-quality, up-to-date and effective resources for successful instruction and study in all areas of the law.

Kluwer Law International supplies the global business community with comprehensive English-language international legal information. Legal practitioners, corporate counsel and business executives around the world rely on the Kluwer Law International journals, loose-leafs, books and electronic products for authoritative information in many areas of international legal practice.

Loislaw is a premier provider of digitized legal content to small law firm practitioners of various specializations. Loislaw provides attorneys with the ability to quickly and efficiently find the necessary legal information they need, when and where they need it, by facilitating access to primary law as well as state specific law, records, forms and treatises.

Wolters Kluwer Law & Business, a unit of Wolters Kluwer, is headquartered in New York and Riverwoods, Illinois. Wolters Kluwer is a leading multinational publisher and information services company.

About the Authors

Joelyn D. Marlowe has been a career prosecutor for more than twenty years. She began prosecuting misdemeanor crimes at the Tucson City Prosecutor's Office as an intern while still in law school. Thereafter, at the Pima County Attorney's Office in Tucson, she prosecuted felony offenses and specialized in prosecuting child and adult sexual abuse cases. She currently is an Assistant United States Attorney at the United States Attorney's Office for the District of Arizona in Tucson, where she has dedicated the greater part of her legal career to prosecuting federal crimes.

Her first career was teaching research and essay writing to college-bound students in a Nebraska high school. Thus, once she became an attorney, it was no surprise that she endeavored to combine her legal knowledge and experience with her teaching skills. Accordingly, for many years, Joelyn simultaneously maintained a part-time position as an adjunct professor at Pima Community College, where she taught the Federal Rules of Evidence to paralegal students. She employed her unique sense of humor, her love of the substantive law embodied in the rules of evidence, and her experience in the courtroom to enhance her students' appreciation and understanding of evidentiary law.

When she is not working, Joelyn often spends her free time traveling the world. Her special love and seemingly second home is in a small countryside village in Tuscany, Italy.

Suzanne Cummins teaches full time about ethics and law in the Eller College of Management at the University of Arizona. She received her Juris Doctorate from Hastings College of the law in 1979 and practiced law until 1990. From 1984 to 1989, she served as in-house counsel for Nicolet Instrument Corporation, which was then publicly traded on the New York Stock Exchange. Although no longer practicing law, she was admitted to the state bars of California, Wisconsin, and Arizona during her legal career.

Suzanne has written or collaborated in several textbooks. She has won both Eller College and University awards for her teaching and service, including the prestigious UA Foundation's Leicester and Kathryn Sherrill Creative Teaching Award.

In memory of loved ones who have been called home, and in celebration of those who remain

—and especially for you, Roo—you were such a good friend.

jdm

Summary of Contents

Table of Contents

Foreword

In the present volume, Joclyn Marlowe and Suzanne Cummins have drawn on their rich and diverse legal experience to provide an eminently readable and useful exposition of trial evidence for paralegals and legal assistants. Replete with practical, easily graspable examples, case extracts, end-of-chapter summaries, and chapter review questions, the book can be read cover to cover or kept on the desk as a reference. I would recommend doing both.

This book explores the rules of evidence to just the right degree. It also contains helpful hints on such matters as gathering evidence, interviewing witnesses, and researching and fashioning evidentiary arguments, all tasks likely to be performed by paralegals and legal assistants.

Stressing the crucial role of legal argumentation, the authors accurately impart a feel for the imperfect and chancey process by which judges arrive at evidentiary decisions. The degree of elasticity of the rules emerges clearly. Ethical limits are conveyed well.

Not only those engaged in litigation work will benefit from this knowledge of evidence. The benefit extends also to those working on any legal matter that potentially could wind up in court. Paralegals and legal assistants are involved in planning, organizing, and drafting many documents, arrangements, and transactions. They work on tax planning; wills and estates; formation of corporations, partnerships, and other business entities; corporate mergers; pre-nuptial agreements; real estate deals; commercial contracts; securities issues; financial reorganizations; business loans; and so on.

Whatever your role may be, some knowledge of evidence is desirable. You should always have an eye on the practicalities of proof—on whether and how clients could marshal admissible evidence needed to vindicate their rights if the matter had to go to court. Your rights are hollow if you cannot prove your case. The prospect of what would happen if transactions went to court is the practical measure of a client's rights.

Good planning takes account of what admissible proof the client could produce; may provide for the accumulation and keeping of such proof; and may even prescribe what shall be sufficient proof in certain circumstances. Proper planning in these respects is probably the best way to keep the matter out of court. Those who would like to take advantage of your firm's client will be considerably discouraged from trying to do so if they know the client's case could be proved.

A knowledge of evidence can also guide you through a myriad of office functions and communications, particularly those involving potential adversaries of the firm's clients. For example, it is useful to know that a contemporaneous note on a calendar may be admissible evidence of the meeting or conversation it records; that a failure to respond to a letter can in certain circumstances be admissible evidence of acquiescence in the facts stated in the letter; and that legal assistants and paralegals might be treated as agents not only of their law firms but of the law firm's clients, for some evidentiary purposes. Their statements may be usable against the client in a number of situations. In some circumstances (but not others), communications to or from a paralegal or legal assistant may be privileged.

Knowing these things, you may be able to avoid mistakes; actively fortify your firm's clients' evidentiary positions; and appreciate better the strengths and weaknesses of a potential adversary's evidentiary position. Forewarned is forearmed!

Marlowe and Cummins are to be congratulated for providing a clear and concise roadmap in an area of the legal landscape where it is easy to go astray.

The book is also quite enjoyable.

Paul F. Rothstein
Professor of Law
Georgetown University
Washington, D.C.

Acknowledgments

I am ever grateful to the many people at Wolters Kluwer for their enthusiasm and dedication to *Evidence for Paralegals*. In particular, I had the pleasure to benefit from Melody Davies's profound insight and guidance. As always, I owe special gratitude to Elizabeth "Betsy" Kenny, my west coast developmental editor. Also, my sincere appreciation goes to Troy Froebe, my east coast editor, whose e-mails always seem to have a smile, and to Emily Bender (editor), Barbara Roth (managing editor), and Carol McGeehan (publisher).

To my brother, Dr. Charles Marlowe, whose incisive intellect always amazes me. To Gary Ford Spector for his astute legal mind, his sagacious support, and his friendship. To my friends, Claire and Alex, for their enduring love and encouragement.

Finally, but most heartfelt, for Roo who kept watch over me as long as she was able before being called to puppy heaven. *Sempre nel mio cuore.*

Joelyn D. Marlowe

Evidence
for Paralegals

1

Introduction

1.1 Overview

This textbook is intended to assist nonlawyers, specifically those studying to become paralegals or legal assistants, with the study of the law of evidence. It will focus on the practical application of the rules of evidence, referring primarily to the Federal Rules of Evidence, but also noting variations in the states. The authors have attempted to concentrate on, and provide insight into, those areas specifically relevant to paralegal practice.

Like all law, the rules of evidence gain far more meaning when viewed as how they work in "real life." Therefore, this book will not only explore the meaning of the rules, but will provide examples, hypothetical situations, and applications. Since the ability to understand the law correlates to the ability to extract the law from cases, examples of case law are provided throughout. This book will ask the student to think and to solve problems with the information learned. We hope this will advance the student's analytical skills while gaining insight into this exciting area of substantive law.

1.2 Historical Development of the Rules of Evidence

Until the 1970s, almost all rules of evidence were made by the courts through case law. There was wide resistance to uniform evidentiary rules being imposed on the judiciary in the early years of American jurisprudence. The absence of evidence codes allowed a great deal of flexibility for the courts, but inconsistencies abounded. In July 1975, Congress adopted the first set of Federal Rules of Evidence, and these rules have been revised and refined since then. They are found in Title 28 of the United States Code. Most states have now adopted their own evidence codes, using the Federal Rules as a guideline. These are found in the various state statutes.

Since this is a textbook geared to practical application, there will not be a substantial amount of time spent providing historical analysis of the rules of evidence. However, there are times when such historical information is critical to understanding and applying the evidentiary rules as they exist today. Rules of evidence evolved from and have been interpreted by the courts, and many cases include terms that can only be understood in terms of their historical context.

FRE 401, P. 264

On a practical note, when the authors refer to specific rules in the Federal Rules of Evidence, they use the citation FRE before the rule number. For example, relevancy is defined in FRE 401. Notes in the margin will appear each time a Federal Rule is cited, and the notes will refer the reader to the page in the appendix where the full text of the rule can be found.

Although the authors consistently refer to the rules with the FRE notation, the courts do not necessarily use the same format. In the cases cited, you may see citations to the federal rules using the notation Fed.R.Evid., or F. R. Evid. Each of these notations refers to the Federal Rules of Evidence.

Advisory Committee
Committee that proposed first FRE.

Advisory Notes
Comments accompanying the FRE proposals.

Throughout the book, the authors refer to the **Advisory Committee** and the **Advisory Notes.** The Advisory Committee was first appointed in 1965 by Chief Justice Warren, to draft Rules of Evidence for the federal courts. The Advisory Committee proposed rules and circulated comments along with the proposed rules. These comments are referred to as the Advisory Notes. The Advisory Notes provide historical context and explanation of the rules, and they are discussional in nature. They are quoted throughout this book.

1.3   Ethics and Advocacy

Admissible
Evidence allowed to be considered by the trier-of-fact.

Excludable
Evidence that may not be presented to the trier-of-fact.

We caution that if the authors appear irreverent at times with regard to the rules and their application, this is never our intention. It is important to keep in mind that the paralegal or legal assistant works in an adversarial system of justice, where each side attempts to present evidence in the manner most favorable to its client. Our approach for the paralegal, then, is to explore all avenues and to consider all desirable evidence as potentially **admissible** and all undesirable evidence as potentially **excludable,** while keeping in mind the constraints in the rules.

Although at times it may appear "unethical" when the authors talk about getting evidence in through the "back door," when it is inadmissible through the "front door," keep in mind that ultimately it is the court's decision whether to admit it. The job of the paralegal is to assist in considering all the options and to aggressively pursue avenues that help the attorney zealously represent the client.

There is one ethical consideration, however, that underlies everything presented in this textbook. It is never the job of the legal assistant or the attorney to fabricate evidence or to change a witness's testimony. It is unethical and unlawful to ask witnesses to lie, or to corrupt or destroy evidence. It is the paralegal's job to help present the evidence as it exists, in the manner most favorable to the client. It is within this context that the authors present the material.

1.4   Reasons for the Rules of Evidence

When a child gets into trouble, usually a parent or caregiver is called on to ascertain truth and assign blame. Generally this "trial" process involves the child's giving his or her "side of the story" and the truth-seeker/parent's deciding a reasonable outcome. In assessing the situation, the parent generally considers some or all of the following factors:

1. Statements made by the child;
2. Statements made by others;
3. The circumstances surrounding the event;
4. Physical things at the scene;
5. Parental insight into the nature and past conduct of the child involved.

The margin of error in this system is wide. As children, we probably all experienced being blamed for conduct of which we were innocent because of negative conduct in our own past, or the unsubstantiated accusations of a hostile adversary (usually our obnoxious kid brother or sister). The parent has been diverted from the truth in such circumstances and has made a mistake in assigning blame. Luckily, the consequences of such mistakes are minimal and tolerable because they are generally made in an atmosphere of love, by people whose overall interests are the same as the child's.

In a judicial system serving an entire society, where the consequences of incorrect outcomes can be catastrophic to individuals and groups of individuals, we must depend on a more formalized and reliable method of assessing truth. All sides need to be able to present their "side of the story," but to avoid injustice, the system must constrain the presentation of information in such a way as to both promote truth and avoid mistakes to the greatest extent possible. Rules of evidence exist to safeguard, as much as possible, against injustice. The Federal Rules of Evidence, by their own statement of purpose and construction, seek to secure "fairness in administration, elimination of unjustifiable expense and delay, and promotion of growth and development of the law . . . to the end that the truth may be ascertained." FRE 102.

FRE 102, P. 261

Trier-of-Fact
Person who determines the facts in a legal proceeding also known as the factfinder.

Since the way in which all sides present the "truth" to the **trier-of-fact** is with the use of evidence, the remainder of this chapter will focus on

- What constitutes "evidence";
- What forms it may take; and
- What should be considered when preparing a "trial story."

1.5   What Is Evidence?

Before studying the rules as to the admissibility or excludability of evidence, it is important to understand in general what constitutes evidence in a court of law. This may be easier to understand by first looking at what does not qualify as evidence:

Testimony
The statements of a witness made under oath in court, or in a deposition.

- Statements, arguments, questions, or objections made by the attorneys are not evidence.
- Information obtained outside the courtroom by the judge or jurors, which is not part of the proceeding, is not evidence.
- **Testimony** that the court specifically strikes or excludes is not evidence.
- Testimony or exhibits admitted for limited purposes by the court are not evidence for anything other than the limited purpose for which the court admitted them.
- **Jury instructions** given to the jury by the judge are not evidence.

Jury Instruction
Statement by the court to the jury instructing the jury on the law.

Now that we have identified what evidence is *not*, we will undertake the more difficult task of identifying what evidence is.

Evidence comes in four different types, each of which is explained in more detail below. Evidence includes

1. **Witness testimony**, given under oath.
2. **Exhibits** that are **tangible** items admitted at the proceeding.
3. **Stipulated** facts to which the lawyers have agreed.
4. **Judicial notice** of facts that are common knowledge.

Exhibits
Physical items that are shown to the trier-of-fact.

Tangible
Something physically material, i.e., something you can touch.

Stipulated
Facts that are agreed to.

Judicial Notice
Facts the court admits are true without evidence, because they are common knowledge.

FRE 201, P. 263

Demonstrative Exhibits
Exhibits that illustrate or demonstrate something, but are not the "real" thing.

Documentary Evidence
Evidence in the form of documents.

1. Witnesses come in two varieties: They can be either lay witnesses or experts. A lay witness is one who testifies as to matters of which the witness has personal knowledge. An expert witness gives testimony about conclusions he has drawn based on his expertise.
2. Exhibits come in three varieties.
   a. Exhibits can consist of "real evidence," such as an actual gun or a torn piece of clothing.
   b. Exhibits can be **demonstrative**. Demonstrative exhibits are created evidence, as opposed to "real" evidence. Examples of demonstrative evidence include photographs, charts, and diagrams. An intersection where an accident occurred cannot be brought into the courtroom as real evidence. However, photographs of that intersection may be admitted, which provide the trier-of-fact with a visualization of the accident scene.
   c. Exhibits can be **documentary**. Business records, diaries, letters, and court transcripts are just a few of the types of documents that may be used as exhibits in the course of a proceeding. Documentary exhibits are something of a hybrid in that they contain testimony, but they are "tangible" and available for the trier-of-fact to scrutinize.
3. Stipulated facts are evidence. When there is no factual dispute about certain information, the proper way for the information to be offered is by stipulation. Stipulations are entered into between parties through counsel and are reviewed by the court. Stipulated facts are provided in writing or are read to the trier-of-fact.
4. Judicial notice is taken of those items the court believes are "common knowledge." Such information is presented to the trier-of-fact, without any proof. The court does not take judicial notice often, but it does occur. The following example illustrates the use of judicial notice.

Sharkey met some foreign students at a bar. The students seemed fascinated with the Chicago Cubs. Sharkey encouraged them to place bets with him on an "upcoming" Cubs National League playoff game between the Cubs and the Yankees. Sharkey gave the students great odds, allowing them to win if the Cubs lost to the Yankees by less than 10 runs. The students agreed to make the bet and Sharkey told them he would hold the money until payoff time.

In the case against Sharkey for fraud, the court took judicial notice that the Chicago Cubs play for the National League, while the Yankees play for the American League. This allowed the inference to be drawn that Sharkey knew there was no upcoming game at the time he took the bet money, since teams from the different leagues do not play against each other during the National League playoffs.

Judicial notice is a method used only rarely. "Common knowledge" that may be noticed judicially includes only that information generally known by society as a whole, and not merely information commonly known by members of the judicial system.

For the most part, to introduce evidence, there must be either a qualified witness to talk about it, a way to display it, or a stipulation from the opposing counsel agreeing to it. These types of evidence will be discussed throughout this textbook.

1.6   Role of the Paralegal

How to present evidence in court can involve some of the most creative aspects of trial work, and will be the subject of further discussion throughout this book.

As a paralegal, you may be called on to help determine which evidence is needed before a case goes to trial. You may be asked to assist in gathering the evidence, researching its admissibility, and developing arguments for admissibility. Likewise, you may be asked to assist in assessing the opposition's evidence, researching its excludability, and developing arguments for excludability.

In a later section of this chapter we will discuss gathering evidence by interviewing witnesses. Paralegals are often asked to assist in preparing a "trial book," which is an orderly presentation of the witnesses, testimony, and exhibits in a case. Paralegals are often also asked to assist in the preparation of pretrial evidentiary motions and **memoranda** in support of such motions.

Memoranda
Brief legal essays that provide the court with facts, law, and argument as to why the legal point being argued should be decided in the favor of the party on whose behalf the memorandum is written.

Understanding the rules of evidence allows a paralegal to prepare for trial knowledgeably and to accumulate evidence that is admissible. If evidence is not admitted, then lawyers cannot argue the evidence before the jury. Juries are instructed by the judge that the arguments of the attorneys are not evidence, but that the lawyers are permitted to make reasonable inferences from the evidence. Obviously, if the evidence is not admitted at trial, it cannot be used to draw reasonable inferences by the attorneys during closing argument.

Cases are often won or lost during preparation. A paralegal competent in assisting with trial preparation can be an invaluable asset. Throughout this textbook, issues specifically relevant to paralegal work in trial preparation will be addressed and discussed.

1.7   Direct and Circumstantial Evidence

Direct Evidence
Evidence that directly proves
a point.

Circumstantial Evidence
Evidence from which
inferences can be drawn to
prove a point.

**FRE 401 and 402,
P. 264**

Evidence can be either **direct or circumstantial.** Direct evidence includes such things as eyewitness testimony or the confession of a criminal. An admission of liability of a defendant is direct evidence in a civil suit.

Much more common than direct evidence is circumstantial evidence. Circumstantial evidence is indirect and is used to prove facts by implication or inference. It may surprise the reader to find out that pursuant to the Federal Rules of Evidence regarding relevancy (FRE 401 and 402), both types of evidence are fully admissible. Most of us have seen "television lawyers" argue as a "defense" that the evidence against their client is purely "circumstantial." Such a comment, however, is without legal consequence because either circumstantial or direct evidence can support a verdict of guilty. This makes sense from a policy perspective, since rarely do torts or crimes occur in plain view, and even less frequently are criminals or tortfeasors caught in the middle of commission of the unlawful act.

Law school professors love the following example regarding persuasive circumstantial evidence.

A mother walks into her kitchen and notices that her freshly baked blueberry pie is missing. Shortly thereafter she sees her young son, whose face and hands are covered with blueberry stains, and who is complaining of a stomach ache. When asked what happened to the pie, the child claims ignorance as to its disappearance.

The evidence that the child stole the pie is purely circumstantial. Nobody saw him take the pie. He didn't admit taking the pie. Nonetheless, the evidence is persuasive of the child's guilt. Such evidence can be equally persuasive in a court of law.

Circumstantial evidence is extremely important as a tool for building a case. Any given item of evidence may have alternative meanings. For example, when you leave a building, and there are puddles outside on the ground, you might assume that it has recently rained. However, alternative explanations are possible. A hydrant may have burst. A fire truck may have extinguished a fire. Still, the puddles are circumstantial evidence of rain. If you also perceive people walking with wet umbrellas, raincoats, and boots, you have used several indicia of circumstantial evidence to build a stronger case from which you can draw reasonable inferences that it has rained.

In a jury trial, the judge will generally instruct the jury that the law allows the jury to give equal weight to both direct and circumstantial evidence, but that it is their decision how much weight to give any evidence. As noted above, circumstantial evidence is often all there is.

1.8   How Is Evidence Obtained?

Often, much of the evidence in a case is acquired prior to the file ever reaching the paralegal. For learning purposes, however, let us assume that we are "at the scene" of an incident to see what evidence is available from the beginning of a case, through its evolution. Consider the following situation:

You are driving westbound behind several cars, and the traffic light is green in your direction. Suddenly you observe that a car has entered the intersection from the north heading south, and that this car has hit a westbound car in front of you, broadside. You hear the loud screech of tires and the sounds of the collision. You and the other drivers barely avoid the accident. It looks as if there are injured people in both of the vehicles. You dial 911 on your car phone to call for help and wait for police and emergency medical vehicles to arrive. You observe a large bus and several other vehicles caught in the traffic jam around the accident. Police and emergency vehicles arrive and clear up the scene. Just prior to leaving, you overhear an officer comment that he believes the driver of the southbound car is inebriated.

What is the evidence that you need to acquire to prove that the driver of the southbound car was driving under the influence of alcohol? Who are potential witnesses at this accident scene? Obviously, under this hypothetical situation, you are an eyewitness to the accident; however, at this scene there are many other possible witnesses who can offer valuable testimony. They include the bus riders, pedestrians, and other drivers who may have observed part or all of the accident. The police officers and paramedics who arrived at the scene will also be able to give valuable testimony. Although they were not eyewitnesses to the accident, they have observed the positions of the vehicles and the condition of the suspect, and they may have spoken with the suspect and perhaps gotten statements from the other injured parties.

Tangible evidence from the accident scene may include the accident debris, the road, and the cars.

As the suspect and other injured victims of the accident are taken away in ambulances and brought to the hospital, more evidence is developed. The admitting clerk, emergency room personnel, doctors, nurses, aides, and laboratory technicians all have the opportunity to observe the suspect and other injured parties, to hear their statements, and to acquire tangible evidence. Tangible evidence of the suspect's clothing, purse or pocket contents, and other items can be relevant. A cocktail napkin from a local tavern left in a pants pocket may take the investigator to a place where the suspect was drinking just prior to the accident. Perhaps there are medications in the suspect's purse that might provide information about her condition at the time of the accident.

Tangible evidence created at the hospital is also very important. Blood samples taken, other medical tests given, and medical reports can all provide valuable information.

Evidence can be created from other evidence. Demonstrative evidence such as photographs, diagrams, and reconstructions is essentially "created" evidence, which is governed under the rules. Experts can "reconstruct" an accident from the evidence acquired at the accident scene.

Experts can give testimony based on their special knowledge in a variety of areas. Blood analysts can ascertain alcohol or other intoxicants in the blood of a suspect at the time of the accident. Chemists can examine various components in the blood, such as over-the-counter medications and prescription medications, and can testify as to their interactions. Police experts can testify as to symptoms of driving under the influence of an intoxicant.

The purpose for obtaining and developing all this evidence, and trying to ensure its admissibility, is fundamental. The jury was not an eyewitness to the event. The only way the trier-of-fact can determine what occurred is through the evidence admitted. Therefore, the more complete picture you can paint, the more likely a just outcome will result.

Keep in mind that the evidence discussed in this section relates to the hypothetical situation presented. Each case is unique, and the types of evidence you gather will depend on the individual characteristics of the case on which you are working.

1.9   Interviewing Witnesses

It should be clear by now that witnesses, both eyewitnesses and experts, will play an enormous role in the outcome of any case. Properly conducting witness interviews is probably one of the most important jobs that paralegals do. Frequently, you are given a case file with the names of witnesses and their phone numbers. Your job then is to ascertain all the relevant information that the witnesses know and can testify about.

Throughout this textbook, as the rules of evidence are explored, the authors will suggest certain questions or types of questions that should be asked of witnesses during interviews to obtain the necessary information for trial. For purposes of this introduction, there are some general guidelines to good interviewing practice that are worthy of mention.

Open-Ended Question
A question that does not suggest an answer or put words in the witness's mouth.

First, a good interviewer listens more than he or she speaks. Ask **open-ended questions** and then wait while the witness responds.

Sometimes you may think the witness is going into irrelevant territory, but it is never a good idea to cut him or her off too quickly. You may find that the witness has something to offer in a way you had not anticipated. For example, early in her career one of the authors had the opportunity to interview a police officer who was to testify regarding a DUI (driving under the influence of an intoxicant) case. Through casual discussion, the interviewer discovered that the officer was not only an expert on the symptoms of drunk driving because of his police work, but had worked as a bartender for sixteen years prior to becoming a police officer. This information was valuable in giving credibility to the officer's testimony and allowing him greater breadth to testify as an expert from more than one perspective on the subject of alcohol impairment.

Leading Question
A question that suggests an answer.

Another caveat to the interviewer is to avoid asking **leading questions**. If you ask, "You beat your wife, don't you?" you will, at best, be given either a "yes" or "no" answer. You may end up with a witness who refuses to answer altogether. Open-ended questions (which are required during direct examination) allow the interviewee to answer in his or her own words rather than in yours.

Listen closely to the answers. Although you don't want to interrupt your witness, you may note areas that you wish to examine more thoroughly after the interviewee is finished answering a question. If you listen closely, each answer may give rise to more questions.

Finally, avoid arguing with the witness. An already hostile witness won't be made less hostile if the interviewer becomes argumentative. More disturbingly, a friendly witness may become hostile if the interviewer argues with her. If the witness does not answer a question directly, try to ask the question a different way, or come back to it later in the interview. It is possible to be persistent without being argumentative.

Ultimately, you depend on your witnesses, and the information they provide you, to win your case.

1.10 Discovery Devices

Discovery
The process by which parties in a lawsuit obtain information and evidence from others, including their opponents.

Acquiring evidence requires knowledge of the **discovery** rules found in statutes relating to civil and criminal procedure. Students using this textbook may not have yet studied the discovery rules; so, although we will not cover discovery procedure in general, which is beyond the scope of this textbook, it is important to list some of the frequently used discovery methods. When discovery terms appear in the cases, you will have a reference here to use for context. In very brief summary, then, the following tools are available to the litigant to compel others to provide evidence or information that may yield evidence:

- Subpoena: A witness can be compelled by subpoena to appear in court and testify.
- Subpoena duces tecum: A witness can be compelled to appear in court and to bring specified documents along.
- Deposition: A witness can be compelled to answer questions in an extrajudicial (out-of-court) proceeding called a deposition, where the witness testifies under penalty of perjury, and the witness's testimony is recorded.
- Orders of examination: A party can be compelled to come to court and provide evidence about the amount and location of the party's assets. The court can use its power to find a party in **contempt of court** for failing to appear or provide the requested information.
- Request to produce documents: A party may be requested to produce documents, and to make copies available to the opposing party.
- Disclosure requests: The defendant in a criminal proceeding may request the government to disclose records, exhibits, and certain other items intended for use by the government as evidence at trial, and the government may request disclosure of evidentiary documents and certain other evidentiary items from the defendant.
- Motions to compel production of documents: When a party refuses to produce documents, the court can order the party to do so, and can use contempt proceedings to enforce its will.
- Requests for admissions and denials: A party can be asked to admit or deny certain facts. Facts admitted are considered stipulated facts.
- Interrogatories: Parties may be sent written questions to which they must provide written answers.

Other types of discovery proceedings are available to give access to information and evidence, but are of generally less importance than those listed above.

1.11 Evidentiary Procedures

In the Wizard of Oz, Dorothy asks the scarecrow, "What would you do with a brain, if you had one?" The paralegal might well ask the attorney, "What would you do with an evidentiary problem, if you had one?" Evidentiary procedures provide the answer to that question. Once you have gathered the evidence in a given case, there are a variety of procedures that deal with how to admit, exclude, or limit

Contempt of Court
A finding by a judge that a person has disobeyed a court order, and is consequently subject to fine and imprisonment.

the use of that evidence in the courtroom. Some of those procedures are described here.

Objection
In court, counsel objects to testimony believed to be inadmissible, and counsel states the basis for the objection.

The **objection** is the most well-known method by which a party asks the court to exclude certain evidence. An objection is made when testimony or other evidence is offered that is inadmissible on one or more legal grounds. The bases for objections will be discussed throughout this textbook. A party loses his or her right to appeal if an objection is not made when the "bad" evidence is **proffered.**

Proffered
Evidence tendered or offered.

Motions in Limine
Motions made before trial on the admissibility or excludability of specific evidence.

Pretrial motions called **motions in limine** are made to secure rulings on the admissibility or excludability of evidence, before the trial begins. A motion in limine is based on the expectation that the opposing party will offer specific objectionable evidence during the trial. A motion in limine is therefore like an objection made in advance of the evidence actually being proffered. Motions in limine may include motions to **suppress** evidence for constitutional reasons, or to exclude highly prejudicial evidence. Paralegals often draft motions in limine or responses to motions in limine.

Suppress
Keep out of court.

FRE 103, as amended December 1, 2000, now provides that once the court has made a definitive ruling on the record either admitting or excluding evidence, a party does not need to renew the objection or offer of proof in order to preserve his or her right to appeal the ruling.

FRE 103, P. 261

Limiting Instruction
An instruction given by the judge to the jury to restrict their use of a specific item of evidence.

Once the trial begins, the paralegal may be asked to research issues regarding jury **limiting instructions.** Jury instructions, generally, are directions given by the judge to the jury informing the jury of the law it must use when reaching its conclusions. Limiting instructions are given by the judge to limit the jury's use of evidence to the specific purpose for which the evidence was admitted. Limiting instructions are necessary because there are times when evidence is admitted for one purpose, but would be excluded if offered for another purpose. Consider the following example:

Jacko is charged with fraud. He has two prior criminal convictions for the crime of perjury. He testifies in the fraud trial that he did not defraud the alleged victim. His two prior perjury convictions are admissible to show that Jacko is a liar, but not to show that he committed the fraud with which he is currently charged. (Reasons for this will become clear as you study the material in this textbook.)

Under the circumstances in the above example, the defense may request that the judge give the jury a limiting instruction, ordering the jury to consider the evidence of the prior perjury convictions only for the purpose of assessing Jacko's truthfulness, and not as evidence of whether he committed the charged crime. You may well assume that such a limiting instruction might not have much effect on the manner in which a jury might use the evidence of the prior convictions. Limiting instructions are not necessarily effective; however,

Mitigate
Reduce or lessen.

they are considered to be better than nothing, and sometimes they are all that is available to **mitigate** the effects of admissible, prejudicial testimony.

1.12   In Summary

- Whether a litigant has been able to acquire "good" evidence has an enormous impact on the outcome of a case.
- The potential admissibility or excludability of evidence is a problem to be ultimately reconciled by the court and should not be allowed to act as a barrier to your investigation.
- A good advocate zealously attempts to admit evidence that is favorable and to exclude evidence that is unfavorable; however, it is unethical and unlawful to attempt to change evidence to win a case.
- Evidence consists of witness testimony, exhibits, stipulated facts, and facts of which the court takes judicial notice.
- The federal and state rules of evidence have, for the most part, replaced the common law rules from which they were derived. However, the common law provides a context in which to understand the rules as they are currently drafted. Not all state rules follow the federal rules.
- Direct evidence and circumstantial evidence bear equal importance in the law. Direct evidence is evidence that directly proves a point, such as a confession, or an eyewitness report. Circumstantial evidence is evidence from which inferences can be drawn.
- Paralegals are important contributors in the litigation field. Paralegals assist in gathering evidence, preparing for trial, drafting motions, writing memoranda in support of or in opposition to motions, and in other important ways.
- Evidence is frequently obtained by interviewing witnesses or by using discovery devices.
- Objections, motions in limine, and jury limiting instructions are the most often used evidentiary procedures when evidence is problematical.
- It is no longer necessary for a party to renew an objection or an offer of proof once the court makes a definitive ruling on the record.

End of Chapter Review Questions

1. What are the limitations of being a good advocate, when gathering evidence?

2. What are the three main types of evidence?
3. What types of information do not constitute evidence?
4. What types of things might a paralegal be asked to do in regard to evidence?
5. What is direct evidence?
6. What is circumstantial evidence?
7. How is evidence obtained?
8. What evidentiary procedures are available when evidentiary problems arise?

Applications

Consider the following hypothetical situation:

Veronica went out drinking with a male friend. After several rounds of drinks, her friend left and Veronica walked to her own vehicle, intending to drive home. At her vehicle, a man named Stu, who had been conversing with Veronica and her friend at the bar, assaulted Veronica and then dragged her into his vehicle against her will. Veronica was punched several times in the face, and she bled profusely all over Stu's car, all over herself, and all over Stu. Stu threatened to rape Veronica; however, eventually Veronica was able to persuade Stu to release her, and she was not raped.

Based on this hypothetical, answer the following questions.

1. What tangible "real" evidence would be important to gather?
2. What witnesses might you attempt to interview?
3. Assume you are working on the side of the victim (Veronica) in this case. What demonstrative evidence might you use to assist in presenting your evidence?
4. What direct evidence is available to prove Veronica's story?
5. What circumstantial evidence is available to prove Veronica's story?
6. What experts might you call for this case, and for what reason?
7. What questions would you ask the male friend with whom Veronica was drinking prior to the incident?

2

Relevance

2.1 Common Law Rules of Relevancy and Materiality

Most jurisdictions no longer follow the common law definition of relevancy, but instead follow the more comprehensive definition found in the Federal Rules of Evidence. Nonetheless, the concepts found in the common law are integrated into the Federal Rules, and understanding those concepts allows understanding the law of relevancy today in greater depth.

The common law definition of relevancy is broad, and to some degree, imprecise. Generally, evidence is relevant under common law if it sheds light on a contested matter, or if reasonable inferences can be drawn from the evidence regarding a fact at issue. This definition is so inclusive, however, that over time additional constraints have been placed on relevancy in the cases.

Material Evidence
Evidence that affects the
outcome of the case.

Immaterial evidence
Evidence that is not material.

Adversary System
A system of justice where the
parties work in opposition to
each other, and each party tries
to win a favorable result for
itself.

Proponent
The party who proffers or
presents the evidence.

First, in order for evidence to be admissible, the cases hold that the evidence must not just be relevant, but must also be **material.** Although this term is somewhat vague, generally it is taken to mean that the evidence must matter, or in some way potentially affect the outcome of the case. If the evidence sheds light on an issue in the case, but really can't affect the outcome of the case, it is **immaterial.** The difference between materiality and relevancy is often difficult to define.

The concept of materiality is most often applied in the cases when one of the parties attempts to introduce evidence in order to inflame the jury against the opposing party. Keep in mind that a majority of the evidence presented in an **adversary system** is introduced to prejudice the factfinder in favor of the **proponent.** The evidence becomes immaterial when the prejudice it creates is related to an issue that has either been thrown out of court, or already decided.

Frequently, the concept of materiality is raised after the parties have entered into a stipulation. Consider the following hypothetical example.

Assume a lawsuit is based on allegations that defendant took the plaintiff's car without the plaintiff's permission and thereby committed a trespass. Assume further that the defendant stipulates that he took the plaintiff's car. The only remaining issue is whether the defendant had the plaintiff's permission to do so. If the plaintiff tries to present evidence that his car was seen (after it had been taken) at a movie theatre where an "X" rated movie was being shown, this evidence would be relevant to show that the defendant left the car at the porno movie, but it would be immaterial to any issue existing in the case. This is because the defendant already admitted taking the car. The sole purpose of such evidence would be to inflame the jury.

The following case illustrates a situation where the court found that the issue of the defendant's being drunk at the time of the accident was immaterial because the defendant had already admitted being liable for damages caused in the accident. The court did not rule the evidence irrelevant but reasoned that since the defendant had already admitted he was responsible for damages, anything tending to prove liability was immaterial. Evidence that the defendant was drunk at the time of the accident was also considered inflammatory.

Jarvis v. Hall

210 N.E.2d 414 (Ohio 1964)

This action was commenced in the Common Pleas Court of Scioto County by Gladys Jarvis against Clell Hall seeking damages for personal injuries alleged to have been sustained in an automobile collision on December 16, 1961, in the city of Portsmouth. The parties will be referred to herein as the plaintiff and defendant in the same relation they appeared in the trial court.

The petition alleges in substance that the plaintiff was operating her husband's automobile in a westerly direction on Gallia Street; that she stopped for a traffic control light; that the defendant was operating his automobile on the same street in the opposite direction, under the influence of alcohol; that defendant crossed the center of the street and collided with the automobile the plaintiff was driving; and that as a result of the defendant's negligent act plaintiff sustained serious and permanent injuries.

The defendant filed an answer admitting the collision but denying all other allegations of the petition. The case came to trial on January 30, 1964, and on that date the defendant was granted permission to amend his answer, admitting that defendant was negligent in driving his automobile on the left of the center line of the highway and that such negligence was the proximate cause of the collision of the two vehicles. In other words, the defendant admitted liability, leaving the question of damages, if any, the only issue to be determined by the jury.

The trial by jury resulted in a verdict in favor of the plaintiff in the sum of $5,000 upon which judgment was entered, the motion for a new trial was overruled, and the defendant now seeks a reversal of the judgment.

Under the first assignment of error the defendant claims that the court erred in overruling defendant's motion to withdraw a juror and declare a mistrial. The record shows that before the jury was empanelled and after the defendant had been granted permission to amend his answer admitting liability, counsel for plaintiff inquired whether the defendant would admit that the defendant was driving his automobile under the influence of alcohol. Upon receiving a negative reply, the plaintiff made a motion to amend her petition to include in the prayer of the petition a sum for punitive damages because of the operation of the automobile under the influence of alcohol. This motion was overruled.

The plaintiff began the introduction of testimony by calling the defendant for the purpose of cross-examination. So far as pertinent to this assignment of error the record reads:

Q: How fast were you driving, Mr. Hall, when your car collided with that car occupied by Mrs. Jarvis?
A: Well, I would say around 30 or 35.
Q: Was there anybody in the car with you?
A: No sir.
Q: Do you remember this accident clearly?
A: Yes sir.

Q: Isn't it a fact that you were under the influence of alcohol, or intoxicated?

Objection

Mr. Howland: May I finish my question?

Q: Mr. Hall, had you had anything intoxicating to drink?

Thereupon the defendant moved to withdraw a juror and declare a mistrial. This motion was overruled, and the jury was instructed to disregard the question. The defendant contends that liability having been admitted by the defendant, the attempt to inject intoxication into the case by the plaintiff was prejudicial and the court's instruction to disregard it was ineffective: that the damage had been done. In *Cleveland Ry. Co. v. Kozlowski*, . . . Stephenson, J., says:

> An admission of liability in a personal injury case sends the pleadings to the four winds except as to the nature and scope of the injuries on the one side and the denial thereof on the other. Negligence and proximate cause go out of the case as if by magic and nothing remains for the jury to do except fix the amount of damage. This is the sole and only issue left in the case.

In the colloquy between the court and counsel, in the absence of the jury, the court had expressly advised counsel that the only issue to be determined was the nature and extent of the injuries, if any, sustained by the plaintiff and that the question of whether the defendant was intoxicated was removed from the case.

The court said: "The only issue now is the question of money damage."

The purpose of pleading is to define the issues to be determined, to inform the respective parties of the claims of each and the nature and scope of the trial. [citation.] The plaintiff, by propounding the question relating to defendant's intoxication, not only attempted to inject an immaterial and inflammatory issue into the case, under the pleadings, but violated the instructions of the court in regard to the issues to be submitted to the jury. Regardless of the motive in asking the question, it served only to improperly influence the minds of the jury in determining the only issue in the case, i.e., damages.

*   *   *

For the reasons above set forth the judgment is reversed and this cause is REMANDED to the Common Pleas Court of Scioto County for a new trial.

Since Mr. Hall was willing to pay for his negligence in this case, the only thing left for the jury to decide was how much he would have

Probative
Assisting in the exploration for truth; informative.

to pay. Mr. Hall's drunken state wasn't **probative** of the dollar value of Mrs. Jarvis's damages. The plaintiff's purpose in introducing such evidence was to get the jury angry at Mr. Hall, so they'd be more inclined to award Mrs. Jarvis more money.

The appellate court concluded that the attempt by plaintiff to inject into the case evidence that was immaterial and inflammatory warranted that the matter be reversed and remanded for a new trial. This is an unusual result in that ordinarily the appellate court will not overturn a trial judge's ruling unless there has been an abuse of discretion on the part of the trial judge. In this case, the trial judge did instruct the jury to disregard the inflammatory question, but the appellate court felt the damage had already been done, and the jury had been unfairly prejudiced by hearing about the allegation of alcohol consumption.

The result might be the same under the Federal Rules of Evidence today, but the reasoning would be slightly different, as discussed in the next section.

2.2   Relevancy under the Federal Rules of Evidence

Under the Federal Rules of Evidence, materiality is not an issue. This is because the federal rules and most state evidence codes have eliminated the concept of materiality by merging it with the concept of relevancy. Although in courtrooms (especially television courtrooms) it is not uncommon to hear, "Objection, Your Honor! Irrelevant and immaterial!" the reality is that only the relevancy objection has legal meaning in most jurisdictions today.

FRE 401, P. 264

The Federal Rules of Evidence define relevancy in FRE 401, as "evidence having any tendency to make the existence of any fact that is of consequence to the determination of the action more probable or less probable than it would be without the evidence." The result is that materiality is now incorporated into the definition of relevancy. Under an FRE 401 analysis, Mr. Hall's inebriated state in the *Jarvis* case, above, is simply irrelevant. It is not related to a fact of consequence to the determination of the action, because the issue of liability has already been determined.

Reconsider the hypothetical example in Section 2.1 involving the plaintiff who was suing the defendant for taking his car without permission. In that hypothetical, the defendant admitted that he had taken the car, but plaintiff wanted to introduce evidence that after the car was taken, it was seen at a porno theatre. The only remaining issue to be determined in that action, however, was whether or not the defendant had plaintiff's permission to take the car. Since the place where the car was seen has no relationship to any fact that was "of consequence to the determination of the action," this evidence was irrelevant under the Federal Rules. Under common law, it would have been relevant to show where the car was seen, but immaterial to any outstanding issue in the case.

In all other respects, the definition of relevancy under the Federal Rules either reflects or expands common law applications. In early common law, to be relevant, evidence had to relate to an **ultimate issue** in the case. An ultimate issue is one that must, in the final analysis, be answered in the lawsuit. For example, an ultimate issue in an automobile accident case is whether or not the defendant was negligent. Under the FRE definition of relevancy, all evidence having any tendency to prove any fact of any consequence to the determination of the action is relevant. According to the Advisory Notes, "The fact to be proved may be ultimate, intermediate, or evidentiary; it matters not, so long as it is of consequence in the determination of the action." Consider the following example.

Dave, the noncustodial parent of a four-year-old boy, took his son from preschool one day and did not return him to Mary, the custodial parent. Dave was arrested two weeks later for child-stealing, and the child was then returned to his mother. At the time of his arrest, Dave had a cocktail napkin in his pocket with Mary's address and phone number on it. This cocktail napkin would not be relevant to the ultimate issue of his guilt in that it would not go to prove whether Dave actually "stole" his child away from the mother. It might, however, be probative of his state of mind. If Mary gave Dave the cocktail napkin, this might create inferences that she and Dave were negotiating about the child. If Dave wrote the information himself, it might be probative that he was intending to return the child. The cocktail napkin would be relevant because inferences can be drawn from that evidence, which, in the context of other evidence presented, might be of consequence in the determination of the action.

Although the concept of "ultimate issues" is still important in some areas of evidence law, for purposes of relevancy, whether or not evidence relates to an ultimate issue does not affect its admissibility under FRE 401. Therefore, such things as a defendant's financial condition prior to the robbery, or a defendant's attempt to flee after the issuance of a warrant, or love letters written to the spouse of a murder victim, are all potentially relevant pieces of evidence.

For the most part, the Federal Rules of Evidence are extremely liberal. It is noted in the Advisory Notes that the success of showing the relevance of a particular item to a fact in the case is often coextensive with the ingenuity or creativity of the lawyer. If a lawyer wants the evidence to come in, she has wide berth to argue that it is relevant.

Ultimate Issue
A legal question that must be answered to resolve the case.

2.3   Admissibility of Relevant Evidence

FRE 402, P. 264

Evidence must be shown to be relevant before the court will allow it to be admitted for consideration by the factfinder. Once relevancy is established, FRE 402 indicates a predisposition to accept rather than reject relevant evidence. However, after establishing relevancy, the proponent may have to overcome various other obstacles before the evidence is admitted. Relevancy is only the essential first step. FRE 402 states:

> All relevant evidence is admissible, except as otherwise provided by the Constitution of the United States, by Act of Congress, by these rules, or by other rules prescribed by the Supreme Court pursuant to statutory authority. Evidence which is not relevant is not admissible.

The words "except as otherwise provided" are operative in this rule. Exceptions to the admissibility of relevant evidence are the subject of a large number of evidentiary rules relating to such things as character, habit, hearsay, unfair prejudice, authentication, and identification. These exceptions will be discussed at length in this textbook.

Laws from sources other than the rules of evidence may also require the exclusion of relevant evidence, as is acknowledged under Rule 402.

- Federal Rules of Civil and Criminal Procedure require the exclusion of relevant evidence in some instances. For example, if a party refuses to produce documents when requested to do so by the opponent, the document is inadmissible if proffered by the party who refused to produce it.
- The Constitution may require that relevant evidence be excluded. For example, a confession given without proper Miranda warnings is certainly relevant, but inadmissible to prove a crime for Constitutional reasons.
- Relevant evidence may be excluded based on legal privilege. For example, statements by a client made to a paralegal while working as an agent of an attorney may be relevant to a proceeding, but are inadmissible because they are protected by the attorney/client privilege.
- Other exceptions can be found throughout the law.

Finally, notwithstanding the predisposition in the rules to accept rather than reject relevant evidence, the courts do recognize that certain evidence is so unfairly prejudicial that were it to be admitted simply because it is relevant, the outcome would likely be an unjust result. Rules relating to highly inflammatory or unfairly prejudicial evidence are presented in the next section of this chapter.

2.4   Evolution of the Unfair Prejudice Objection

The courts grapple a great deal with issues surrounding evidence that is likely to create unfair prejudice against a party in the eyes of a jury, or evidence likely to inflame a jury and cause it to reach its decision on improper grounds. Before the Federal Rules of Evidence existed, the courts constructed legal theories through which they were able to exclude certain evidence that would have caused unfair prejudice. Evidence that was relevant but inflammatory was considered "logically relevant" but "legally irrelevant." In other words, such evidence could not be construed as factually irrelevant, so the courts ruled the evidence irrelevant as a matter of law. The Federal Rules have replaced the concept of legal relevancy with Rule 403.

FRE 403, P. 264

Discretionary Provision
A rule that is not absolute and gives the court latitude to decide.

FRE 403 is a **discretionary provision** through which highly prejudicial evidence may be found inadmissible. If you work for a prosecutor or in a criminal defense firm, you might hear Rule 403 referred to by some cynical members of the bar as the "whiner's objection." This comes from the perception that if the opposition doesn't want certain evidence to come in, it may be anticipated that they will "whine" about it to the judge, pursuant to Rule 403.

Rule 403 is actually extremely important in the courtroom, as it allows the judge a certain amount of discretion to keep out evidence that might lead to an unjust result. FRE 403 states:

> *Although relevant, evidence may be excluded* if its probative value is substantially outweighed by the danger of unfair prejudice, confusion of the issues, or misleading the jury, or by considerations of undue delay, waste of time, or needless presentation of cumulative evidence. [Emphasis added.]

Rule 403 requires that the court exercise discretion in balancing the conflicts that certain proffered evidence may cause. Rule 403 assumes that the evidence is relevant, but gives the court discretion to exclude it anyway. The court is under no obligation to exclude evidence under this rule. It is merely required to balance the competing interests. Under this rule, the court must first examine the evidence to consider its probative value. The more probative value a given piece of evidence has, the less likely it is to be excluded under this rule.

Probative value is weighed against several criteria for ultimate determination of the admissibility of evidence under Rule 403. The court must look at whether the evidence will unfairly prejudice, confuse, or mislead the jury. In addition, the court must consider whether the proffered evidence will cause undue delay, waste of time, or needless presentation of **cumulative evidence.**

Cumulative Evidence
Evidence repetitive of other evidence.

FRE 403, P. 264

Rule 403 is the result of a long history of concern by the courts regarding fairness in the admission of inflammatory or extremely burdensome material. As discussed previously, at common law, evidence that was highly inflammatory or unfairly prejudicial would be excludable as logically relevant, but not legally relevant. Under the Federal Rules of Evidence, the same evidence would now be described as "relevant under Rule 401 but not admissible because of Rule 403." See Roger C. Park, *Trial Objections Handbook: Trial Practice Series* (1991).

2.5   What Constitutes Unfair Prejudice

Keeping in mind that in a criminal case, any evidence offered to convict a defendant may well prejudice the jury against the defendant, the operative word to be considered under FRE 403 is "unfair." The prejudice caused by the admission of the evidence must be *unfairly* prejudicial against the party who objects to it. Even where there is a possibility of unfair prejudice, this is not sufficient to exclude the evidence if it is extremely important to the proffering party's case. The use of the evidence may be **limited**, or partially **expurgated** to accommodate some of the objecting party's concerns, but if it is extremely probative, it is likely to come in. The following is an example of testimony admitted over an objection of unfair prejudice, pursuant to Rule 403, in a court trial.

Limited
Restricted.

Expurgated
Cleared out or removed.

FRE 412, P. 267

D was a coach for a high school basketball team. Two boys alleged that D molested them. D's attorney offered evidence that the alleged victims were gay. Prosecution objected on the grounds of unfair prejudice. (Also, prosecution objected on the grounds that prior sexual history of a victim is generally inadmissible—see Rule 412.) D's attorney argued that the information regarding the boys' sexual preference was probative to D's defense that the allegations made by the boys were the result of a vindictive conspiracy they had entered into after the coach's son had rebuked the boys' sexual advances. D's defense was that the alleged victims had made up their story to strike back at the coach's son by accusing the coach.

In this case, the court admitted the evidence of the alleged victims' sexual preference. The sexual preference of the alleged victims was critical to the accused's defense, and therefore the potential prejudice against the alleged victims was outweighed by the probative value of the evidence.

The following is an example of evidence that was excluded upon objection by prosecution under Rule 403, because of its highly prejudicial nature.

Richard Byfar, a 19-year-old man, was charged with one count of robbery, based on his stealing a purse from Bambi, a middle-aged woman. The defense attempted to introduce evidence that Bambi

was extremely wealthy, on the grounds that this was probative of Byfar's defense that the woman gave him her purse willingly.

Prosecution argued that raising the issue of the victim's wealth would unfairly prejudice the jury. There was risk that the jury would decide out of sympathy for the indigent defendant and against the wealthy woman who could afford the loss.

In this case, the court found that the probative value of evidence of the victim's wealth was outweighed by its prejudicial effect, and the evidence was excluded.

The case below provides another example of a court exercising its discretion in precluding inflammatory evidence. After the September 11, 2001 terrorist attacks, Awadallah was called to testify before a federal grand jury and subsequently indicted for perjury. The indictment charged that Awadallah had lied to the grand jury when he denied knowing Khalid Al-Midhar's name and then again when the Government showed Awadallah a photocopy of his own college exam booklet, in which the name "Khalid" was written, and Awadallah claimed that the handwriting was not his.

United States v. Awadallah

202 F. Supp. 2d 17 (S.D.N.Y. 2002)

Awadallah is a lawful permanent resident of the United States and a citizen of Jordan. Awadallah entered this country in April 1999, at the age of 19, with the goal of becoming a United States citizen. In the Fall of 2001, Awadallah was living in San Diego, and beginning his second year at Grossmont College, studying English as a Second Language.

On September 20, 2001, a group of FBI agents investigating the terrorist attacks of September 11, 2001 approached Awadallah at his home. Awadallah was a subject of the investigation because agents had found a scrap of paper with the words "Osama 589-5316" inside a car abandoned by Nawaf Al-Hazmi, one of the hijackers of American Airlines Flight 77. . . at Washington Dulles International Airport on the afternoon of September 11. The FBI had subsequently matched this number to a phone at a residence where Awadallah had briefly lived nearly two years earlier. . . .

During the course of Awadallah's grand jury testimony, the prosecutors repeatedly asked Awadallah about his knowledge of Al-Hazmi. Awadallah answered that he had met Al-Hazmi while working at a gas station in San Diego in the Spring of 2000, and had last seen him in December 2000, and described a number of innocuous encounters with Al-Hazmi. The prosecutors also asked Awadallah about another man whom Awadallah had seen in

Al-Hazmi's company-Khalid Al-Midhar, another of the hijackers. Awadallah described Al-Midhar's appearance, but said that he did not know the man's name. The Government then showed Awadallah a photocopy of his college exam booklet, in which Al-Midhar's name was written. Awadallah claimed that the handwriting was not his.

*   *   *

. . . [Awadallah] asks the Court to strike the references to three videotapes found in his car and to certain computer-generated photographs found in his apartment, both of which are found at paragraph six of the Indictment. Two of the videotapes concern the 1993 war in Bosnia and the other concerns the Koran. The photographs are of Osama bin Laden. It is beyond cavil that this material is highly inflammatory when our country is currently engaged in a war against terrorism in Afghanistan, a prime purpose of which is to arrest Osama bin Laden. Moreover, the material has no relevance to the narrow perjury charges of this Indictment.

The government has not specifically addressed this material. Rather, it asserts the general proposition that the information known to the grand jury at the time defendant testified is relevant to the charges. . . . Because the challenged material is not relevant to the crime charged, and it is inflammatory and prejudicial, it is hereby stricken.

Even though the court above did not refer to FRE 403 or even engage in a discussion of the balancing test provided in the rule, it would be difficult to imagine that any court would have ruled differently.

Conventional wisdom would provide the following rule of thumb when dealing with Rule 403 objections based on unfair prejudice, confusion of the issues, or misleading the jury. Evidence will most likely be excluded if it is really going to be used for an impermissible purpose. If the reason for wanting the proffered evidence is not an allowable one, the court will most likely refuse to admit it, notwithstanding clever arguments by counsel. It is frequently the job of the paralegal to draft memoranda stating reasons supporting the admission or exclusion of evidence that is subject to FRE 403 objection.

2.6   Undue Delay, Waste of Time, or Needless Presentation of Cumulative Evidence

Rule 403 objections may be made to evidence that if admitted would unduly burden the court or litigants. The court will balance the time and expense that would be consumed in the presentation of the evidence against such things as whether other evidence has already been introduced that adequately covers the subject or whether the evidence possesses only minimal probative value.

The following example illustrates where the court precluded the introduction of certain evidence because the evidence would be needlessly cumulative.

James was charged with assaulting John. James denied the charges. The prosecution indicated that it intended to call 16 witnesses to testify that each of them had heard James threaten John some days prior to the assault This evidence was admissible to prove James's state of mind. The court ruled that only 4 of the proffered witnesses would be allowed to testify. Although the evidence was admissible, the testimony from 16 witnesses would have been needlessly cumulative and unduly burdensome on the court. In addition, the repetition of such testimony might have confused the jury. So much repetition might cause the jury to improperly believe that the evidence had much greater importance than establishing the accused's state of mind.

2.7 Objection for Unfair Prejudice Where Evidence Is Admissible for a Limited Purpose

FRE 403, P. 264

FRE 403 and comparable state evidentiary rules against unfair prejudice may be used by counsel to keep out evidence admissible for one purpose, but inadmissible for another.

Ordinarily, when evidence is admitted on one ground although objectionable on another, the court will give a limiting instruction to the jury to consider the testimony only for the purpose for which it was admitted. However, if the probative value of the evidence is outweighed by its prejudicial effect, even though admitted for only a limited purpose, the courts have the discretion to exclude the evidence, pursuant to FRE 403.

For example, in general terms, hearsay (which will be discussed at length later in this book) is inadmissible to prove the truth of the matter asserted. Certain hearsay evidence, however, may be considered nonhearsay and admissible when offered for some other reason. Consider the following hypothetical.

Plaintiff Jimmy sued Defendant ChemCo for failure to warn users that exposure to their chemical, Agent X, might be toxic. Jimmy suffered brain damage after using Agent X in a poorly ventilated indoor area. ChemCo denied that Agent X was the cause of Jimmy's injury. Jimmy attempted to introduce into evidence a letter written

to ChemCo from another Agent X user. The letter said, in relevant part, "When used for even brief periods in an unventilated area, Agent X causes our employees to become ill. This product appears to be extremely dangerous."

The proffered letter is inadmissible hearsay to prove that Agent X is really extremely dangerous. It is admissible, however, to show that ChemCo had, in fact, been informed of a potential health problem in connection with the product.

Rule 403 can be used to argue that the letter in this example, even though technically admissible to show that ChemCo had been notified of potential health risks connected with the use of Agent X, should be excluded because of the danger that the jury will be unfairly prejudiced by it. There is a high risk that the jury will consider the letter as evidence of the danger of the chemical, notwithstanding a limiting instruction by the court. The court must weigh the probative value of such a letter against the danger of unfair prejudice to determine whether the letter should be admitted.

Once the trial court has made its determination in a situation such as the one in the above hypothetical, the appellate court will rarely tamper with the trial judge's ruling, even when the appellate court questions the trial court's reasoning.

The following case illustrates an instance when the 7th Circuit Court of Appeals was sympathetic to an argument that the probative value of certain evidence, when viewed in terms of the limited purpose for which it was admitted, was outweighed by its prejudicial effect. Nonetheless, the appellate court refused to superimpose its own judgment over that of the trial judge, and deferred to the district court's determination.

United States v. Moore

845 F.2d 683 (7th Cir. 1988)

A jury convicted Kathryn Joy Moore of one count of conspiring to transmit and present altered postal money orders and five counts of transmitting and presenting altered postal money orders. Moore appeals from her conviction arguing that the admission into evidence of seventeen exhibits, which only remotely tended to prove her state of mind, constituted reversible error. We find the district court did not commit reversible error in admitting the exhibits, and therefore affirm.

During February and March of 1982, defendant-appellant, Kathryn J. Moore, received six money orders in two letters from Frank Baker, Jr., an inmate at the Michigan City State Prison in Indiana. Each money order was payable to Moore in the apparent amount of $261.00. Moore, then living in Texas, negotiated the money orders at her local post office and two stores by endorsing the money orders using her own name and social security number.

In 1982, postal agents, investigating a massive money order scheme involving altered money orders originating primarily from the Michigan City prison, met with Moore and informed her that the money orders she had cashed had been altered from $1.00 to $261.00. Moore agreed to cooperate with the government's investigation.

Moore admitted that she had endorsed the six money orders she received from Baker but claimed she did not know they were altered. She provided the government with six letters from Baker, written between January 26, 1982, and March 8, 1982, in which Baker referred to a "money scheme." Two of the 1982 letters contained the altered money orders. Moore also turned over seventeen other letters from Baker, written between April 24, 1981, and December 17, 1981, in which Baker made no reference to money orders but in which he asked Moore to procure drugs.

At trial, Moore conceded that she received and cashed the money orders which formed the basis of the charges against her. Moore argued, however, that she did not know they had been altered and thus, she could not be found guilty of a crime which required proof of specific intent to negotiate altered money orders.

In an attempt to prove Moore knew the money orders were altered, the government introduced not only the six letters from Baker, written in 1982 and referring to a money scheme, but also the seventeen letters sent in 1981 containing references to drugs—but no references to a money scheme. Moore objected to the introduction of the 1981 letters. [Moore pointed out in the proceeding that the 1981 letters predated the conspiracy alleged in the indictment.]

*   *   *

The court found that the letters were admitted not to prove Baker's numerous requests for drugs, but rather, to prove the effect those letters had on Moore's state of mind. In other words, the district court permitted the introduction of the letters as evidence of Moore's knowledge of Frank Baker's propensities.

*   *   *

Moore alleged that the introduction of the 1981 letters would cause the jury to evaluate her actions on the basis of her association with Baker. Thus, she asserted the harmful effect of the evidence greatly outweighed the probative value of the evidence. Moore's contention that the jury might find her "guilty by association" was not without some plausibility. No evidence was introduced that Moore ever responded to Baker's 1981 requests for drugs by procuring them. She testified that she may have written and stated she would look into it, but that she never did and never had any intention of doing so. Moreover, the letters contained quite a bit of personal information which could easily have portrayed Moore as a less favorable person in the eyes of the jury.

As Moore argued, the harmful effect of evidence seemingly outweighed the only slightly probative value of the 1981 letters (especially given the ample evidence the government had already introduced to prove Moore's knowledge). Yet we do not reverse a district court simply because we would have decided an evidentiary issue differently.

On appeal, we will not find error in a district court's evidentiary determination unless the court "clearly abused its discretion in admitting the challenged evidence." [citations omitted.]

In this case, as we have said, the 1981 letters were relevant to Moore's state of mind and we defer to the district court's determination that any harm of introducing those letters was outweighed by their probative value.

*   *   *

AFFIRMED.

In the above case, the appellate court found that the letters admitted over the objection of defense counsel had only slight probative value, and the harmful effect of the letters most likely outweighed their probative value. Nonetheless, finding no clear abuse of discretion, the appellate court refused to find error. The fact that the appellate court would have decided the evidentiary issue differently is insufficient to cause it to reverse a district court ruling.

2.8   Rule 403—Inapplicability

For the most part, whenever evidence is proffered, it is subject to review under FRE 403. The probative value must outweigh the prejudicial effect of the evidence for it to be admissible. There is, however, one exception where the court is not permitted to "balance" the prejudicial nature of the evidence against its probative value. Rule 609(a)(2) mandates that evidence of a prior conviction for a crime which requires proof of dishonesty or false statement, when offered to attack the credibility of any witness, is absolutely admissible without

Judicial Discretion
Latitude of choice in the
part of the trial judge.

subjection to Rule 403 consideration. There is no **judicial discretion** allowed in this situation.

To illustrate, consider the following situation.

Jerome is an excellent security guard at Hitech, Inc. While on duty, he noticed an employee leaving the building with a large package. He asked the employee about the contents of the package, but the employee refused to answer. The next day, it was discovered that one of Hitech's minicomputers was missing. Jerome implicated the employee, who was later found with the missing computer.

Unfortunately, five years prior to this incident, Jerome plead guilty to a misdemeanor charge of welfare fraud. This prior conviction will undoubtedly prejudice the jury against Jerome, and taint the veracity of his testimony against the employee who allegedly took the minicomputer. The embezzlement conviction is admissible notwithstanding its prejudicial effect, pursuant to FRE 609(a)(2).

FRE 609(a)(2), P. 274

This exception is a minor one. It doesn't cover all criminal convictions, only those involving dishonesty. Other evidence that may be offered to impeach a witness is generally subject to FRE 403 review. This will be discussed at length in a later chapter in this textbook.

2.9 In Summary

- Under the common law, evidence had to be both relevant and material to be admissible. Under the FRE, materiality is included in the definition of relevancy.
- All relevant evidence is admissible unless it is subject to an exception in either the Rules of Evidence or some other body of law.
- Under the common law, evidence that was logically relevant could be deemed irrelevant as a matter of law, if the evidence was inflammatory and caused unfair prejudice. Under FRE 403, if evidence is highly prejudicial, its probative value must outweigh its harmful effect to be admissible.
- Evidence that causes undue delay or is cumulative may be excluded under FRE 403.
- When evidence is admitted for a limited purpose, its probative value in that limited purpose must outweigh its prejudicial effect, or it is subject to exclusion pursuant to FRE 403.
- FRE 403 does not apply to the admission of prior convictions for crimes which require proof of dishonesty or false statement, when offered to prove credibility (or lack thereof). Even though extremely prejudicial, these prior convictions are admissible and not subject to judicial discretion.

End of Chapter Review Questions

1. What is relevancy under the FRE?
2. What is materiality under the common law?
3. What is unfair prejudice?
4. What is probative evidence?
5. Who is the proponent?
6. Must relevant evidence pertain only to the ultimate issue?

Applications

Consider the following hypothetical situation.

Danielle rear-ended Charisse, who was stopped at a red light. Charisse sued Danielle for negligent driving. In the back seat of Danielle's car at the time of the accident, there was a magazine wrapped in a brown paper wrapper.

1. Is the magazine in the back seat of the car relevant evidence? Why or why not?
2. Suppose that the magazine was in the wrapper, but in the front seat. Is the magazine relevant evidence now? Why or why not?
3. Suppose that the magazine was unwrapped in the front seat, and that it was filled with child pornography. Is the magazine relevant evidence now? Why or why not?
4. Suppose that the magazine is lying open on the front seat to a page of a picture of a nude child. Is the magazine relevant evidence now? Why or why not?
5. Suppose the magazine is taped open to the steering wheel. Now, is the magazine relevant evidence?
6. Assume that the child pornography magazine is relevant evidence. What is the likely objection that opposition will make to the introduction of the magazine into evidence in the auto accident case? Present arguments for and against admissibility.
7. Suppose in other places in this magazine, there are very explicit pornographic pictures of young children performing sexual acts. These pictures were not on the exposed page at the time of the accident. Does the presence of these pictures make the entire magazine inadmissible as highly prejudicial? Why or why not? What might you do to mitigate the prejudicial affect of the magazine?
8. Charisse's lawyer wants to present evidence of Danielle's prior conviction for lying to a grand jury. Is it relevant? Would it be admissible?

CHAPTER

3

Character

3.1 Character Evidence Defined

Character can be defined as the nature or disposition of a person, or the particular traits that identify the way he or she would probably act under certain circumstances. For example, a person can be characterized as "hot tempered," or "inconsiderate," or he can be said to "always yell at the neighbor's kids." All these statements would fall under the definition of "character evidence." Common law and state evidence codes are generally in accord with the Federal Rules on the treatment of character evidence.

FRE 404(a), P. 265

Pursuant to FRE 404(a), evidence of character is generally inadmissible to prove that an individual acted accordingly. The following hypothetical is illustrative.

Wanda (Harry's wife) awakes in the middle of the night and has to use the bathroom. She goes to sit down on the toilet seat and unceremoniously falls in. She screams, "Darn you, Harry! You never put the toilet seat down!" Evidence of Harry's propensity to leave the toilet seat up is character evidence that is *inadmissible* to prove that he left the seat up on this particular occasion.

This particular hypothetical not only clearly illustrates the application of FRE 404(a), it also serves to explain why, when working in a criminal law setting, you might hear FRE 404(a) referred to as "the toilet seat rule."

Character evidence is usually excludable under FRE 404(a) even though it may appear to meet standards for relevancy. This is because character evidence is really excluded for **public policy** reasons, not because it is necessarily irrelevant.

For example, assume a defendant is on trial for shoplifting. Evidence that she previously shoplifted may be considered relevant circumstantial evidence from which an inference can be drawn that she is guilty of shoplifting in the current case. It isn't **conclusive** circumstantial evidence, but it does seem to be probative. People who have shoplifted before are probably more likely to be guilty of shoplifting than people who haven't. The problem is that the jury is likely to overestimate the importance of the past shoplifting. A jury might well be inclined to convict the defendant based not on the evidence of the current crime, but on the assumption that "she did it before so she's probably done it again."

The 8th Circuit Court of Appeals in *U.S. v. Mothershed*, 859 F.2d 585 (8th Cir. 1988) summed up the policy issue with the following comments: "We do not convict people of crimes simply because of their propensities; we do so because of what they have actually done."

Consider our "toilet seat" hypothetical one more time. Suppose Harry had had a poker party the evening of Wanda's "accident." In fact, it wasn't Harry who'd left the toilet seat up, but one of his poker buddies. Wanda incorrectly assumed Harry was the perpetrator because of his past conduct. FRE 404(a) attempts to exclude the kind of evidence that might yield this type of incorrect assignment of blame.

The proscription in FRE 404(a) against the admissibility of character or a character trait to prove present conduct is the general rule in both criminal and civil cases. As always in the law, the general rule is just that—general. There are exceptions that are applicable in

Public Policy
The general principle that law should work for the public good.

Conclusive
Evidence that is irrefutable, or allows only a single inference to be drawn.

both criminal and civil cases which we will discuss throughout this chapter. For instance, FRE 404(a)(1) and (2) provide exceptions for the admissibility of character evidence of both the accused and the victim in a criminal case. FRE 404(a)(3) relates to impeachment by character evidence of a witness in either a civil or a criminal case. FRE 404(b) describes, but does not limit, situations when a person's prior conduct, that is, "crimes, wrongs, or acts" may be used for purposes other than to prove if the person did it before, then the person must have done it again! FRE 405(b) permits character evidence both in a criminal and a civil case when character or a character trait is an element of the case or an element of the defense. FRE 412 limits the admissibility of a sexual assault victim's prior sexual conduct in both the criminal and civil context. Similarly, FRE 413 through FRE 415 govern the use of the defendant's prior sexual conduct in adult sexual assault cases and child molestation cases in both a criminal and a civil case. Finally, if character evidence is admissible under one of the exceptions, then FRE 405, 412 through 415, 608, and 609 authorize the proper method or way in which the person's character may be proved.

FRE 413, 414, 415, PP. 269, 270

3.2 Character Evidence in Civil Cases

FRE 404(a)(1) and (2), P. 265

For many years, evidence of an individual's character generally was not permitted in civil cases to prove conduct, even though the same evidence might be admissible in a criminal case under one of FRE 404(a)'s exceptions. (FRE 404(a)'s exceptions for criminal proceedings are discussed in detail in Section 3.3.) The exceptions under FRE 404(a)(1) and (2) are written exclusively for criminal proceedings. They apply to the "accused" and the "victim," which are terms used to describe parties in a criminal setting. So, for example, where an accused might be able to introduce evidence of a pertinent trait of character to help establish his innocence of a crime, a defendant in a civil action generally had no such mechanism.

Although the language in FRE 404(a)(1) and (2) explicitly refers to the use of character evidence in criminal proceedings, courts across the country had been in conflict about whether there were types of civil cases in which character evidence should be admissible to prove conduct. Some courts, doing what some courts do, that is, make their own rules, decided to create their own exception in order to permit character evidence in civil cases. In those instances, the courts reasoned that there were some issues in civil cases which were akin to issues in criminal cases. To illustrate, consider the following case in which the Tenth Circuit reasoned accordingly.

Perrin v. Anderson

784 F.2d 1040 (10th Cir. 1986)

This is a ... civil rights action for compensatory and punitive damages arising from the death of Terry Kim Perrin. Plaintiff, administratrix of Perrin's estate and guardian of his son, alleged that defendants, Donnie Anderson and Roland Von Schriltz, members of the Oklahoma Highway Patrol, deprived Perrin of his civil rights when they shot and killed him while attempting to obtain information concerning a traffic accident in which he had been involved. The jury found in favor of defendants.

In this appeal plaintiff contends that the district court erred in admitting: (1) testimony by four police officers recounting previous violent encounters they had had with Perrin. . . .

A simple highway accident set off the bizarre chain of events that culminated in Perrin's death. The incident began when Perrin drove his car into the back of another car on an Oklahoma highway. After determining that the occupants of the car he had hit were uninjured, Perrin walked to his home, which was close to the highway.

Trooper Von Schriltz went to Perrin's home to obtain information concerning the accident. He was joined there by Trooper Anderson. They knocked on and off for ten to twenty minutes before persuading Perrin to open the door. Once Perrin opened the door, the defendant officers noticed Perrin's erratic behavior. The troopers testified that his moods would change quickly and that he was yelling that the accident was not his fault. Von Schriltz testified that he sensed a possibly dangerous situation and slowly moved his hand to his gun in order to secure its hammer with a leather thong. This action apparently provoked Perrin who then slammed the door. The door bounced open and Perrin then attacked Anderson. A fierce battle ensued between Perrin and the two officers, who unsuccessfully applied several chokeholds to Perrin in an attempt to subdue him. Eventually Anderson, who testified that he feared he was about to lose consciousness as a result of having been kicked repeatedly in the face and chest by Perrin, took out his gun, and, without issuing a warning, shot and killed Perrin. Anderson stated that he was convinced Perrin would have killed both officers had he not fired.

At trial the court permitted four police officers to testify that they had been involved previously in violent encounters with Perrin. These officers testified to Perrin's apparent hatred or fear of uniformed officers and his consistently violent response to any contact with them. For example, defendants presented evidence that on earlier occasions Perrin was completely uncontrollable and violent in the presence of uniformed officers. On one occasion he rammed his head into the bars and walls of his cell, requiring administration of a tranquilizer. Another time while barefoot, Perrin kicked loose a porcelain toilet bowl that was bolted to the floor. One officer testified that he encountered Perrin while responding to a public drunk call. Perrin attacked him, and during the following struggle Perrin tried to reach for the officer's weapon. The officer and his back-up had to carry Perrin handcuffed, kicking and screaming, to the squad car, where Perrin then kicked the windshield out of the car. Another officer testified that Perrin attacked him after Perrin was stopped at a vehicle checkpoint. During the ensuing struggle three policemen were needed to subdue Perrin, including one 6'2" officer weighing 250 pounds and one 6'6" officer weighing 350 pounds.

Defendants introduced this evidence to prove that Perrin was the first aggressor in the fight-a key element in defendants' self-defense claim. The court admitted the evidence over objection, under Federal Rules of Evidence provisions treating both character and habit evidence. Plaintiff contends this was error.

Section 404(a) of the Federal Rules of Evidence carefully limits the circumstances under which character evidence may be admitted to prove that an individual, at the time in question, acted in conformity with his character. This rule is necessary because of the high degree of prejudice that inheres in character evidence. . . . In most instances we are unwilling to permit a jury to infer that an individual performed the alleged acts based on a particular character trait. The exceptions to Rule 404(a)'s general ban on the use of character evidence permit criminal defendants to offer evidence of their own character or of their victim's character. Fed. R. Evid. 404(a)(1)-(2). Not until such a defendant takes this initial step may the prosecution rebut by offering contrary character evidence. . . . Although the Advisory Committee on the Rules of Evidence has observed that this rule "lies more in history and experience than in logic," . . . it does seem desirable to afford a criminal defendant every opportunity to exonerate himself. In offering such potentially prejudicial testimony, the defendant of course proceeds at his own risk. Once he offers evidence of his or his victim's character, the prosecution may offer contrary evidence. . . .

*   *   *

Although the literal language of the exceptions to Rule 404(a) applies only to criminal cases, we agree with the district court here that, when the central issue involved in a civil case is in nature criminal, the defendant may invoke the exceptions to Rule 404(a). . . .

In a case of this kind, the civil defendant, like the criminal defendant, stands in a position of great peril. . . . A verdict against the defendants in this case would be tantamount to finding that they killed Perrin without cause. The resulting stigma warrants giving them the same opportunity to present a defense that a criminal defendant could present. Accordingly we hold that defendants were entitled to present evidence of Perrin's character from which the jury could infer that Perrin was the aggressor. The self-defense claim raised in this case is not functionally different from a self-defense claim raised in a criminal case.

As you can see, the court in the *Perrin* case above recognized that FRE 404(a) was intended to restrict the use of character evidence to prove conduct in conformity with the character trait to criminal cases. Nevertheless, the court created its own exception by reasoning that the facts and circumstances in the *Perrin* case were analogous to a criminal case.

Recently, however, Congress enacted an amendment to FRE 404(a), effective December, 2006, to end the inconsistent and inaccurate application of FRE 404(a). The amendment adds only a few words to FRE 404(a)(1) and (2), but by those few words, Congress ended the dispute and clearly expressed that circumstantial use of character evidence to prove conduct in civil cases is prohibited. It will be interesting to follow the case law to see whether the courts will adhere to the clear congressional intent or whether the courts will continue to make their own rules!

This does not mean, however, that the paralegal does not have to be concerned with character evidence in civil cases at all. The prohibition against the admission of character evidence relates to the use of such evidence to prove conduct on a particular occasion. Character evidence is both relevant and admissible for other purposes.

For example, FRE 404(3) refers to the impeachment rules (FRE 607, 608, and 609) that provide that evidence of the character of a witness is admissible when relevant to prove a witness's character for truthfulness. In other words, where character evidence is specifically related to a witness's propensity for honesty or dishonesty, the evidence may be admissible as probative of whether that witness's testimony should be believed. FRE 404(3) is applicable both in civil and criminal proceedings. Impeachment rules will be discussed at length in a later chapter. They specifically address how evidence, including character evidence, can be used to either **discredit** or **rehabilitate** a witness.

Another important exception regarding the admissibility of character evidence in both criminal and civil actions is FRE

FRE 404(a)(1) and (2), P. 265

FRE 404(a)(3), P. 265

FRE 607, 608, 609, P. 273 et seq.

Discredit
To cause the witness to be doubted or found not to be believable.

Rehabilitate
To establish a witness's credibility after it has been damaged.

FRE 405(b), P. 265

Essential Element
An integral part of the cause
of action.

405(b), which provides for the admission of character evidence when character is an **essential element** in the case. An essential element in a case is like an ultimate question: something that must be resolved for a determination of the outcome of a case to be made. FRE 405(b) and its applications are discussed at length later in this chapter.

3.3 Character of the Accused in Criminal Proceedings

Important exceptions allowing for the admissibility of character evidence are found in FRE 404(a)(1) and (2), which relate to the treatment of the accused in criminal proceedings. The defendant in a criminal prosecution is permitted to present evidence of his or her own character as part of the defense, and is allowed to present pertinent character evidence regarding the victim as well. The prosecution has certain rebuttal rights but cannot be the first to raise the issue of the defendant's character. Understanding the evidentiary rules requires something of an understanding of the criminal trial process itself.

Direct Questions
Questions that do not suggest an answer (opposite from leading questions), which are asked during direct examination, during which time the witness is being questioned on the merits for the first time.

In a criminal trial, the prosecution presents its evidence first. The prosecutor calls the government's witnesses and interrogates them with **direct questions**. The prosecutor thereby presents the government's **case in chief**. Absent the raising of character by the defense in either opening statement or cross-examination, no provision under the Federal Rules of Evidence, or under any state rules, allows the prosecution to initiate an attack on the defendant's character during the government's case in chief.

Case in Chief
The presentation of evidence by the party who has the burden of proof, after which the party rests its case.

After the prosecution has presented its case in chief, the accused may but is not required to present his defense. Under most circumstances, this is the first time in the trial that character evidence is admissible, because it is at this point that the accused may, pursuant to FRE 404(a)(1), elect to bring in evidence of his own **pertinent character traits**. In other words, ordinary character evidence doesn't come in until the accused brings it in. This is often referred to as "opening the door."

FRE 404(a)(1) and (2), P. 265

Pertinent Character Traits
Character traits related to or relevant to the charges at issue.

The accused is allowed to bring in testimony of his own pertinent character traits to try to establish his innocence. For a character trait to be pertinent and admissible under 404(a)(1), it must generally relate to the charges for which the defendant is being tried. For example, in a "bad check" case, character evidence regarding the manner in which the defendant handled his finances would be pertinent. Conversely, in a case where the accused is charged with driving under the influence of alcohol, evidence that the accused donated money to his church each year would not be pertinent.

The following case illustrates character evidence found by the court not to be pertinent, and therefore not admissible to show the accused's character.

United States v. Santana-Camacho

931 F.2d 966 (1st Cir. 1991)

A grand jury charged the appellant with [2 counts of] illegally bringing Dominican citizen(s) into the United States . . . , and with [1 count of] transporting an alien already, and illegally, within the United States. . . . After trial a jury convicted the appellant on the first two counts and acquitted him on Count III. He appeals his two convictions and his sentence.

Our reading of the record convinces us that appellant's . . . claims of trial error, in respect to his two convictions, lack merit. First, he argues that the trial court erred in refusing to admit into evidence testimony of his daughter, Damaris Santana, whose testimony, he says, showed his "reputation" in respect to his "character for truthfulness or untruthfulness." See Fed. R. Evid. 608(a). We find nothing in that testimony that refers to any reputation for truthfulness. Damaris simply talked about her father having sent her money when she lived in New York and having lived with her when she was in Boston, facts that had nothing to do with the present case. Conceivably, appellant thought her testimony relevant as showing he was a kind person or a good family man. See Fed. R. Evid. 404(a). But traits of character "pertinent" to the crime charged must be relevant. Here, evidence that appellant is kind or a good family man would not make any fact " 'of consequence to the determination of the case [significantly] more or less probable than it would be without evidence of the trait." See Fed. R. Evid. 401. Therefore, the district court had more than sufficient discretionary power to strike the testimony as not worth (in terms of relevance) the potential confusion, or potential prejudice, that it might bring. See Fed. R. Evid. 403.

*   *   *

AFFIRMED. . . .

Note that in the above-cited case, the court not only found that the character evidence proffered by the accused was not pertinent and therefore not relevant, it found further that the introduction of such evidence might confuse or prejudice the jury and was therefore excludable under FRE 403. It is important to remember that whenever character evidence is at issue, FRE 403 is a rule to consider. Character evidence can be extremely prejudicial and is excludable when its probative value is outweighed by its harmful effect.

When the accused does successfully introduce pertinent character evidence, either through his own testimony or with the testimony of

Cross-Examination
Examination of an opponent's witness to test the truth of the witness's testimony or to further develop it.

Rebuttal
Evidence given to explain or contradict testimony given by opposing party.

FRE 404(a)(1) and (2), P. 265

FRE 405(a), P. 265

FRE 404(a)(1), P. 265

other witnesses, then the door is open for the prosecution to bring in the negative aspects of the defendant's character in response. This can be done by **cross-examining** the defense witnesses or by calling in new witnesses for **rebuttal**.

In a trial, after the defense has rested its case, the prosecution is allowed a last chance to call witnesses to rebut the testimony of the defendant's witnesses. Under FRE 404(a)(1), the prosecutor may, during rebuttal, introduce evidence of the accused's character (or lack thereof) to rebut the inferences created by the accused in his own defense. Consider the following example.

Bart is charged with assault. Homer is called by the defense to testify that Bart is always gentle and never loses his temper. During rebuttal, the prosecutor calls Marge to testify that Bart is extremely volatile and has a reputation for being violent when angry.

By introducing character evidence in his own behalf, the accused has opened the door for prosecution to bring in negative character evidence on rebuttal.

In addition, pursuant to FRE 405(a), the prosecutor may inquire into specific instances of conduct on cross-examination of character witnesses. In other words, if there are specific incidences of conduct in the defendant's past that belie the depiction of character presented by defendant or defendant's witnesses in his behalf, these incidences may be inquired into when the prosecutor cross-examines the defense's character witnesses.

Consequently, a criminal defendant must be very careful when deciding whether to open the door to character evidence. If neither the accused nor any witnesses for the defense introduce evidence of the accused's character, the prosecution is precluded from presenting any evidence regarding the accused's character traits under FRE 404(a)(1). Thus, if the defendant never brings up his or her character, the prosecutor's hands are tied, and character evidence about the defendant ordinarily is not admissible. One exception has been recently created as we will discuss in Section 3.4 below—when the defendant introduces a trait of character of the victim, then the prosecutor can rebut with the same character trait of the defendant. There are times when silence is golden, and sometimes being silent on the issue of character is the best strategy for a defendant.

3.4 Character of the Victim in Criminal Proceedings

FRE 404(a)(2), P. 265

The prosecution may not introduce evidence about the character of the victim until the defendant does so first. FRE 404(a)(2) deals with evidence of pertinent character traits of the victim.

If character evidence about a victim is to be proffered by the defendant, it will generally be presented to try to make the victim appear to be the bad guy or somehow at fault. (The defense certainly isn't going to try to offer evidence to make the victim look like the good guy.) For example, in an assault case, the defense might introduce character evidence to show that the victim is "hot-headed" or has a quick temper, in order to provide an inference that the assault was provoked by the victim or that the defendant was acting in self defense. The prosecution may, on rebuttal, introduce "good" character evidence about the victim in response.

As we said above, the defendant must be careful when deciding to present his or her own character trait. Now, the defendant also must be circumspect when deciding whether to introduce character evidence about the victim. Prior to the amendment to FRE 404(a)(1) effective December 1, 2000, the prosecution was not permitted to launch a counter attack against the accused with "bad" character evidence in response to the defendant's offering "bad" character evidence about the victim. The prosecution could only rebut with character evidence about the victim. Pursuant to the amendment, the prosecution now may attack the accused with the same type of character trait that the defendant offered against the victim. For example, if in an assault case, the accused claims that the victim actually struck the first blow, the accused might present a character trait of the victim's violent disposition. Before the amendment, the jury was not permitted to hear evidence from the prosecution about the same type of character trait, a violent disposition, of the accused. The jury would not have had the complete picture to determine whether the accused or the victim was the first aggressor. The amendment remedies that inadequacy.

In an **unpublished opinion**, the Tenth Circuit discussed the amendment to FRE 404(a)(1) but did not have to decide the issue presented in the case based on the interpretation urged by the defendant-appellant. The ways in which the parties employed the new rule have some interesting twists.

| FRE 404(a)(1), P. 265 |

Unpublished Opinion
A court opinion not selected for publication and therefore cannot be cited for precedential value.

United States v. Herder

2003 WL 245092 (10th Cir. 2003)(unpublished opinion)

The charges in this case arose out of a fight in a trailer located on Navajo land at Shiprock, New Mexico, where the victim, 17-year-old Sheila James, was living with Mary Jane Redhouse's son, Wilfred. On July 28, 2000, 62-year-old Mary Jane Redhouse, her daughter, 40-year-old appellant Cynthia Redhouse, and Cynthia's two daughters, 23-year-old appellant Rachel Herder, and 14-year-old Candace Prendergast, drove to Wilfred's trailer to retrieve from Sheila keys to a car owned by Mary Jane but being used by Wilfred. Earlier that day Mary Jane and the three other women had seen Sheila with Mary Jane's car stopped by police for a traffic violation. Apparently, Mary Jane had not known Wilfred was allowing Sheila to drive Mary Jane's car, and she disapproved.

*   *   *

After the altercation Mary Jane, Cynthia, Rachel and Candace left in their truck. Sheila, worried about a miscarriage . . . went into the bathroom. . . . It was then that she discovered severe bleeding from a wound in her back. . . .

The injury consisted of a rounded gouge out of her flesh, about three inches in length, and a puncture wound at least three to four inches deep in the lower right side of her back. . . .

*   *   *

At trial, counsel for Rachel Herder elicited testimony from Michael Prendergast that Sheila had a reputation in the community as a violent and untruthful person. (Citation to record omitted) The purpose of the evidence was to support the claim—asserted by both defendants—that Sheila was the first aggressor and that the defendants were acting in self-defense.

On rebuttal, the government called Officer Dwayne Vigil who testified that the defendant, Cynthia Redhouse (Rachel's mother), had a reputation in the community as a person "prone to violence." (Citation to record omitted) Neither counsel for Cynthia nor counsel for Rachel objected to that testimony.

*   *   *

Rachel contends that under a plain language reading of Rule 404(a)(1), the government can only introduce character evidence against "the accused" who offered character evidence against the victim. Thus, since Cynthia was not "the accused" who offered character evidence against Sheila, the court committed plain error by admitting rebuttal evidence about Cynthia's character. Put another way, since Rachel was the one who elicited reputation testimony against Sheila, then Rachel was the only defendant against whom the government could offer rebuttal character evidence.

In response, the government argues that "the accused" can be read collectively to apply to all co-defendants or, in any case, the drafters did not think of a co-defendant situation and could not have intended the limitation envisioned by Rachel since it would allow counsel for co-defendants to manipulate the Rules. Because the present wording of the Rule in question has only been in effect since the year 2000, it has not been interpreted in any prior case. . . .

*　　　*　　　*

[Rachel] contends she was prejudiced by evidence of Cynthia's character trait of being "prone to violence" since the jury could draw the inference of "like mother, like daughter."

*　　　*　　　*

To avoid the harm Rachel alleges, all that was required was that the jury not speculate that because Cynthia was "prone to violence," Rachel must also be prone to violence, and then further speculate that, as a result, she was the first aggressor. Considering the instructions given to the jury, and an examination of the full record, we are unconvinced that the evidence that Cynthia was "prone to violence" seriously affected the fairness or outcome of the trial as to Rachel.

In the case above, the defendant Rachel attempted to support her self-defense theory by introducing character evidence that the victim, Sheila, had a reputation for violence. Pursuant to the 404(a)(1) amendment, the prosecution rebutted with character evidence that the co-defendant Cynthia, who was Rachel's mother, also had a reputation for violence. The Tenth Circuit Court of Appeals grappled with whether the amendment was properly implemented but did not decide the question because Cynthia had not objected at trial and was not raising the issue in the appeal. Although the case is an unpublished opinion and it cannot be cited as precedent, it does demonstrate that the rules are subject to interpretation. Moreover, it raises the question whether the amendment to FRE 404(a)(1) intended to permit the prosecution to introduce rebuttal character evidence against a co-defendant other than the defendant who first introduced the character evidence about the victim.

There is one situation where the prosecutor gets to go first in introducing pertinent character traits of a victim rather than waiting for rebuttal. FRE 404(a)(2) allows the prosecution to introduce evidence of the peacefulness of a homicide victim when the defendant has raised a claim of self-defense. The defense need not say anything about the character of the victim. If the defendant is claiming that the victim was really the first aggressor, the prosecutor is allowed to present evidence of the victim's peaceable character traits. This is allowed under the rules because the victim is unable to testify in her own behalf or to make an impression on the jury—the victim in this situation is dead.

FRE 404(a)(2), P. 265

3.5   Prior Sexual Conduct Evidence in Civil and Criminal Sex Offense Cases

FRE 412, P. 267

Prior to the introduction of FRE 412 in the Federal Rules and similar protective statutes, the introduction of evidence about a rape victim's prior sexual conduct was permitted without restraint. The result was that the crime of rape was one of the most seriously underreported crimes, and in those instances where the victim had the courage to come forward, she was usually "tried" much more harshly than the accused. She had, after all, fewer constitutional protections. She was often victimized in the very courtroom that was supposed to be there to protect her against the accused.

FRE 412 was introduced to limit the use of a victim's prior sexual history in criminal sexual assault cases. It narrowly allows evidence to be admitted in order to protect the defendant's constitutional rights, while it rigorously protects the victim. All evidence of prior sexual history that the defense intends to proffer must be presented before trial and analyzed by the court for admissibility. Reputation and opinion evidence are specifically prohibited. The following example is illustrative.

FRE 412, P. 267

Ferdinand was charged with raping Raquel. Ferdinand tried to introduce evidence that Raquel had a reputation in the community for promiscuity. This reputation evidence was inadmissible pursuant to FRE 412.

Ferdinand also attempted to introduce evidence that approximately six months prior to the alleged rape, Raquel left a local tavern with a man previously unknown to her and that she had sex with the stranger that night. This evidence was also inadmissible under FRE 412.

FRE 412(b)(1), P. 268

FRE 412(b)(1) defines narrow areas where past sexual conduct of the victim might be admissible in a criminal case. These are:

1. Evidence of specific instances of sexual behavior by the alleged victim offered to prove that a person other than the accused was the source of the semen or other physical evidence;
2. Evidence of past sexual conduct between the accused and the alleged victim, to show consent; and
3. Evidence that, if excluded, would violate the defendant's constitutional rights.

The same type of evidence would be admissible in civil proceedings, subject to rule 403 review for undue prejudice. Furthermore, in a civil case, if an alleged victim places her own reputation into evidence, this evidence may be rebutted by the defendant. Consider the following example.

Vanessa sued Harold based on a rape claim. Vanessa, in the civil trial, introduced evidence that her reputation was pristine and that she was known to be sexually pure. After the introduction of this evidence, Harold may introduce reputation evidence that Vanessa was reputed to be sexually promiscuous.

Even evidence offered for these purposes must be reviewed by the court prior to trial.

For the legal assistant who is interviewing witnesses, this is an especially sensitive area. Given the current trend, it is generally not necessary or appropriate to interview a victim/witness on the issue of her prior sexual history. If the defense gives notice of an intention to raise any such factual issues, the legal team as a whole is best suited to assess the extent to which it is appropriate to interview the victim/witness in this regard. This is one of the few instances where extra rigor in interviewing a witness is undesirable.

FRE 412, P. 267

Although protections offered to victims under FRE 412 have removed some of the obstacles that previously prevented victims from charging sex crimes, the fact remains that rape and other forms of sexual assault have continued to be extremely difficult to prosecute. Incidences of repeat child molestation offenders and adult rapists escaping conviction in the past have been numerous. In response to the unique and especially troublesome problems associated with trying rape and child molestation cases, former Congresswoman Susan Molinari introduced legislation that dramatically changed the law as it relates to the admissibility of evidence in sex-related crimes. The rules allow evidence to be admitted as part of the prosecution's case in chief regarding other offenses committed by the accused.

FRE 413, P. 269

FRE 413 provides that in a criminal case for sexual assault, the defendant's commission of another offense or offenses of sexual assault is admissible and may be considered "for its bearing on any matter to which it is relevant." Although evidence of extrinsic offenses

FRE 404(b), P. 265

are narrowly admissible under FRE 404(b) to show motive or opportunity, and so forth, FRE 413 goes substantially further and, without any limiting instruction, allows the evidence.

FRE 414, P. 269

FRE 414 provides the same standards as FRE 413 for admissibility of extrinsic offense evidence that relates to child molestation cases.

FRE 415, P. 270

FRE 415 provides that evidence admissible under FRE 413 and 414 is also admissible in civil trials.

In each of the new rules, there are safeguards that require that the government disclose its intent to use evidence under these statutes and allow the defense time to argue against admissibility. Nothing in the statutes appears to preclude the court from weighing the evidence for its probative value versus its prejudicial effect pursuant to FRE 403, although some argue that the statutes could be interpreted in that manner.

It should be noted that the new statutes, FRE 413, 414, and 415, are extremely controversial. The Advisory Committee indicated its concern (discussed in the Judicial Conference report submitted to Congress) about the inconsistency between FRE 413-415 and FRE 403, 404, and 405. The Judicial Conference requested that Congress reconsider the new rules, or at least clarify them, and make them more specific and congruous with existing rules. Congress declined to take this recommendation.

Although some argue that the new rules conflict with existing rules, FRE 413, 414, and 415 are law; they have been used by the courts since 1995 and upheld on appeal. The following case illustrates one appellate court's approval of the implementation of FRE 412, FRE 413, and FRE 414. Courts generally do not permit the use of a minor's name in legal documents. Consequently, initials denote the minors' names in this case.

FRE 413, 414, 415, PP. 269-270

FRE 403, 404, 405, PP. 264-265

United States v. Withorn

204 F.3d 790 (8th Cir. 2000)

On July 7, 1998, Withorn beat and forcibly raped H.S., a 12-year-old girl, on the Crow Creek Sioux Indian Reservation. Withorn, an enrolled member of the Crow Creek Sioux Tribe, was 19 years old at the time and was on federal probation as a result of a juvenile conviction for a firearms offense.

*   *   *

The jury also heard from Sally Hill, a certified nurse midwife who conducted a sexual assault examination of H.S. early in the morning of July 8, 1998, at the Mid-Dakota Hospital in Chamberlain, South Dakota. Over the defense's objection that portions of her testimony constituted expert testimony offered without adequate foundation, Hill related her observation that H.S. had been "run through the mill." She described swelling, bruises, and scratches on various parts of H.S.'s body apparently resulting from "blunt trauma." Hill testified that during the course of the examination H.S. claimed that she had been struck, choked, and raped by Withorn. Hill stated that the injuries she observed were fully consistent with H.S.'s claim.

The government also called Withorn's cousin, R.M. to testify at trial. R.M. described how, when she was 12 years old, Withorn forcibly raped her in his car and later claimed that she had consented. . . .

*   *   *

As part of the defense, Withorn attempted to introduce evidence of a previous sexual assault accusation made by H.S. several years earlier against Chris Fallis, a teenage friend of Withorn who had committed suicide before the matter could be adjudicated. Withorn believed that H.S.'s allegation of forcible rape against Fallis, who claimed that H.S. had consented to intercourse, suggested a pattern of false accusations by H.S. During the jail-cell conversation with Krietlow, (another witness at trial) Withorn indicated his belief that such a pattern existed by stating that "the same thing happened to Chris Fallis." At trial, the court granted the government's motion to suppress this portion of Withorn's statement to Krietlow and prohibited the defense from introducing any other evidence about the Fallis incident.

*   *   *

The jury convicted Withorn on both counts, and the district court imposed concurrent sentences totaling 20 years' imprisonment.

Withorn argues that it was error to admit evidence of his past sexual assault while simultaneously excluding evidence that another man whom H.S. accused of sexual assault had claimed that she consented. We begin by analyzing these evidentiary decisions individually, and then consider their effect in combination. . . .

*   *   *

R.M.'s testimony that Withorn sexually assaulted her was admitted pursuant to Rules 413 and 414 of the Federal Rules of Evidence, recently enacted provisions that create exceptions to the general rule that evidence of past crimes may not be used "to prove the character of a person in order to show action in conformity therewith." (Citation) Rule 413 expressly permits the use of evidence of any past sexual assault offense "for its bearing on any matter to which it is relevant" in an ongoing sexual assault prosecution. Likewise, Rule 414 permits the introduction of evidence of past child molestation offenses in child molestation prosecutions. (Citation) The district court found the rules applicable in Withorn's case, and we agree.

In considering whether to admit evidence under Rule 413 and 414, federal district courts must still apply the "balancing test" of Rule 403, which calls for the exclusion of evidence whose probative value is substantially outweighed by its potential for unfair prejudice. (Citation) In doing so, however, courts must balance probative value against potential for unfair prejudice "in such a way as to allow the new rules their intended effect." (Citation) Thus, in determining the admissibility of R.M.'s testimony the district court was obligated to take into account Congress's policy judgment that Rule 413 was "justified by the distinctive characteristics of the cases it will affect," and that Rule 414 evidence is "exceptionally probative" of a defendant's sexual interest in children. (Citations)

In light of this "strong legislative judgment that evidence of prior sexual offenses should ordinarily be admissible," (Citation) we conclude that the district court did not abuse its discretion in allowing R.M. to testify. The incident R.M. described was substantially similar to H.S.'s experience with Withorn. The victims were approximately the same age at the time of the rapes, and both assaults involved force and occurred after Withorn had isolated the victims from others. Both victims also testified that immediately after the incident Withorn threatened them not to inform anyone what had occurred, and in each case Withorn's defense was to claim that the victim had consented to the sexual activity. Because of these parallels, R.M.'s testimony was probative evidence showing Withorn's propensity toward the type of behavior H.S. alleged.

*   *   *

In excluding evidence of H.S.'s prior allegation against Fallis, the district court relied on Rule 412, which generally prohibits evidence of the victim's past sexual behavior in sex offense cases. (Citation)

Withorn wished to introduce H.S.'s prior rape allegation against Fallis in the hope that the jury might infer that H.S. was lying based on the fact that both Fallis and Withorn claimed that she had consented to intercourse. A conclusion that H.S.'s unadjudicated accusation against Fallis was untrue, however, would have required the jury to rely on sheer speculation. Moreover, impeaching the victim's truthfulness and showing her capability to fabricate a story "are not recognized exception to Rule 412." (Citations) "In the absence of an applicable exception, Rule 412 specifically bars admission of evidence of the past sexual behavior of an alleged rape victim." (Citation) Accordingly, the district court acted well within its discretion in limiting the cross-examination of Krietlow to exclude Withorn's statement that "the same thing happened to Chris Fallis" and in preventing the defense from introducing any other evidence of H.S.'s allegedly false prior accusation.

*   *   *

The judgment of conviction is affirmed.

This case exemplifies the balancing test that courts will employ to weigh the probative value of any evidence against its prejudicial impact pursuant to FRE 403 which we examined in Chapter 2. But here the appellate court, in addition to assessing the evidence, explicitly deferred to the legislative intent of FRE 413 and FRE 414 and also strictly applied FRE 412. In approving the district court's decision to admit evidence of the prior sexual assault committed by the defendant on his minor female cousin, the appellate court listed the similarities between that sexual assault and offense against the victim in the case. Additionally, the appellate court strictly applied FRE 412. The appellate court was clear that the evidence of the victim's prior unadjudicated sexual assault allegation did not fall within the express exceptions of FRE 412, so the evidence was properly excluded.

As a paralegal, you may be asked to investigate into the accused's prior conduct. The evidence in the above case that the defendant similarly sexually assaulted another minor female surely had a persuasive influence on the jury. Often such evidence will be critical. So, although uncovering such conduct can be a difficult task especially in light of many victims' unwillingness to recall and to discuss the unpleasant experience, a diligent search is imperative.

3.6 Methods of Proving Character

So far in this chapter, we have addressed issues concerning the admissibility of evidence of character and character traits. The next issue we must discuss is how one introduces evidence of a person's character in court. The following paragraphs relate to the general case, and not to the specific exceptions carved out for sex crimes under FRE 413-415. One innovative paralegal student, when given a hypothetical involving an especially diabolical defendant and asked how she would present evidence to convey information about this man's character to the trier-of-fact, suggested drawing a mustache and horns on his photograph and presenting that to the jury as demonstrative evidence of his evil nature. If this was a clever idea, it's one whose time has not yet come. Evidentiary rules are, in general, extremely rigid and narrow on allowable methods of proving character.

FRE 405, P. 265

Methods of proving character are covered under FRE 405, which provides that to introduce evidence of character or a trait of character on direct examination, proof may be made only by testimony as to reputation or by testimony in the form of an opinion. At common law, in some jurisdictions only reputation evidence was admissible. The Advisory Committee opined, however, that reputation is nothing more than what one person perceives the opinion of others to be. Consequently, the Federal Rules of Evidence adopted a rule allowing the introduction of either opinion or reputation evidence to prove character.

You will learn about hearsay evidence and exceptions in Chapters 9 and 10. Because opinion evidence is based on the witness's own opinion regarding the pertinent character trait, the testimony is not hearsay. Reputation evidence, on the other hand, is based on what the witness has heard other people say and thus is hearsay but with an exception as provided by FRE 803(21).

Specific instances of conduct may not be inquired into on direct examination. If the defendant is reputed to be a nurturing person, this evidence is admissible as reputation testimony. The fact that he quit his job to nurse his sick child back to health, however, would not be something about which the defense attorney would be permitted to inquire because it describes a specific instance of conduct.

As mentioned earlier, however, on cross-examination the prosecutor may inquire into the specific acts of the defendant to rebut the character evidence proffered in the defendant's favor. If there are unpleasant incidences in the defendant's past relating to a pertinent character trait, the prosecution will attempt to inquire about these incidences on cross-examination of either the defendant or defendant's character witnesses. Therefore, when interviewing potential character witnesses, the paralegal should first ask questions to determine the witness's qualifications to testify about the party's character. Then, the paralegal should inquire whether the witness is aware of specific instances of conduct likely to be brought out on cross-examination. The following questions suggest the information that at a minimum should be obtained during the interview of a potential character witness.

FRE 803(21), P. 283

1. Can the witness identify the party?
2. How long has the witness known the party?
3. How often and under what circumstances has the witness seen or communicated with the party over the time he has known him?
4. What is the nature of the relationship between the witness and the party?
5. Does the witness know the party well enough to have formed an opinion of his character with respect to truthfulness, reliability, hostility, or whichever trait you wish to prove?
6. Does the witness know other people who know the party?
7. When and where does the witness converse with other people who know the witness about this character trait (or about the party's character)?
8. Does the party have a reputation for being truthful, reliable, or whatever?
9. What is that reputation?

10. Does the witness know of any specific instances of conduct that show this character trait?
11. Does the witness know of any specific instances of conduct that might contradict this character trait?
12. Can the witness provide information regarding such conduct?

Laying a Foundation
Providing preliminary evidence to identify, authenticate, and properly connect evidence to the issues in the case.

The first nine questions are designed to elicit information necessary to **lay a proper foundation** to qualify the witness to testify as to character and to ascertain what the testimony will be. The proponent needs to establish how the witness knows the reputation of the party, or on what basis the witness has been able to form an opinion, before the witness can testify as to what the reputation or opinion is. (Rules regarding witness competency are discussed later in this textbook.)

The last three questions on the list ask about specific instances of conduct, even though such evidence is not admissible on direct examination. However, since the opposing attorney is allowed to inquire about specific conduct on cross-examination, it is valuable to find out what may come out on cross-examination before the decision is made to call the witness to testify.

Recall the women who had the altercation in the unpublished case of *United States v. Herder*. There, the defense presented another witness to testify about the victim's reputation for violence. The testimony was stricken—read and laugh.

United States v. Herder

2003 WL 245092 (10th Cir. 2003)(unpublished opinion)

The defense presented Laura Yazzie as a reputation witness who would testify that Sheila had a reputation for violence in the community. When asked if she knew Sheila James, Yazzie responded, "no." Later she testified that she did not know who Sheila James was. After she was provided with an interpreter she again testified that she did not really know Sheila. She also testified that she did not know how many people she knew who knew Sheila.

After hearing the government's cross-examination, in which Yazzie again denied knowing Sheila, the district court struck Yazzie's testimony for lack of foundation. Appellants argue that this was error because any deficiencies in Yazzie's testimony went to the weight of, and not the foundation for, her testimony. We disagree.

*   *   *

A reputation witness must have "such acquaintance with the [person], the community in which he has lived and the circles in which he has moved as to speak with authority on the terms in which generally he is regarded." (Citations)

Yazzie's testimony, which was rife with equivocations and inconsistencies, evidenced her lack of familiarity with Sheila and her reputation in the community. The appellants did not give the court any additional evidence to suggest that Yazzie was familiar with Sheila or her community. The record supports the trial court's conclusion that there was insufficient foundation for Yazzie's testimony.

Yazzie's testimony is entertaining for us to read now, but imagine the defense attorney's horror upon hearing it at trial. Her testimony illustrates the necessity of thorough pretrial witness preparation. Or, it may illustrate that a witness will not testify as expected! In any event, the case demonstrates that proper foundation for the witness's testimony is a prerequisite to admissibility.

3.7 Character as an Essential Element of the Civil or Criminal Case

As mentioned earlier, there are a small number of causes of action in which character evidence may not be offered to prove conduct, but may be offered to prove character itself. In other words, there are times when character itself is an ultimate issue or an essential element in a case. For example, if there is a lawsuit for defamation of character, the character of the plaintiff is one of the issues that must be determined in order to determine if the plaintiff's character has, in fact, been defamed.

FRE 405(b), P. 239

The Federal Rules of Evidence address this type of character evidence in FRE 405(b). The rule uses the term "essential element." When character is an essential element, the issue of character must be resolved in order for the factfinder to reach a final decision in the case. Pursuant to 405(b), when character is an essential element in a case, proof may be made by reputation, opinion, or by proof of specific instances of the person's conduct.

Students frequently become confused when trying to determine when character is an essential element in a case. Consider the following example.

Assume Fast Eddie is charged with embezzlement. He denies embezzling funds and claims that any incorrect entries in the corporate books were inadvertent. Assume further that Fast Eddie likes to gamble and is reckless with money. Are Fast Eddie's gambling and money squandering character traits an essential element to proving Fast Eddie embezzled the funds?

Fast Eddie's character may appear to be essential to the case against him for embezzlement, but it is not an essential element within that term's legal meaning. The essential element in this hypothetical case is not whether Fast Eddie gambles or squanders money, but whether Fast Eddie embezzled the company money. Fast Eddie may be convicted of embezzlement without presenting one shred of character evidence.

The student should be careful not to confuse situations where character evidence appears to be extremely persuasive and situations where character evidence is an essential element in a cause of action. The quality of the evidence is irrelevant in determining whether or not character is an essential element. One looks to the cause of action itself to make the determination.

The student should be aware that character is only very rarely an ultimate issue in criminal proceedings. The only crime the authors could think of where character might be an essential element is in entrapment cases, and even then sometimes character is raised to the level of an ultimate question, and sometimes it isn't. This depends on whether the defense attempts to use character evidence to show the absence of predisposition on the part of the defendant to commit the charged crime. If the defense does introduce character evidence to try to prove that the defendant wouldn't have committed the crime without the government's inducement, then character becomes an essential element in the entrapment case. If the defendant does not introduce a character defense, character is not raised to an ultimate issue in the case.

Character is an essential issue in more causes of action in the civil domain than in the criminal setting. There are several types of civil cases where character is the essential element on which the outcome is based. For example:

- In a custody dispute where one parent is claiming the other is unfit, the character of the allegedly unfit parent is admissible because the parent's character or "fitness" is the ultimate question to be determined in the lawsuit.
- In an action for defamation, character evidence about the plaintiff is an essential element of the cause of action because truth is a defense to the charge. A person can say terrible things about someone without liability if everything they are saying is true. Assume Mouthy Smith is being sued by Slobbo Sam for defamation of character based on Mouthy's calling Slobbo a "sloppy drunk." Mouthy is allowed to introduce evidence of Slobbo's drunken behavior since whether or not Slobbo is a sloppy drunk is an ultimate issue in the case.
- In an action by an employee for unlawful discharge, when the employer raises as a defense that the employee was terminated for

cause, and if such cause was based on character traits such as tardiness, unreliability, excessive absenteeism, or incompetence, then evidence of such character traits is admissible because those traits are an essential element to the defense's case. (This is common in employment discrimination cases.)

FRE 405(b), P. 265

In each of the above types of cases, opinion and reputation evidence is admissible along with evidence of specific conduct pursuant to FRE 405(b), to prove the pertinent character traits. It should be noted again, however, that circumstances where character is an essential element of the case are not very common.

3.8   General Prohibition against Evidence of Other Crimes, Wrongs, or Acts to Prove Conduct in Civil and Criminal Cases

As mentioned earlier, proof of character ordinarily has to be introduced with reputation or opinion evidence. Inquiry into specific instances of conduct may only be made on cross-examination and only when character is put into issue by the defendant. Even where evidence of specific conduct is admissible on cross-examination pursuant to FRE 405(a), it is admissible only as it relates to proving (or disproving) character. It is not usable to prove conduct.

FRE 404(b), P. 265

In general, then, using evidence of other crimes, wrongs, or acts to prove conduct is prohibited. The Federal Rules of Evidence specifically address this issue in FRE 404(b), which states in relevant part, "(e)vidence of other crimes, wrongs, or acts is not admissible to prove the character of a person in order to show action in conformity therewith." In other words, you cannot use evidence of another wrongdoing to prove the conduct currently at issue except, of course, under the new sex crimes exceptions under FRE 412-415. Consider the following hypothetical.

Suppose defendant Harry were currently charged with unlawfully peeping into his neighbor's window. Evidence of past peeping would not be admissible to prove that Harry peeped this time.

Extrinsic Offense
An offense not charged or directly at issue in the current proceeding.

FRE 404(b) does go on, however, to allow the introduction of evidence of **extrinsic offenses** (other crimes, wrongs, or acts), when offered for "other purposes" than to prove conduct. A non-exhaustive list of other purposes is enumerated in FRE 404(b), and provides substantial openings through which to proffer evidence. We know that the enumerated examples in FRE 404(b) are not exhaustive because the Rule uses the words "such as" before providing specific illustrations.

3.9 Offering Extrinsic Evidence of Crimes, Wrongs, or Act's through the Back Door

FRE 404(b), P. 265

FRE 404(b) provides a very wide back door through which otherwise excludable evidence can be admitted. Under this rule, evidence of extrinsic offenses may be admitted if offering such things as "motive, opportunity, intent, preparation, plan, knowledge, identity, or absence of mistake or accident."

With this rule in mind, let's reconsider our hypothetical about Harry and his propensity to peep into the windows of his neighbor's house. Although his prior peeping would not be admissible to prove that he is guilty of peeping this time, it would be admissible for other purposes, such as to show absence of mistake or accident. Harry's past conduct provides circumstantial evidence that Harry intended to peep and wasn't just standing outside the neighbor's window by accident. The important thing for the prosecution is that if the evidence is allowed, the trier-of-fact has now heard evidence of Harry's prior peeping. The jurors may be given a limiting instruction telling them to only consider the evidence for the purpose for which it was admitted, but jurors, despite such instructions, are believed to incorporate such evidence into their overall impression of the case. By getting the evidence in through the "back door," the prosecution has given the jury evidence likely to create an impression that Harry has definite peeping propensities.

FRE 404(b), P. 265

Note: An example of a limiting instruction for evidence presented pursuant to FRE 404(b) is given in the case *United States v. Adcock*, 558 F.2d 397 (8th Cir. 1977). In this extortion case, the prosecution presented evidence of an extrinsic offense, and the trial court instructed the jury that such "evidence is only admissible to shed light on the possible motive or intent of the Defendant or the possible existence of a scheme or plan." The efficacy in limiting the jury's consideration of the evidence with this type of instruction is unclear.

The following is an excellent example of a case in which evidence of other acts was properly admissible pursuant to rule 404(b) to show intent.

United States v. Hillsberg

812 F.2d 328 (7th Cir. 1987)

On April 27, 1985, Earl Hillsberg spent the afternoon drinking with a number of companions at various bars. They adjourned to the home of one of the party, Charla Lyons, at about five in the afternoon.

At about seven, Hillsberg left in the company of several others. On the way to the next tavern, the driver pulled over to the side of the road to afford the passengers a chance to relieve themselves. Standing outside the car, Hillsberg drew a .22 caliber semi-automatic pistol from his waistband and fired it twice in the air. The driver of the car took the pistol, unloaded it, and returned the pistol and ammunition to Hillsberg. Hillsberg placed the gun and ammunition in separate pockets.

The group then continued to a saloon, the Morning Side. They became embroiled in a brawl with members of the Stockridge tribe. They retreated to the car, where Hillsberg fired twice in the direction of their pursuers. They next returned to a party at the Lyons home, arriving around midnight.

Hillsberg entered the den of the house, where Marvin Pamonicutt was located with several others. Hillsberg asked for some of Pamonicutt's bottle of malt liquor. Pamonicutt demurred at first, then complied. The two began "acting tough," puffing out their chests. Pamonicutt removed his coat. There were no threats or blows exchanged. There was no pushing, jostling, or argument. Abruptly, Hillsberg said, "Don't fuck with me." He removed the gun from his waistband and pointed it at Pamonicutt's face, at the range of less than a foot. The weapon discharged, fatally wounding Pamonicutt.

Hillsberg's memory of the night in question was limited. He testified that beginning with the drive to the Morning Side he felt "like I was just out of my body . . . I was real drunk and I was just like on— I don't know. I was just functioning." He did not recall firing the pistol during the impromptu rest stop or at the tavern. He testified that at the Lyons home Pamonicutt made him angry, but he did not know why. He testified that he did not intend to shoot Pamonicutt, that he took the gun out only to scare him. He testified further that the feeling of being out of his body, of being a spectator to his own actions, disappeared after the shooting.

*   *   *

Hillsberg contends that the court erred in admitting evidence of his two previous uses of the gun on the day of the killing. Under Federal Rule of Evidence 404(b):

> Evidence of other crimes, wrongs, or acts is not admissible to prove the character of a person in order to show that he acted in conformity therewith. It may, however, be admissible for other purposes, such as proof of motive, opportunity, intent, preparation, plan, knowledge, identity, or absence of mistake or accident.

The pivotal issue at trial in the present case was whether Hillsberg intended to shoot Pamonicutt. Hillsberg testified that he "pulled the gun out and brought it up and it went off." He denied intending to kill Pamonicutt. He also testified that he took the gun out only to scare Pamonicutt. Evidence that twice that day he had taken the gun out and fired tended to prove that he again fired it intentionally, that the discharge was not accidental or inadvertent. That he had twice that day demonstrated his control over the firearm tends to negate the possibility that he mishandled it on the third occasion.

AFFIRMED.

This case illustrates an important principle about the use of circumstantial evidence. Remember that in a case in which the prosecution is using circumstantial evidence, the prosecutor can suggest to the jury inferences that can be drawn from the evidence presented. In the *Hillsberg* case, the defendant shot the victim at point blank range. In unrelated circumstances, the defendant had used his gun twice earlier in the day, shooting into the air. In this case, the prosecution was able to successfully argue that the prior acts of shooting provided circumstantial evidence suggesting that when the defendant shot directly at the victim, it was intentional. The evidence came in

FRE 404(b), P. 265

under 404(b) to prove intent and to impeach the witness's own account of his intent at the time of the fatal shooting.

The above case was a criminal case. However, evidence of "other crimes, wrongs, or acts" not offered to prove character but rather offered for "other purposes, such as proof of motive, opportunity, intent, preparation, plan, knowledge, identity, or absence of mistake or accident" under FRE 404(b) may be admissible in both criminal and civil cases. FRE 404(b) refers to the "accused," the "prosecution," and a "criminal case"—but only in the context of the accused requesting and the prosecution providing notice of the prosecution's intent to use the "other purposes" evidence in a criminal case. Therefore, unlike FRE 404(a), which now clearly precludes the use of character evidence to prove conduct in civil trials, FRE 404(b) allows evidence of "other crimes, wrongs, or acts" in both criminal and civil cases.

As a paralegal, you must be careful not to overlook those pieces of information in police reports or witness interviews that may not be obviously or directly relevant. Considering evidence in light of all the options for admissibility, front or back door, under one rule or several rules, for a single or multiple purpose, is strategically essential. In the *Hillsberg* case, the uneventful uses of the gun earlier in the day would, at first glance, seem irrelevant to the murder. The prosecutor, however, used this evidence in a critical aspect of the case to show intent and to impeach the defendant. Had it been overlooked or had the prosecutor not known of it, this evidence would not have been admitted, the prosecutor would not have been able to suggest inferences from it to the trier-of-fact regarding the defendant's intent, and the case might have had a different outcome.

3.10   The Battle between FRE 403 and FRE 404(b)

FRE 403, P. 264

FRE 404(b) is not without limitations. Like other rules we have discussed, it is limited by the court's ability to protect against unfair prejudice pursuant to FRE 403. Countless appellate cases have grappled with the issues surrounding whether the probative value of the admission of evidence of an extrinsic offense is substantially outweighed by the danger of unfair prejudice. It might be said that FRE 404(b) and FRE 403 are designed to battle each other. Whether a proffered extrinsic offense is sufficiently probative to get past a 403 objection depends on factors too numerous and too inconclusive to be worthy of the effort. There are no hard and fast rules, and decisions vary widely from court to court. The paralegal must nonetheless be aware of the issues and know when a problem is likely to evolve, even if the outcome isn't predictable with any certainty. Therefore, the authors present a series of examples to familiarize the reader with the types of situations that may evolve when Rules 403 and 404(b) are in conflict.

FRE 404(b) can be applied in both criminal and civil actions. Although one most often thinks of evidence of extrinsic offenses in the context of criminal trials, it can be extremely important in civil trials as well. Consider the following.

Dr. Bigfake put an ad in the local newspaper advertising a tonic that cures warts forever. Weird Walter has spent his life plagued with warts, and so he inquired about the tonic using the toll-free number provided in the advertisement. He was called back several times by Dr. Bigfake's "wart" consultants who advised him that he needed a year's supply of tonic since his case was so serious. The cost was $1,000, but results were "guaranteed." One year later, poor Weird Walter was still covered with warts and was out his $1,000. He sued for fraud and for punitive damages.

In the course of the lawsuit, Weird's attorney introduced evidence over Dr. Bigfake's objection that Dr. Bigfake had, just two years prior, entered into a "consent decree" (settlement agreement) with the Food and Drug Administration (FDA) barring him from advertising a tonic purporting to remove freckles but totally ineffective to that end.

FRE 404(b), P. 265

Under FRE 404(b), evidence of Dr. Bigfake's consent decree with the FDA was admissible for the limited purpose of showing his knowledge and intent, both of which are required to prove punitive damages. Since the consent decree Dr. Bigfake entered into with the FDA involved practices very similar to those in Weird Walter's case, the consent decree was admissible to show Dr. Bigfake's state of mind, even though it would not have been admissible to prove Dr. Bigfake's conduct with regard to the wart tonic. Since this evidence was extremely probative of intent, it survived an FRE 403 objection as being more probative than unfairly prejudicial.

Extrinsic offense evidence is perhaps more restricted in criminal proceedings than in civil ones, because the danger of unfair prejudice is scrupulously avoided when incarceration of an individual is a potential outcome of the proceeding. Still, the discretion of the trial court is wide, the outcomes vary greatly, and the court's discretion will generally not be disturbed on appeal.

The following is an example of a court's precluding the introduction of FRE 404(b) evidence of a past crime to prove intent because it found the evidence too highly prejudicial.

Sam Slime was charged with defrauding investors in a sham real estate enterprise. Eight years prior, Sam had written $2,000 worth of bad checks to several local vendors and had been charged with two felony counts as a result. These charges had eventually been dropped when Sam was able to pay off the victims, and the matter was considered resolved as a result of a "civil compromise." Evidence of Sam's prior bad check incidents was not admitted in the pending case because of the prejudicial nature of the evidence, the length of time that had elapsed since the time the bad checks had been written, and the limited probative value of the evidence to show intent in the current fraud scheme.

FRE 403, P. 264

In the following example, the court allowed the introduction of 404(b) evidence of a past crime over an objection under FRE 403.

D. Lowlife was charged with the murder of V. Stoolie. In an uncharged prior offense, V. Stoolie and D. Lowlife had allegedly committed a crime together. V. Stoolie was the only one charged, but he was talking to the state about a plea bargain that involved testifying against D. Lowlife. D. Lowlife had motive to kill V. Stoolie if he feared V. Stoolie was going to turn against him in court. Prosecution was allowed to present limited evidence of the uncharged prior offense to show D. Lowlife's motive and state of mind.

The following case is a recent example of one court's analysis of the fight between FRE 404(b) and FRE 403. In this case, the defendant Mohr, a police officer, was charged with conspiracy and with unlawfully releasing her police dog in violation of federal law. She was acquitted of conspiracy in the first trial, but because the jury could not reach a verdict as to the substantive charge, a second trial ensued on the unlawful use of the police dog charge. Defendant Mohr was convicted and appealed. On appeal, she contested the district court's rulings admitting several FRE 404(b) acts, one of which is included in this excerpt of the case.

United States v. Mohr

318 F.3d 613 (4th Cir. 2003)

At approximately 2 a.m., Officer Brantley spotted two men on the roof of the Sligo Press building. He called for assistance and several Takoma Park officers, including Sergeant Dennis Bonn, responded. Bonn then asked for assistance from Prince George's County and specifically requested a K-9 dog. Prince George's K-9 officers Mohr and Anthony Delozier arrived with Mohr's police dog.

*   *   *

As the suspects stood with their hands in the air, Delozier approached Bonn and asked: "Sarge, can the dog get a bite?" Bonn "responded with one word, which was yes." Bonn testified that "[a]t that time, [the suspects] still had their hands in the air and weren't doing anything." Bonn then witnessed Delozier and Mohr have a very, very brief exchange, followed by Mohr releasing the dog. The dog attacked Mendez, who "still had has hands in the air when . . . the dog bit him in the leg. [He] went down screaming and continued to scream."

*   *   *

Mohr also contends that the district court abused its discretion in admitting testimony regarding her threat to release her police dog on Jocilyn Hairston's "black ass" if Hairston lied about the whereabouts of her fugitive brother. Hairston, her mother, and Mohr testified about the incident.

*   *   *

In July, 1998, Hairston, an African-American woman about thirty-seven years old, and her mother lived in Capitol Heights, Maryland. One evening, some time after 11:30 p.m., (sic) three officers arrived at Hairston's home looking for her brother, who had violated his probation in California. Mohr, accompanied by a police dog, was one of these officers. After the officers learned from Hairston that her brother was not here, one of the male officers asked if they could search the house. Hairston replied "sure." While they searched, Mohr and the dog remained on the top step of the stoop and Hairston asked Mohr if she could move because she was "scared of the dog," who was jumping up. Mohr said no. Hairston testified that Mohr then said: "I'm going to let him in. He's going to bite your black ass and your brother if I find out he's in there." Mohr's tone of voice and demeanor were "nasty" when she "said the comment about the black ass."

*   *   *

We again apply the four factors for admissibility of evidence under Rule 404(b). As with the Sneed evidence, (another 404(b) act admitted) Mohr does not contest the reliability of the Hairston evidence. With regard to relevance, she argues that the Hairston incident and the release of the dog on Mendez are not sufficiently similar because Mohr never released her dog on Hairston. But the purpose of the 404(b) evidence in this case was to establish that Mohr possessed the requisite state of mind—willfulness—when she released her dog on Mendez. Mohr's threat to release her dog on an unresisting, innocent citizen goes to that essential question of willfulness, regardless of whether she actually released the dog. . . . (Citation) Thus, the evidence was relevant. We also conclude, for the reasons discussed with regard to the Sneed incident, that evidence of the Hairston incident was necessary and not unfairly prejudicial.

We do address, however, one specific argument that Mohr raises as to the asserted prejudicial nature of the Hairston evidence. Mohr contends that, even if the district court properly found the evidence admissible, the court should have redacted any reference to Hairston's "black ass" as "extremely prejudicial." Of course a district court should, when possible, eliminate inflammatory language. In this instance, however, we agree with the district judge that the "black ass" portion of Mohr's threat cannot be reasonably separated from the threat itself.

Without that phrase, Mohr could argue that Hairston misunderstood her or that she merely issued a legitimate warning. Indeed, in her appellate brief, Mohr argues precisely this: "[A]ll Ms. Mohr did—sans the alleged racism—was warn that she would release the dog if and only if it were established that the residents were lying to police, that they were harboring a known fugitive who was suspected of armed bank robbery." The "black ass" portion of Mohr's remark could not be redacted from the remainder of it without changing the meaning of that remark. Therefore, the district court did not abuse its discretion in not redacting it.

The excerpt above refers to a four-part test used by courts to evaluate and weigh whether evidence should be admissible under FRE 404(b). The evidence must be (1) relevant to an issue in the case; (2) probative of an issue, essential claim, or an element of the offense; (3) reliable; and (4) admissible under FRE 403 in that its prejudicial nature does not substantially outweigh its probative value.

Offering evidence pursuant to the "other purpose" exceptions under FRE 404(b) should always be considered, if offering the evidence directly as proof of conduct is prohibited. The courts are aware, however, of the enormous potential for abuse that exists with exceptions that are as broad as those under 404(b). Therefore, the courts will scrutinize such offers of proof scrupulously. Finally, be mindful that FRE 404(b) requires the prosecution to give notice if it intends to use such evidence.

3.11   In Summary

- Character evidence is evidence that describes the nature or disposition of a person or the way it is anticipated that a person will act under certain circumstances.
- Character evidence is generally inadmissible to prove that a person did, in fact, act in a specific way at a specific time.
- A criminal defendant may introduce pertinent character evidence about himself or about the victim to help prove his innocence.
- Traditionally, in a criminal case, a prosecutor could introduce rebuttal character evidence about the accused only if the accused "opened the door" by introducing a pertinent character trait about him or herself first. Now, if the accused offers a pertinent character trait about the victim, the prosecutor may rebut with the same character trait about the accused.
- Character evidence is inadmissible in civil cases to prove that a person acted in the same way in "question" as the person had acted in the past.
- Character is ordinarily proved by reputation or opinion testimony. On cross-examination, the opponent may question about specific instances of conduct to contradict the character evidence, but generally cannot call new witnesses to testify about specific instances of conduct which refute the character trait.
- In rape cases, evidence of the past sexual behavior of the victim may not be proffered by the accused unless it is screened prior to trial and is relevant to the identity of the alleged rapist or to past sexual behavior by the victim with the accused.

- In rape and child molestation cases, evidence of other similar offenses may be admitted against the accused for any relevant purpose, despite the general rule against "propensity" evidence being admissible to prove guilt.
- If character is an essential element in a case, then specific incidences of conduct are admissible to prove character.
- Evidence of extrinsic offenses (other crimes, wrongs, or acts) is inadmissible to prove conduct but admissible to prove other things, such as motive, intent, preparation, plan knowledge, identity, or absence of mistake.
- Evidence of extrinsic offenses is carefully scrutinized by the courts for potential unfair prejudice.

End of Chapter Review Questions

1. What is character evidence?
2. When is character evidence admissible to prove conduct in civil cases?
3. Who may raise the issue of the accused's character in a criminal case?
4. When may the prosecution present testimony regarding the character of the accused?
5. Who may raise the issue of the victim's character in a criminal case, and under what conditions?
6. Is the prior sexual history of a rape victim generally admissible if proffered by the accused as part of his defense?
7. What are the two methods of proving character?
8. When is character an essential element in a case?
9. Under what circumstances may evidence of extrinsic offenses be admitted in a criminal proceeding?
10. How do FRE 403 and FRE 404(b) interact?
11. When may evidence of extrinsic offenses by the accused be used to prove guilt in sexual assault or child molestation cases?

Applications

Consider the following hypothetical situation.

Brutus is accused of brutally murdering his former girlfriend Ruth. He has denied the charges against him. Brutus has a reputation for having threatened and abused Ruth.

Three emergency 911 calls to the police were recorded prior to the murder. In each of these calls, Ruth can be heard asking for help, having just been threatened, or in one case beaten, by Brutus.

1. What arguments could you make pursuant to the Federal Rules of Evidence described in this chapter to keep evidence of Brutus's reputation out of the courtroom?

   Suppose that Brutus calls a witness to testify that he is a kind and loving parent.

2. What arguments could you make to exclude this character evidence?
3. What arguments could you make to include this character evidence?
4. Would Brutus be wise to introduce character evidence of this sort? Why or why not?
5. As a member of the defense team, what arguments would you make to keep evidence of the 911 calls out?
6. As a member of the prosecution team, what arguments would you make to get evidence of the 911 calls in?
7. If Brutus were accused of both the rape and murder of Ruth, would any of your answers be different? Why or why not?

4

Habit and *Modus Operandi*

4.1 Habit Defined

Habit
One's regular, nearly automatic, response to a repeated situation.

FRE 406, P. 266

Habit can be defined as a persons ordinary, regular response in a situation that repeats itself. Unfortunately, this definition is not easily distinguishable from the definition of character discussed in the previous chapter. We defined character there, in part, as the way a person would probably act under certain circumstances. Although the differences between the definitions of character and habit may be slight, characterizing evidence as relating to one or the other carries substantial legal consequence. Therefore, it is important to be able to differentiate character evidence from evidence of habit. In the Advisory Committee's Notes to FRE 406 (quoting McCormick), there is the following analysis.

> Character and habit are close akin. Character is a generalized description of one's disposition, or of one's disposition in respect to a general trait,

such as honesty, temperance, or peacefulness. "Habit," in modern usage, both lay and psychological, is more specific. It describes ones regular response to a repeated specific situation. If we speak of character for care, we think of the person's tendency to act prudently in all the varying situations of life, in business, family life, in handling automobiles, and in walking across the street. A habit, on the other hand, is the person's regular practice of meeting a particular kind of situation with a specific type of conduct, such as the habit of going down a particular stairway two stairs at a time, or of giving the hand-signal for a left turn, or of alighting from railway cars while they are moving. The doing of the habitual acts may become semiautomatic.

The Federal Rules of Evidence treat "habit" much differently from "character." Under FRE 406, evidence of habit is relevant "to prove that the conduct of the person or organization on a particular occasion was in conformity with the habit or routine practice." This is a huge leap from the limited purposes for which character evidence is admitted under the rules described in the previous chapters. Although the legal treatment of "habit" and "character" are widely different, the definitions of the two phenomena are not always so **distinguishable**.

Distinguishable
Capable of being differentiated or separately identified.

Think back to our "toilet seat" hypothetical in the previous chapter. You may well ask, given the above definition, why we analyzed it in terms of "character" rather than "habit." Recall, after all, Wanda's accusation was that Harry "always" leaves the toilet seat up. The reality is that because of the voluntary, nonroutinized nature of the conduct, the court will simply refuse to identify such conduct as "habit." Had Harry really "always" comported himself that way, Wanda would not have been surprised. Harry's objectionable conduct was undoubtedly repetitive and annoying, but it cannot be legally construed to be habit. In coauthor Marlowe's experience as a prosecutor, she has never been able to convince a judge to raise a character trait, no matter how pervasive, to the level of "habit" for qualification under FRE 406 in a criminal trial.

FRE 406, P. 266

This is confusing to everyone, so don't feel badly if these concepts are troublesome. As a general rule, keep in mind that although the distinction between habit and character is blurred and the cases are inconclusive, the tendency of the courts is to err on the side of "character," where there is an argument to be made.

4.2   **Habit as an Organizational Function**

The clearest application of the habit rule is where an organization, or an individual working for an organization, testifies to the routine process that the organization undertakes under given circumstances.

This is important when you are trying to use the organizations custom, pattern, or practice to circumstantially show that such custom, pattern, or practice was followed in your case. For example, when someone works in the mailroom, she can testify as to how she sorts, records, and distributes mail. It would be unlikely that such a person would be able to remember the specific treatment afforded one particular letter. However, habit evidence would be a good indicator of how a specific item running through that organizational system would have been treated. Habit evidence doesn't conclusively prove that the mail was treated in the habitual manner, but it is good circumstantial evidence to that effect.

FRE 406 specifically eliminates the requirement for **corroborating** evidence or for an eyewitness to testify as to whether a routine was followed on a specific occasion. Given that most people would not be able to recall a single matter out of potentially thousands of routine transactions, injustice would result if the rule required such corroborative testimony.

FRE 406 is silent as to the manner of proof required to introduce habit evidence either for organizations or for individuals. The field is wide open to allow testimony about specific instances of conduct, general routine, or ordinary usage to prove habit. Keep in mind, however, one must always be wary of FRE 403's prohibition against unfair prejudice, which will be discussed below.

In gathering proof of organizational habit, you would look for testimony from competent witnesses (those who are in a position to know), to testify as to the specific nature of the organizational routine that is ordinarily followed. Competent witnesses may not include the actual "doer," that is, the one who put the mail in the chute or stamped the paper with the date. The more remedial the job, the more likely the person who actually performed it is a temporary employee or an individual who has spent little time on that particular job. The witness who is knowledgeable about the routine, such as a supervisor or line manager, is the appropriate competent witness in this situation. During an interview, you would need to find out the following information.

- What position does the witness hold in the organization?
- How long has the witness held that position?
- In that position, has the witness observed the routine or habit of the organization with respect to your area of inquiry?
- What has the witness observed?
- How often has the witness observed this?
- What specific instances of this behavior has the witness observed, if any?
- Has the witness observed variations of this behavior? If yes, what has the witness observed?

FRE 406, P. 266

Corroborating
Other evidence supporting the same point.

FRE 403, P. 264

Although the types of evidence admissible to prove habit are broad, the standard for establishing habit is a tight one. An interesting case, too voluminous to include in this text in its entirety, is summarized and then partly quoted in relevant part below to illustrate how a lower court assumed too much in "interpreting" habit. In its decision to reverse, the Fourth Circuit Court of Appeal gave some stringent guidelines for properly laying a foundation to establish "habit."

Wilson v. Volkswagen of America

561 F.2d 494 (4th Cir. 1977)

SUMMARY

In this case, plaintiff driver sued Volkswagen of America for an alleged design defect in the manufacture and assembly of the Volkswagen vehicle he had been driving at the time of a serious accident. Plaintiff Wilson claimed the design defect caused the vehicle to become unstable, which in turn caused the accident in which he was seriously injured.

Defendants were requested, in the ordinary course of discovery, to produce records and film coverage of all crash tests conducted during a certain time period with regard to steering "flexible coupling." No such evidence was produced, and the court entered a default judgment against Volkswagen. Volkswagen strenuously objected to this, because it claimed that the reason it didn't produce any such test results was because *it didn't have any.* The trial court didn't believe Volkswagen's witnesses, believing instead that pursuant to the trial judge's understanding of German "habits," Volkswagen was concealing or deliberately not producing the flexible coupling tests. The Appellate Court took an opposite view, quoted as follows:

*   *   *

[T]here may have been flexible coupling tests conducted while the Volkswagen Beetle was being developed and prepared for marketing in the 1930s but, if so, those tests had long since been lost or abandoned and were no longer "available." The . . . Motion only called for tests on the Beetle between 1966 and 1972 and the witnesses said that no flexible coupling tests were conducted during this period. The witnesses proceeded to explain that the Beetle had been on the market since the 1930s, over 50,000,000 had been sold, there had never been a claim of any defect in the design or operation of the flexible coupling until this case, and the flexible coupling was substantially the same as that used on other cars. For this reason, the defendants

asserted there would have been no occasion for them, after the introduction of the model, to test later for safety a mechanism that had
been used for decades without any subsequent claim of defect or
danger. In substantial part, this testimony had been confirmed previously in the testimony by deposition of the plaintiff's own expert
witnesses. Despite all this, the findings of the District Court . . . contain no statement of reasons for finding this explanation unconvinc-
ing or incredible . . .

It is true the Court did suggest during the testimony of
[Volkswagen attorney] Ceresney, two reasons why it may have
found the explanation with reference to the flexible coupling tests
untrustworthy. Both reasons dealt with the testimony that any tests
conducted in the 1930s had been lost, discarded, or destroyed. The
Court said, first, that it was not in character for a German organization
ever to destroy or discard anything. In proof of this, it said:

"Don't you know that the Germans have the marching orders
from the Franco-Prussian War and are preserved in the German
Reich? They haven't destroyed anything."

The second reason was that it was, the Court stated, the custom of
automobile manufacturers to retain permanently all records of tests.
When the defendants' counsel expressed some doubt about such a
custom or practice, the Court replied, "I told you what the custom
was." Neither of these reasons assigned by the Court for disbelieving
the defendants' explanations is persuasive. The mere fact that the
German War Office may have retained for many years certain
military records does not support a finding that all German
commercial organizations preserve permanently all their records
any more than do any other commercial organizations. Nor can a
custom be established on the part of automobile manufacturers,
without proof, merely on a judicial ["I said so"].

*   *   *

. . . Existence of usage or custom can only be proved by numerous
instances of actual practices, and not by opinion of a witness. A
person seeking to establish custom or usage has the burden of proving
it by evidence so clear, uncontradictory, and distinct as to leave no
doubt as to its nature and character.

*   *   *

REVERSED and REMANDED.

This case is important for two reasons. First, it was refreshing to
read the sentence in this case, "Nor can a custom be established on the

part of automobile manufacturers, without proof, merely on a judicial [I said so]." Coauthor Marlowe has been told by more than one judge, "I am the rule, Ms. Marlowe." Its nice to know that the Fourth Circuit Court of Appeal disagrees.

Second, this case gives clear guidelines as to what must be established in order to prove "habit."

- The habit must be proved by numerous instances of actual practices.
- It cannot be proved by opinion evidence.
- The evidence must be clear, uncontradictory, and distinct.

As you might imagine, the burden of proving habit is not one to be met lightly.

4.3   Proving the Habit of an Individual

FRE 406, P. 266

The standards for proving habit or custom are extremely rigorous where habit is being used to try and prove individual conduct in criminal cases. As noted above, in practice it is extremely difficult to introduce such testimony about an individual under FRE 406. The court expects proof of habit to reflect a "regular practice of meeting a particular kind of situation with a certain type of conduct, or a reflex behavior in a specific set of circumstances." *Frase v. Henry,* 444 F.2d 1228 (10th Cir. 1971).

There are many examples of cases in which "habit" has not been allowed, even though it appears logical that such evidence should have been admitted. The following example might be typical.

Homeless Harry is frequently seen walking around town talking to himself. He has been arrested five times in the past two years for public intoxication. This has been held to be inadmissible to prove a "habit" of public drunkenness.

However, there are occasions where the court has allowed testimony to prove conduct in accordance with habit, and therefore the legal assistant cannot overlook that possibility when organizing a case for trial. In each of the following two situations, the court allowed individual "habits" to be introduced under FRE 406 to prove the current charges.

1. D. Deadbeat was charged with tax evasion for the years 1974 and 1975. In the case brought against him, testimony about Mr. Deadbeat's failure to file tax returns in 1971, 1972, 1976, 1977, and 1978 was admissible as habit evidence tending to show that the defendant failed to file tax returns in the charged years.

2. In a case charging Brutus Jones with assaulting a police officer, the court allowed evidence under FRE 406 that the defendant had a "habit" of reacting violently to uniformed police officers, even though the court recognized that such an admission of testimony was extraordinary. In this case, there were eight officers willing to testify that on numerous different occasions, when Mr. Jones was approached by a uniformed police officer, he had become extremely violent. The court allowed only four of the officers to testify, believing this to be sufficient to establish "habit." This was affirmed on appeal.

FRE 404(b), P. 265

In both of these cases, some evidence might be admissible under FRE 404(b), which, as discussed in Chapter 3, allows evidence of "other acts" to prove such things as motive, intent, and so on. If, for example, Mr. Deadbeat in the first example tried to imply that his failure to file tax returns was unintentional or a result of oversight, evidence of the "other acts" of failing to file during the noncharged years might well be admissible to show intent. However, under FRE 404(b), character evidence may not be introduced to show that the defendant acted in conformity therewith. The judge allows the evidence under Rule 404(b) with a limiting instruction distinguishing its use from the ordinary use of evidence to prove conduct. The benefit to the prosecution of introducing habit evidence is that habit evidence is relevant to show that the conduct of the person on a particular occasion was in fact in conformity with the habit you've proved.

Obviously, the testimony in the above two examples would be extremely influential in a jury trial. One would be hard-pressed to hear such evidence and not find a guilty verdict given the habitual histories presented. It is logical to wonder, then, when such evidence *wouldn't* be "unfairly prejudicial," pursuant to FRE 403. It could be argued that the court should always exclude such evidence under FRE 403.

FRE 403, P. 264

Keep in mind, however, that the individual still has the opportunity to show that in the particular instance charged, she or he did not act in conformity, with usual habit. The court can give the jury a limiting instruction, reminding the jurors that although the evidence suggests certain things, it is not conclusive. The court can also mitigate the effects of the habit evidence by controlling the amount of testimony that comes in so as not to overwhelm the jury. For example, in the preceding hypothetical involving Mr. Jones, the court allowed only four officers to testify to establish habit, rather than allowing all eight of the available witnesses to give testimony.

Also, keep in mind that the purpose of all the Rules of Evidence is to assist a trier-of-fact in ascertaining the truth, while using as many safeguards as reasonable. Although the habit evidence in the preceding hypotheticals is extremely prejudicial, given the "clear, uncontradictory, and distinct" evidence about the character of the individuals in question, it isn't necessarily *"unfairly"* prejudicial. The safeguards can reasonably be said to be in place even though the evidence has been allowed.

4.4   Proving the Habit of an Individual Who Follows a Professional Routine

There are many instances where professional routine is admissible as habit evidence. Frequently this occurs with witnesses who are employed in the medical profession. When medical testimony is introduced in a case, it is often necessary to rely on FRE 406 to ascertain the treatment a physician or other medical practitioner has used in a given situation.

Assume you work for Attorney Jackson who is representing client Clyde, who claims that he was poisoned by eating tainted food in a local restaurant. Dr. Green was the examining physician at the emergency room, who first saw Clyde after he became ill. Dr. Green administered several tests in the emergency room, and Attorney Jackson wishes to question her about the specific procedures she employed in administering those tests. Dr. Green has no specific recollection of the exact procedure she followed with regard to Clyde. She has seen literally hundreds of patients and administered some or all of those same tests to emergency patients on an almost daily basis. She can therefore testify as to the procedure she generally uses, without needing to specifically recall the procedure she used on your client.

This type of habit evidence is not without restriction, however. In order to be admissible, it must be shown that the physician administered the same tests in the same way with each patient as she did with the plaintiff. The following is an interesting case where evidence was found not to be admissible since it failed to adequately establish habit.

Weil v. Seltzer

873 F.2d 1453 (D.C Cir. 1989)

*   *   *

We do not believe the evidence of Dr. Seltzer's treatment of five former patients constitutes habit as envisioned by Rule 406. In deciding whether conduct amounts to "habit" significant factors include the "adequacy of sampling and uniformity of responses." Fed. R. Evid. 406 Advisory Committees note. Thus, one of the concerns over the reliability of habit testimony is that the conduct at issue may not have occurred with sufficient regularity making it more probable than not that it would be carried out in every instance or in most instances. This concern is not allayed by the former patient testimony because none of the former patients had ever observed Dr. Seltzer with another patient. Before the former patient evidence could be properly admitted as habit evidence the witnesses "must have some knowledge of the practice and must demonstrate this knowledge prior to giving testimony concerning the routine practice. Where a witness cannot demonstrate such knowledge, he cannot testify as to the routine nature of the practice." . . . Each witness who testified against Dr. Seltzer only knew of the way Dr. Seltzer treated his own allergies. Although they each saw Dr. Seltzer on more than one occasion, he was treating the same patient (the testifying witness) on each occasion. None of the patients were able to testify concerning Dr. Seltzer's method of treating others. Dr. Seltzer's actions might constitute habit only if he reacted the same way each time he was presented with a new patient with allergies. For the former patient testimony to be at all probative it must show that Dr. Seltzer responded the same way with each patient as he did with the testifying patient.

Weil's estate emphasizes the failure to contradict the testimony of Dr. Seltzer's former patients, noting that evidence concerning Dr. Seltzer's treatment of his other patients was within appellant's control. We note, however, that the admissibility of habit evidence under Rule 406 does not hinge on the ability of the party seeking exclusion of the evidence to disprove the habitual character of the evidence. Rather, the burden of establishing the habitual nature of the evidence rests on the proponent of the evidence.

Evidence concerning Dr. Seltzer's treatment of five former patients is not of the nonvolitional, habitual type that ensures its probative value. Rather the former patient evidence is the type of character evidence contemplated under Rule 404(b). This evidence of Dr. Seltzer's treatment of the former patients was clearly an attempt to show that Dr. Seltzer treated Weil in conformity with his treatment of the five testifying patients. Thus the evidence was admitted for an improper purpose and was undoubtedly prejudicial to appellant's defense.

We note that under Rule 404(b) the former patient evidence may have been admissible for other purposes, i.e., to show plan, knowledge, identity, or absence of mistake or accident. Indeed, Judge Oberdorfer ruled in the first trial that the evidence could be introduced for that purpose. We, of course, express no view on the correctness of that ruling since that issue is not before us in this case.

Accordingly, the admission of this prejudicial evidence under the standard of "habit" requires us to vacate the district court's judgment.

*   *   *

REVERSED and VACATED.

In the above case, the doctor had died after the lawsuit started, so obviously he was not available to testify about his regular medical routine. None of the witnesses called could testify, "Dr. Seltzer always did it this way." They could testify only as to how Dr. Seltzer performed in their individual presence. In this court's view, the plaintiff needed a witness to testify that he or she was in a position to observe the doctor always comporting himself in a certain way. A nurse or medical assistant might be an appropriate witness in these circumstances. This may seem unfair. If several witnesses can testify they were all treated identically, it is not unreasonable to assume that the physician habitually so treated his patients. However, the fact that the proponent can show numerous instances of a certain practice is, in itself, insufficient to prove habit.

As can be expected, courts will disagree on what evidence is sufficient to establish admissible "habit" evidence. The case below illustrates that a sole, uncorroborated witness's testimony is sufficient to establish his own habit in his business practice and that the "habit" testimony is sufficient to convict a defendant.

United States v. Ware

282 F.3d 902 (6th Cir. 2002)

*   *   *

This case arises from [defendant] Ware's role in a scheme designed to defraud insurance companies. Ware participated in the scheme by intentionally providing false information on applications for hospital indemnity policies. The type of policy in question pays a fixed-dollar benefit directly to the insured for each day that the insured spends in the hospital. Ware and his girlfriend, Marie Long, eventually obtained 12 such policies that listed Ware as the insured. Long later filed false claims under the policies that she and Ware had fraudulently obtained.

*   *   *

Turning now to the jury's guilty verdict on Count 10, Ware contends that the government failed to prove beyond a reasonable doubt that he submitted a false insurance application to Mutual of Omaha. Ware acknowledges that Mutual of Omaha received a false application in his name, but he maintains that Long forged his signature on that application.

To prove that Ware completed and personally signed the Mutual of Omaha insurance application, the government offered the testimony of Mitch Wilson. Wilson, an insurance agent, testified that he processed an application for a Mutual of Omaha hospital indemnity policy that bore Ware's signature. Although he conceded that he could not recall personally meeting with Ware during the application process, which occurred approximately four years prior to Ware's trial, Wilson nevertheless explained that it is his "standard procedure" to meet with every insurance applicant. He testified that, during such a meeting, he asks the applicant each of the questions on the insurance application, fills in the answers given by the applicant, and then witnesses the applicant's signature. Wilson further stated that he had no reason to believe that this standard procedure was not followed with regard to Ware's application.

Ware argues that Wilson's testimony was insufficient to prove that he submitted the application to Mutual of Omaha. We disagree. Wilson testified that he routinely interviews insurance applicants and observes them sign their applications. The jury could have reasonably inferred from this testimony that Wilson followed his standard procedure in processing Ware's application, and that Ware therefore signed the application. . . .

For the reasons set forth above, we hold that the district court correctly determined that the jury's guilty verdict on Count 10 is supported by sufficient evidence.

The court in Dr. Seltzer's case may have similarly ruled if Dr. Seltzer had been alive to testify as to his medical routine.

FRE 404(b), P. 265

As evidence is assembled, the paralegal may well not be able to anticipate whether it will be admissible under FRE 404(b) as evidence of extrinsic acts or under FRE 406 as habit. When looking to establish habit, it is critical to find witnesses who have the foundational information necessary to establish the habit you are trying to prove.

To Lay a Foundation Generally, to provide testimony that identifies evidence and ties it to the issue in question.

More discussion about **laying a foundation** to introduce evidence will follow later in this book. Laying a foundation basically means introducing the preliminary information that is required in order to allow the evidence that you want to come in. When laying a foundation to introduce professional habit evidence, the witness must be able to testify as to his knowledge of a large "sampling" of the recurrent situations, and the uniformity of response in each incident. The interview questions proposed in Section 4.2 can be adapted to get the necessary foundational information to introduce professional habit evidence.

4.5   *Modus Operandi*

Modus Operandi
The mode of operation, or repetitious conduct of a criminal in the course of committing similar crimes.

FRE 404(b), P. 265

Although most authors would have included a section on *modus operandi* in a chapter covering FRE 404(b), this complex common law doctrine goes beyond Rule 404 (b) in some of its more interesting applications. *Modus operandi* literally translates to mean "mode of operation." When similar methods are employed by a single perpetrator of multiple crimes, the perpetrator is said to have a *modus operandi*. In popular television shows, this is sometimes referred to as an "M.O." In legal circles, the perpetrator is said to operate with a "common scheme or plan."

Evidence that a defendant has a *modus operandi* is admissible under FRE 404(b) to show identity. A killer, for example, may carve the letter "Z" on the backs of all his victims. Under Rule 404(b), the prosecutor can introduce evidence that the letter "Z" was carved onto the back of a victim in another crime to show that the identity of the perpetrator is the same person as the one charged in the current case.

Sometimes, however, evidence of *modus operandi* is admissible to help prove the crime itself. Under such circumstances, it doesn't genuinely fit into the exceptions under 404(b), although that is where the court generally tries to reconcile the admissibility of the evidence. There are circumstances where the "habitualness" of the crime is what makes the case prosecutable—none of the cases in isolation would be sufficient to allow a conviction. Although *modus operandi* evidence is generally inadmissible under FRE 406, there are elements of "habit" worth exploring in this fascinating common law doctrine.

A famous *modus operandi* case, commonly known as the "Brides of Bath" case, involved a 1914 murder trial in which the defendant's wife had been found dead in the bathtub. *Rex v. Smith,* All E.R. Rep, 262. There was no proof that the defendant was with his wife at the time of the drowning. The victim had previously complained of having seizures that could have accounted for an accidental drowning. There were no signs of a struggle at the murder scene. The defendant, however, was undoubtedly guilty.

It seems that the victim was defendant's first in a line of three "wives." He had married her under an assumed name shortly after she had inherited some money. Soon after the newlyweds had made out their joint wills, wife number one was found dead in the bathtub, as described in the previous paragraph.

Wife number two, to whom defendant became wed shortly after the death of wife number one, also turned up dead in the bathtub after having taken out a life insurance policy and making out her will naming defendant as beneficiary in both instances.

Wife number three made out an appropriate will and took out a life insurance for her new beloved, and then died a mere 24 hours later—you guessed it—in the bathtub.

When defendant was on trial for the murder of the first wife, the evidentiary issue before the court was whether evidence of the subsequent drownings of the second and third wives was admissible to prove defendant was guilty of murdering wife number one. Remember that in the case of wife number one, there was no clear evidence supporting the conclusion that there was a murder, let alone that defendant was present at the time of death or in any way involved.

In this situation, the case could not have been won without the evidence of the subsequent other acts. The evidence was admitted, the defendant convicted and hanged.

Although the courts try to reconcile this outcome under the language of 404 (b) to reason that the evidence is being admitted in this type of case for an unenumerated "other purpose" under that rule, this appears to be a stretch. In this case, other wrongdoings are definitely being introduced for the purpose of showing that the defendant acted in accordance with the uncharged conduct. Nonetheless, the courts find such evidence is properly admitted because the evidence is not being received to show a "mere propensity" on the part of the defendant to commit the crime.

In a more recent case, *United States v. Woods,* 484 F.2d 127 (4th Cir. 1973), a foster mother was charged with the death of her eight-month-old pre-adoptive foster son who had allegedly died from smothering. Investigation revealed that nine other children or foster children of the defendant had suffered from cyanotic episodes (turning blue) and seven of those children had died. Although the defense rigorously objected to the introduction of evidence of the death or cyanotic episodes of the other children, the court allowed the evidence to be admitted, and the appellate court affirmed. Although the court allowed the evidence pursuant to Rule 404(b) (after a substantial amount of legal manipulation), the language of the court speaks to pattern or practice of behavior that looks very much like the language used in "habit" cases. The court said,

> As we stated at the outset, if the evidence with regard to each child is considered separately, it is true that some of the incidents are less conclusive than others; but we think the incidents must be considered collectively, and when they are, an unmistakable pattern emerges. That pattern overwhelmingly establishes defendant's guilt.

FRE 413, 414, and 415 were enacted because habit evidence is so difficult to admit and sex crimes are so difficult to prove. The *modus operandi* evidence discussed above would be directly admissible under the exceptions of FRE 413 et seq., in a case of sexual assault or child molestation.

4.6   Procedural Information

Where character evidence is admitted, it is usually admitted for a limited purpose. The court instructs the jury with a limiting instruction, and the evidence is supposed to be considered only for the purposes admitted. When habit evidence is admitted, it is admitted to prove conduct and is therefore not limited.

As you might imagine, both character and habit evidence, when controversial, are likely to be objected to by the opposing party. Although FRE 406 does not require disclosure of an intent to introduce habit evidence, if the opposing party becomes aware that such evidence will be proffered at trial, there will usually be motions made in limine (before trial) to try to keep the evidence out, or at least limit its use.

FRE 406, P. 266

The paralegal is usually a very key figure at this stage of the proceeding, since it is frequently part of the responsibility of the paralegal to either draft or answer evidentiary motions in limine. Imagine if a motion in limine, brought in the Brides case, had resulted in the courts precluding admission of the evidence of the other two wives' deaths? It is at this phase of the proceeding that the trial may be won or lost.

4.7   In Summary

- Habit can be defined as one's regular response to a repeated, specific situation.
- Habit is most easily proved in an organizational setting, where a specific routine is followed as a matter of custom, pattern, or practice.
- Habit must be proved by numerous instances of actual practice, cannot be proved by opinion evidence, and the evidence must be clear, uncontradictory, and distinct.
- Proving a habit of an individual requires that the evidence show that the individual has a regular and unvaried practice of meeting a particular type of situation with a certain type of conduct or reflex.
- Proving a habit of an individual or of an organization does not require corroborating evidence of the habit or an eyewitness to the habit.
- Habit is extremely useful as a tool to prove conduct on the part of a professional, such as a physician, who testifies as to a routine

practice. When the physician cannot remember treating a specific patient, for example, habit evidence can be used circumstantially to show how the patient was likely to have been treated.

- *Modus operandi* relates to a criminal who comports himself in a habitual manner in the commission of repetitive crimes. Although evidence of extrinsic offenses is admissible under FRE 404(b) for limited purposes, there are times (although rare) when the courts have stretched the rules to accommodate admitting extrinsic offense evidence to prove guilt.

FRE 404(b), P. 265

End of Chapter Review Questions

1. What is habit evidence?
2. What is the difference between habit and character evidence?
3. What is an example of organizational habit?
4. What is an example of professional routine habit?
5. What is *modus operandi*?
6. How is habit proved?

Applications

Consider the following hypothetical situation.

Charlene was accused of welfare fraud. On her monthly statements to the Department of Social Services, she failed to report that she was working part time and earning income while receiving Aid to Families with Dependent Children (AFDC) benefits. At trial, the social worker in charge of Charlene's case testified that she always advises all AFDC recipients that they must report any and all earned income on their monthly statements, and that failure to do so is a crime. She testified that she works with a case load of approximately 800 recipients. On cross-examination, she testified that she could not specifically remember telling Chariene about her obligation to report income.

1. Under which Federal Rule of Evidence is the testimony of the custodian of records admissible?
2. Is the custodian's testimony conclusive proof that Chariene was advised of her obligation to report income? Discuss. Consider the following hypothetical situation.

Dangerous Dan is arrested and charged with the crime of aggravated assault. He has two prior convictions for aggravated assault and there are several other incidents in Dan's past that were never charged, but would have been grounds for a charge of aggravated assault.

3. Is evidence of Dan's prior assaults, both charged and uncharged, admissible to prove the current charge of assault pursuant to Rule 406? Why or why not?

4. Consider the rules you have studied so far. Is there any other rule under which you may be able to introduce evidence of Dan's prior assaults? Which rule(s) and under what conditions?

Witnesses and Competency

5.1 Common Law Rules of Competency

Competent
Legally qualified to give testimony.

Litigants
The parties in the litigation.

Incompetent
In the evidentiary context, this simply means not legally qualified to testify.

In early common law, a person who was not **competent** to testify could not be a witness. As a matter of law, a long list of individuals were deemed incompetent to testify. Included in this list were children, felons, individuals interested in the outcome of a case, atheists, and people with mental illness.

Imagine, then, the limitations these common law competency requirements placed on the **litigants** in a proceeding. Consider the common law rule that all children were **incompetent** to testify. If a child were not competent to testify, how could a successful prosecution be brought in a child molestation case?

In drug cases, frequently the only means with which to acquire evidence is through the use of a confidential informant. Often, such confidential informants are criminals in their own right. If felons were not competent to testify, as was true at common law, it would be extremely difficult to prosecute drug-related crimes today.

Interested Parties
Parties who have an interest in
the outcome of the case.

Likewise, consider the common law rule against **interested parties** testifying. In civil litigation, the interested parties are usually those in the best position to offer testimony—they are the ones with the most direct knowledge. The common law rule prohibiting all interested parties from testifying was prone to result in extreme injustice.

5.2   Who Is Competent to Testify under the FRE?

FRE 601, P. 272

Modern rules of evidence regarding competency bear little resemblance to these prohibitive rules of the past. Over time the common law rules eroded, and the courts shifted away from excluding witnesses for competency reasons. One can see the result of this policy shift in FRE 601, which begins with the opening statement "Every person is competent to be a witness except as otherwise provided in these rules." Under FRE 601, the exceptions are truly rare, and almost all witnesses are deemed competent to testify.

The only witnesses specifically excluded under the Federal Rules of Evidence are the presiding judge in the case and members of the trial jury. According to the Advisory Notes, the opening statement of FRE 601 comprised the entire rule as originally proposed to Congress. However, the rule as finally enacted contained one additional provision. The second statement in FRE 601 states, "However, in civil actions and proceedings with respect to an element of a claim or defense as to which State law supplies the rule of decision, the competency of a witness shall be determined in accordance with State law."

Diversity Jurisdiction
Federal subject matter
jurisdiction based on litigants'
being citizens of different
states from each other.

Contrary to how you might feel, this second provision was not added specifically to torture lawyers and legal assistants. This provision applies to those cases that are being tried in federal court because of **diversity jurisdiction.** Although jurisdiction is ordinarily the subject of a course on civil procedure, a brief explanation of diversity jurisdiction is necessary here in order to fully explain the second part of FRE 601.

Generally, federal courts have subject matter jurisdiction only over those matters based on a federal statutory scheme or the federal Constitution. However, the federal court is also allowed to take jurisdiction in civil cases where the litigants are all citizens of different states and the alleged damages exceed $75,000. This is called diversity jurisdiction, and its purpose is to ensure that no litigant is subject to unfair treatment in a state court that might be biased in favor of its own citizens. For example, in a breach of contract case where damages are claimed to be in excess of $75,000 and where all the parties are citizens of different states, any party in the action has the right to remove the case to federal court.

When the federal court takes jurisdiction based on diversity, then state law governs the outcome of the case or provides the "rule of decision." The matter is simply heard in federal court to protect against bias. In such circumstances, pursuant to FRE 601, state rules govern witness competency. The rationale for this is fairness. Were it not for citizenship diversity, these cases would not be in federal court at all, and they would be tried in state court. Consequently, it would be inappropriate for witness competency in federal court to be different from state court.

FRE 601, P. 272

Although most states do generally follow the Federal Rules of Evidence, they do not necessarily follow the liberal views of competency found in FRE 601. To determine whether state or federal competency rules will govern when assessing the competency of a witness in a federal civil case, the paralegal must consider whether a case is in federal court because the matter raises a federal question or whether it is in federal court for diversity jurisdiction purposes.

5.3 Modern Competency Rules in the States

Most states have eliminated the prohibitive common law competency requirements discussed in the opening paragraphs of this chapter; however, there are state rules excluding witnesses for incompetency that are distant relatives of those common law rules. For example, many states still have on their books evidentiary rules referred to as "Dead Man's Statutes." Generally speaking, these statutes prohibit a witness in a case against a decedent's estate from testifying against the dead person about prior transactions or conversations with that dead person. Since nature has sealed the lips of the decedent, who can no longer speak in his or her own defense, these statutes seal the lips of the adverse party to even out the playing field. This type of rule is a descendant of the interested party incompetency rule found in the common law.

Many states still regulate the competency of children. Children under a certain age, in those states, are legally incompetent to testify. Likewise, the mentally ill or insane may be deemed incompetent pursuant to state rules.

New areas of incompetency sometimes evolve in the state rules. In recent years, hypnosis has been deemed by the courts to cause a witness to give unreliable testimony since suggestions made while the witness was under hypnosis may be what the witness actually remembers, rather than the events themselves. In some states, witnesses who have been hypnotized are deemed incompetent to testify in related proceedings.

As a paralegal, when you are working on a case in state court or are dealing with a diversity case in federal court, you should inquire whether your witness:

■ Intends to testify about words spoken by a dead person;
■ Is a young child;
■ Is mentally impaired;
■ Is insane;
■ Has been hypnotized with regard to the testimony to be offered.

If any of the answers to these inquiries is yes, there may be a question whether the witness will be allowed to testify under state law.

Consider the following hypothetical situation.

Devon, an Arizona resident, purchased a toaster through a mail order catalog from a company in New York. While he was in another room, his schizophrenic mother-in-law, Freida, tried to place some bread in the toaster. The toaster short-circuited, and Freida was severely burned. In a suit brought in Arizona in federal district court, the Arizona Rules of Evidence will apply to determine whether Freida is competent to testify. Pursuant to Arizona Revised Statutes §12-2202, in civil actions, "persons who are of unsound mind at the time they are called" cannot testify. Although at the time of trial Freida remembers the accident, she believes that she has been the victim of a government plot, and she hears voices that confirm her theory. Freida refuses to take medication. She would not be competent to testify in a civil matter in Arizona.

(Please note for future contemplation, however, that even though Freida may not be able to testify, statements she made to Devon at the time of the accident may be admissible under hearsay exceptions that we will discuss later in this textbook.)

You may legitimately ask why the Federal Rules don't exclude as incompetent the same witnesses that many of the states exclude. If, for example, a person is insane, shouldn't he or she be deemed incompetent to testify? The courts under the Federal Rules of Evidence clearly favor allowing witnesses to testify, believing that the jury will give appropriate weight to the testimony based on the credibility of the witness. A juror is not likely to give as much credibility to a witness who testifies that he speaks to space aliens each morning as to a person of sound mind. Even though hearing voices, the witness may be entitled to testify.

In other words, the Federal Rules do not specify a minimum level of mental competence that a witness must have to be permitted to testify. Although there is law holding that a judge *may* exclude a witness who lacks **minimum credibility** due perhaps to the witness's

Minimum Credibility
The ability to give testimony that is at least potentially believable.

youth or mental deficiencies, this occurs very rarely. Under the Federal Rules, the jury is permitted to see and weigh more evidence than under many of the state rules because only rarely are witnesses precluded from testifying for lack of competency.

5.4   Personal Knowledge of the Witness

FRE 602, P. 272

FRE 602 provides that in general, a witness can testify only as to his or her personal knowledge of the matter. As we study hearsay and its exceptions in later chapters, it will become clearer how this rule operates. Basically, however, FRE 602 requires a witness to testify only as to what he or she knows and not what he or she has been told by others. Ordinarily, this rule goes unchallenged and is considered unambiguous, but there can be some muddling when the hearsay rules and FRE 602 seem to be inconsistent with each other. It is important to note that although personal knowledge is required under FRE 602, a witness who has had the opportunity to observe and form a belief is considered to have personal knowledge. A person need not be absolutely sure. Testimony that begins with words such as "I think" or "I believe" is not inadmissible as long as there is a basis for the testimony.

One of the most interesting cases involving FRE 602 is *United States. v. Mandel*, which is summarized and partially quoted below.

United States v. Mandel

591 F.2d 1347 (4th Cir. 1979)

PROCEDURAL SUMMARY

This case involved charges against the then governor of Maryland, Marvin Mandel, and others, for racketeering and mail fraud. At trial in Federal District Court, Governor Mandel and the other defendants were convicted on several of the counts charged. The first appellate panel of the Fourth Circuit reversed the convictions, and the following analysis regarding FRE 602 comes from that decision.

However, this case didn't stop after this Fourth Circuit opinion. Its path had more factual and legal twists than a mountain road, and continued for more than ten years after this decision. Following this panel's decision to reverse and remand, the prosecution requested another appellate hearing "en banc." The *en banc* Fourth Circuit reinstated the convictions and the defendants all served their sentences. Ten years later, however, the Fourth Circuit granted a special writ and affirmed the District Court's second removal of the convictions based on a Supreme Court decision in a different case that would have been dispositive in favor of defendants had it been decided earlier.

FACTUAL SUMMARY

The story began when Governor Mandel vetoed a bill which would have allowed certain race track investors a greater interest in the Maryland racing industry. The Maryland House of Representatives overrode the veto. The governor was accused of manipulating the members of the Maryland House of Representatives into overriding his own veto, by not giving them information about who the investors were, and by allegedly indicating verbally to some state senators that he wouldn't mind if his veto were overridden. Allegedly, the governor had received money or gifts from some of the race track investors.

The state senators who testified that the governor implicitly encouraged the override of his own veto based their testimony on what they had heard said by others.

The above-summarized facts and testimony were reviewed and analyzed by the first reviewing panel of the Fourth Circuit Court of Appeal. This Court opined:

> A final category of testimony involves the distinction between the rule against hearsay (FRE 802) and the rule requiring personal knowledge (FRE 602). Senators who were present testified to their own general feelings or beliefs as to Governor Mandel's position on the veto override. While this testimony is not hearsay in form, the feeling and beliefs expressed therein were often based in whole or in part on impermissible hearsay. To the extent it was based on hearsay, this testimony is inadmissible because the witness lacked the requisite first-hand knowledge.
>
> While the distinction between such evidence and hearsay is sometimes formal, and the line between the rules often is blurred in practice, the rules do demonstrate that testimony based on hearsay is equally inadmissible as direct hearsay testimony. Therefore, if a senator testified that he did not believe that Governor Mandel wanted his veto overridden, and if that belief were based on inadmissible hearsay statements, then the senator lacks any personal knowledge of the event and his testimony should have been excluded.
>
> The more difficult problem arises when the witness' belief is based in part on admissible testimony. We think this problem is one of degree. If the belief is primarily based on hearsay, it is inadmissible. But, if the belief is substantially based on admissible evidence, such as direct statements or acts by one of Governor Mandel's agents, then it should be admitted. The basis for the belief should be explored in each instance and a ruling on admissibility made when those facts are before the trial court.

FRE 602, P. 272

This case makes clear that knowledge is personal pursuant to FRE 602 when it is based on information that, if offered, would itself be admissible. Knowledge isn't personal under FRE 602 when the information from which the witness's knowledge is derived is based on inadmissible hearsay. This case provides valuable information for the paralegal who is interviewing a witness who might testify with regard to someone else's specific intentions or the witness's own "belief" about a certain situation. In the interview, it is important to question the *basis* of the witness's knowledge. It is not only important for your witness to tell what she or he knows; the witness must also explain how and on what basis she or he knows it. Consider the following example.

Assume you are working on a case in which your firm is representing Pablo, who claims he has been defrauded out of a great deal of money by Mr. E. There are two witnesses who know the alleged perpetrator, E, and who believe that E misled Pablo in order to get his money.

The following questions should be asked in your interview of these two witnesses who know E.

- Do you believe E intended to defraud Pablo?
- On what do you base your impression?
- Can you think of any specific comments made to you by E relevant to this matter? If yes, what were those comments?
- Can you think of any specific comments made to you by anyone else that caused you to believe E intended to defraud Pablo? If yes, by whom were the comments made? What were those comments?
- Can you remember observing any specific conduct by E that caused you to form your belief? If yes, what was that conduct?
- Can you remember any specific conduct by anyone else that caused you to form your belief? If yes, to whose conduct are you referring? What was that conduct?

By asking these types of questions, you not only provide the attorney with sufficient information to prepare a proper foundation for the introduction of the evidence, you also give the attorney a "feel" for the reliability of the witness. An **unsupported opinion,** even if admissible, will carry little credibility in a courtroom.

Unsupported Opinion
An opinion without a sound factual basis.

Be aware that although the credibility of the witness may be important strategically in a case (the attorney on the case may well decide not to use a witness whose claim to personal knowledge is weak), this is not a legal issue under FRE 602. It doesn't matter whether the judge believes that the witness has the personal knowledge to which the witness is testifying. Whether to believe the witness

FRE 602, P. 272

is up to the jury. FRE 602 deals with the substance of the testimony rather than its believability. If the witness is speculating or merely offering an unfounded belief rather than testifying as to his or her personal knowledge, then the testimony is inadmissible pursuant to this rule. If, however, the witness is testifying as to personal knowledge, even though unlikely, it is generally admissible under Rule 602.

The following example illustrates this point.

Vicky is suing Greedy in a civil case for fraud. Greedy's girlfriend Ginger wishes to testify that she has personal knowledge that Vicky frequently intentionally incurred economic losses to avoid paying taxes, and that Vicky was aware that she would lose money in Greedy's scheme, but did so intentionally. She claims Vicky confided these things to her.

Ginger's personal knowledge in this hypothetical is highly suspicious. She is Greedy's girlfriend and has an interest in a successful outcome for him in the case. Furthermore, losing money is never profitable, even with the resulting tax breaks, and so the logic espoused by Ginger as the basis of Vicky's conduct is questionable. However, technically under Rule 602, this evidence is admissible, and it is up to the trier-of-fact to determine its credibility. Keep in mind, however, that all evidence is subject to Rule 403, and if the evidence is highly prejudicial, this will be measured against its probative value to determine its admissibility.

5.5   The Oath or Affirmation

As we all know, before testifying a witness must raise his or her right hand and promise to tell the truth. Historically, the witness was required to swear to God on a Bible to tell the truth. As you might imagine, this was either offensive or meaningless to a witness who was an atheist.

FRE 603, P. 272

FRE 603 was therefore crafted to take the religious underpinnings from the swearing-in process. The rule simply states

> Before testifying, every witness shall be required to declare that the witness will testify truthfully, by **oath** or **affirmation** administered in a form calculated to awaken the witness's conscience and impress the witness's mind with the duty to do so.

Oath
A solemn promise to be truthful, accompanied by a swearing to God.

Affirmation
A solemn promise to tell the truth.

According to the Advisory Notes, "The rule is designed to afford the flexibility required in dealing with religious adults, atheists, conscientious objectors, mental defectives, and children. Affirmation is simply a solemn undertaking to tell the truth; no special verbal formula is required." 56 F.R.D. 183, 263.

The courts take the requirement of truthfulness of a witness very seriously. Perjury by a witness is a felony. As a paralegal, you may be asked to describe to the witness the courtroom procedure she will encounter. Although you are not allowed to give legal advice to the witness, you can certainly inform her about the oath or affirmation that she will have to take prior to testifying and the fact that perjury while under oath is a crime.

In those cases where the witness you are interviewing does not speak English, you may need to use an interpreter to interview your witness. An interpreter will be required in court to translate for the proceeding. Pursuant to Rule 604, an interpreter in a courtroom must take an oath or affirmation that he or she will make a true translation. It is critical that you work carefully with the interpreter that you use during the interview so that you get precisely the same interpretation that will be given by a court interpreter later in trial who is under oath. An interpreter from your office, for instance, may feel inclined to abbreviate or summarize the interview statements made by the witness or to leave things out that the interpreter might find personally offensive. This unprofessional editing could leave your attorney open to unwanted surprises during trial when the courtroom interpreter translates verbatim information perhaps previously given but left uninterpreted during the interview.

FRE 604, P. 273

5.6   Judges and Jurors as Witnesses

FRE 605 and 606, P. 273

Rules 605 and 606 describe the only two types of witnesses who, under the Federal Rules of Evidence, are incompetent to testify: judges and jurors in the case. These rules are strictly construed. The judge need not take the witness stand to "testify;" he or she need only assume the role of a witness. Factual statements made by a judge from the bench during trial may be grounds for a mistrial if they are prejudicial. For example, in a jury trial the judge cannot comment to a witness, "I think you are lying." This would be "testifying." Only the jury has the right to determine the credibility of a witness.

As a paralegal, legal assistant, or law clerk in a courtroom, you function as an extension of the court itself. An interesting case that illustrates this point involved a trial judge's paralegal who talked to a defendant when the defendant telephoned the judge's office. The paralegal subsequently testified against the defendant in his trial. The case is unpublished, but it cites an analogous published case in which a judge's curious law clerk testified about his investigation of a slip-and-fall case. Both cases resulted in reversals because the paralegal and the law clerk, as extensions of their judges, were incompetent to testify.

Frailey v. Commonwealth of Kentucky

2005 WL 1993452 (Ky. App. 2005)(unpublished opinion)

Lowell Frailey, Jr. brings this appeal from a March 23, 2004, judgment upon a jury verdict finding him guilty of first-degree burglary and sentencing him to ten years' imprisonment. We vacate and remand.

In this appeal, we are faced with a particularly troublesome legal issue. Appellant raises as error the admission of testimony from the sitting trial judge's paralegal, Sandra Bryant. After having been identified as the trial judge's paralegal, Bryant testified regarding a phone call she received from appellant on February 3, 2004, at the judge's office. Appellant requested to speak with the trial judge, but Bryant informed him that the judge could not speak to a party outside the courtroom. Thereafter, Bryant testified that she and appellant carried on a conversation for sometime. . . . Of particular importance, Bryant testified that appellant told her that he was guilty of the crime alleged and thus, needed good trial counsel. Additionally, a substantial portion of this conversation was recorded on the judge's answering machine.

After the conversation, Bryant immediately prepared and signed an affidavit regarding the conversation and filed the affidavit in the court record. Bryant advised the court of the conversation and the parties by way of a copy of her affidavit. At trial, Bryant referred to the affidavit during her testimony. In the affidavit, Bryant affirmed that part of the conversation was recorded upon the trial judge's answering machine and that "[w]e have saved that portion of the telephone call that was recorded and it is in our office." Appellant testified at trial and vigorously denied admitting guilt to Bryant. He testified that he was talking fast during the conversation, and she must have misunderstood him.

Appellant alleges as error the introduction of Bryant's testimony. . . . For reasons hereinafter elucidated, we conclude the admission of Bryant's testimony constituted palpable error.

Although not bound by *Kennedy v. Great Atlantic & Pacific Tea Co. Inc.*, 551 F.2d 593 (5th Cir. 1977), we view it as both instructive and persuasive. In *Kennedy*, the Court was faced with a similar issue—whether the district court erroneously admitted the testimony of the district judge's law clerk during trial. The trial involved injuries allegedly suffered by plaintiff as a result of a slip and fall on a slick floor at a grocery store. Upon his own initiative, the district judge's law clerk went to the grocery store to view the actual location where the fall allegedly occurred. The law clerk observed standing water on the floor at the accident site. During trial, the law clerk testified about his observation of standing water on the floor at the grocery store.

In determining whether the testimony of the law clerk constituted reversible error, the [Fifth Circuit] concluded:

> Any challenge of [the law clerk's] credibility or reliability as a reporter of facts would probably be totally unavailable, but more particularly, under our adversary system of justice, it was unacceptable that the most damaging evidence against the defendants in this case was brought about by the intervention of a court official in the accumulation of evidence. The law clerk learned of the litigation and of the disputed issues by virtue of his employment as law clerk to the trial judge. It was his duty as much as that of the trial judge to avoid any contacts outside the record that might affect the outcome of the litigation. . . .
>
> Appellants also cite as support for their argument Rule 605 of the new Federal Rules of Evidence. . . .
>
> It is impossible to believe that the jury must not have attached some special significance to this testimony of the judge's law clerk. . . .
>
> In addition, there was the imprimatur of character, credibility and reliability that was automatically implied as coming from the court itself when the trial judge introduced the witness as his present law clerk.

*   *   *

In the case at hand, it is axiomatic that the jury did "attach some special significance" to Bryant's testimony. It is also reasonable to assume that the jury transferred the "character, credibility and reliability . . . [of] the court itself" to Bryant. We are also struck by the fact that the most incriminating evidence admitted against appellant was the testimony of Bryant concerning appellant's alleged confession of guilt. Taken together, it is difficult to conceive of testimony with a more compelling and with a more prejudicial effect upon a jury. Thus, the admission of Bryant's testimony affected the substantive rights of appellant and resulted in manifest injustice to appellant.

We liken Bryant's role and position to that of a law clerk. . . . And, we likewise recognize that a law clerk is forbidden to engage in any conduct that is prohibited a judge.

*   *   *

In sum, we conclude Bryant's testimony should have been excluded because of its obvious prejudicial effect upon the jury and by reason of [Kentucky Rule of Evidence] 605. . . . For the above stated reasons, we hold the admission of Bryant's testimony constituted palpable error.

Undoubtedly, seeing your own name in an opinion such as above would be excruciatingly unpleasant! Consequently, remember that the bar against a judge testifying in a proceeding over which he presides is absolute. The judge is unequivocally incompetent to testify, and no objection need be made in order to preserve this point on appeal. In the above case, the judge never testified, but the testimony by his paralegal gave the appearance of judicial testimony. This was sufficient for reversal.

FRE 606(a) and 606(b), P. 273

The rule with respect to jurors is a bit more complex. Pursuant to FRE 606(a), "[a] member of the jury may not testify in the trial of the case in which the juror is sitting." In this regard, the incompetency of the juror is the same as that of the judge—it is absolute.

However, after the trial is over, the rule changes slightly. According to FRE 606(b), "a juror may not testify as to any matter or statement occurring during the course of the jury's deliberations or to the effect of anything upon that or any other juror's mind or emotions as influencing the juror to assent to or dissent from the verdict or indictment or concerning the juror's mental processes in connection therewith. But a juror may testify about (1) whether extraneous prejudicial information was improperly brought to the jury's attention, (2) whether any outside influence was improperly brought to bear upon any juror, or (3) whether there was a mistake in entering the verdict onto the verdict form. A juror's affidavit or evidence of any statement by the juror may not be received on a matter about which the juror would be precluded from testifying." The distinctions between what a juror can and cannot testify to after trial are critical in order to determine when there has been actual jury misconduct that can lead to a mistrial.

For example, suppose that Hannah the Horrible is the jury foreperson in a trial where Fingers Johnson is charged with shoplifting. Suppose that during a post-trial interview, she admits that she entered the jury room and began deliberations with a prayer to smite all evil-doers. She would not be able to testify about this because it relates to her state of mind rather than any extraneous information brought into the deliberation.

However, suppose that Gary Gossip is on the same jury. He tells the other jurors that he saw Fingers in a department store just the week before trial, busily stuffing baubles into her pockets. This information was never introduced during the trial. The jurors would be able to testify about this because Gary's comments contained extraneous prejudicial information.

FRE 606(b) recently was amended effective December 2006. The rule always has prohibited inquiry into the jury's mental processes and emotions in arriving at a verdict unless there is prejudice or misconduct as excepted by the rule and as exemplified in the example above. As you would expect, the rule was amended because courts were conflicted about the application and scope of the rule. Prior to the amendment, some courts allowed a juror to be questioned about an erroneous understanding affecting the jury's verdict. The newly added language permitting inquiry about "a mistake in entering the verdict onto the verdict form" restricts inquiry to clerical mistakes and forbids inquiry invasive of the jury's deliberation process. Consequently, the amendment now clarifies for courts that the scope of the rule is to be applied narrowly.

Frequently, federal judges and state court judges will instruct the jurors after they have returned the verdict that the jurors are permitted to talk about the case but are not required to do so. The judge will tell the jury that no one is permitted to ask about the jury deliberations. The judge will also tell the jury to report to the judge if someone persists in attempting an unwanted interview. Typically, the trial lawyer will try to interview the jurors. But if you are tasked with the responsibility, your approach must be toward uncovering misconduct or prejudice that occurred during the trial or deliberations. For example, you should ask about any extraneous resources or information brought into the jury room such as dictionaries, resource books, newspaper and magazine articles about the case or the trial. Ask whether any of the jurors conducted their own research or investigation about the case. It helps to remember that the jury must decide the case based solely on the evidence and testimony admitted at the trial—you will be trying to find out if they did.

5.7   In Summary

- Under the Federal Rules of Evidence, every person is competent to testify unless subject to an exception under the rules. State rules frequently differ, and people suffering from mental illness, children under certain ages, or other classes of people may be deemed incompetent to testify pursuant to various state rules.
- In diversity cases, the state rules regarding competency are applied in place of the Federal Rules of Evidence.
- Witnesses are competent to testify only on matters about which they have personal knowledge. Personal knowledge does not require absolute certainty on the part of a witness, who can testify as to his belief, as long as the belief is well founded in personal observation.
- Judges who preside over the proceeding and jurors who deliberate in the proceedings are legally incompetent to testify. A juror who brings information into the deliberations may be unlawfully giving testimony, thereby causing a mistrial.

- A juror will not be permitted to testify about the jury deliberations when the validity of the verdict is at issue except if they were presented with outside information or outside influence, or if a clerical mistake occurred in recording the verdict.

End of Chapter Review Questions

1. In early common law, what types of individuals were incompetent to testify?
2. Under the FRE, who is competent to testify?
3. If a matter is in federal court due to diversity jurisdiction, do the Federal Rules of Evidence govern competency?
4. If a witness believes but is not certain that a fact is true, but the belief is based on his or her personal observation, is that witness competent to testify to that fact?
5. Must a witness swear on the Bible to tell the truth before testifying?
6. May the judge comment about the facts of the case from the bench?
7. May a juror share information that wasn't presented in court but is known to the juror to be true, and is pertinent to the deliberations?

Applications

Consider the following hypothetical situation.

Maria is a six-year-old Native American child. She lives on a reservation in the Southwest. She was sexually molested by Enrique, another Native American who lived on the reservation. Enrique was charged in Federal Court for child molestation. (Federal law governs this matter.)

1. Is Maria competent to testify?
2. Assume that Maria is unable to accurately describe what occurred at the time she was molested. Does this make her incompetent to testify? If not, what is the consequence of her inability to accurately describe the incident?

Consider the following hypothetical situation.

Jordan is standing on a street corner when he hears shots ring out. He hears someone yell, "Oh no! Carmen just shot Abel!"

3. Can Jordan testify that Carmen shot Abel? Why or why not?

Impeachment

6.1 Impeachment—An Explanation

Impeachment
Attacking a witness's credibility.

The nonlawyer generally thinks of **impeachment** as something that happens to a president when Congress gets seriously irritated by the chief executive's misconduct. Impeachment in the evidentiary sense simply means to attack the credibility of a witness. This is done in a variety of ways, to be discussed in this chapter.

The Federal Rules of Evidence do not enumerate every permissible method of impeachment. Instead, the rules provide a flexible framework through which attorneys can use a variety of methods to impeach witnesses in court. The methods of impeachment that are used in court will be examined in this chapter, so that the paralegal

Rehabilitate
To restore or rebuild after an attack.

will gain an understanding of how a witness's credibility (and therefore his testimony) can be attacked or **rehabilitated** during trial.

The methods listed below are commonly used to attack or rehabilitate the credibility of a witness or the witness's testimony. The first three methods listed are expressly addressed by the Federal Rules of Evidence. The remaining areas have rooted precedent for attacking or rehabilitating the credibility of a witness or a witness's testimony and are generally analyzed under the relevancy rules.

Prior Inconsistent Statements
Statements made previously that either contradict or depart from the current testimony.

- Character for truthfulness; FRE 608
- Prior convictions; FRE 609
- **Prior inconsistent statements**; FRE 613
- Other acts; FRE 401-404(b)
- **Personal bias,** prejudice, or self-interest; FRE 401-403
- Capacity to perceive, recall, or relate; FRE 401-403
- Intentional lying; FRE 401-403
- Other contradictory evidence; FRE 401-403

Personal Bias
A witness's beliefs or prejudices that might influence the witness's perception of the facts.

6.2   Who May Impeach?

FRE 607, P. 273

Pursuant to Federal Rule of Evidence 607, "The credibility of a witness may be attacked by any party, including the party calling the witness." This rule represents a substantial departure from the common law, under which a party was not entitled to impeach his own witness. The logic of the common law rule was simply that if you don't believe your own witness, you shouldn't call him or her to testify. However, the Advisory Notes reflect the Advisory Committee's perception that the common law rule was based on false premises. According to the Advisory Note to Rule 607, "A party does not hold out his witnesses as worthy of belief, since he rarely has a free choice in selecting them. Denial of the right [to impeach] leaves the party at the mercy of the witness and the adversary."

Under Rule 607, then, it is allowable to call up a witness and then impeach that witness's credibility. Strategically, at first glance this would seem counterproductive. If you call a witness and then introduce evidence to indicate the witness you've called is not believable, it is difficult to understand initially how you've bettered your position. The utility of impeaching your own witness is best understood by considering those situations in which it would be necessary to do so.

For example, there are times when your witness does not testify as anticipated or is hostile and unwilling to cooperate on the stand. It is not uncommon for a witness to provide information during an interview and then testify very differently in court. The party calling the witness is then unpleasantly surprised and must impeach its own witness in order to attempt to repair the damage. Consider the following hypothetical situation.

During an interview, Debbie said that she saw a large woman exit the building right after a robbery. The defendant, Melvin, is a short man. The defense called Debbie to testify at trial, at which time Debbie identified Melvin as the person she saw leave the building right after the robbery. FRE 607 allows the defense to impeach Debbie with her prior inconsistent statement about the large woman and thereby try to mitigate the effects of having called a witness who incriminated instead of exonerated the defendant.

FRE 607, P. 273

Additionally, there are times when the only testimony you are able to produce is from a witness who has a credibility problem. At such times, you impeach your own witness to narrow the credibility problem and reduce its impact. In other words, you impeach your own witness to mitigate the harm that opposition will be able to do to your witness on cross-examination.

Consider the following example.

Wanda is to be a witness for the plaintiff in a civil action against Mr. Jones. Wanda said in an interview, "I saw Mr. Jones drive his car into the front window of Mrs. Brown's house." Wanda also said that she testified in the related criminal action against Mr. Jones on charges of felony destruction of property. She further stated that she had agreed to testify in the criminal matter in exchange for the government's agreement not to prosecute her for painting graffiti on Mrs. Brown's house that same night.

Wanda's cooperation agreement with the government could be used by the opposing party to create an inference that Wanda's testimony against Mr. Jones is not completely disinterested and might therefore lack credibility. Your attorney may well wish to bring up Wanda's cooperation agreement with the government before the opposition tries to use it to discredit Wanda in cross-examination. Under FRE 607, this is permissible. A proponent is allowed to point out the flaws in the credibility of its own witness before the opposition has the opportunity to use those same flaws to more thoroughly diminish the witness's credibility in the eyes of the trier-of-fact.

FRE 607, P. 273

6.3   Impeachment Based on Character for Truthfulness

In Chapter 3, we learned that evidence of a person's character or character trait generally is inadmissible to prove that the person acted in conformity. FRE 404(a)(3), however, refers you to the exceptions provided in FRE 607, 608, and 609. In this section, we will discuss FRE 608 which governs the admissibility of character evidence for the limited purpose of proving a witness's character for truthfulness or untruthfulness.

FRE 608(a), P. 273

FRE 608(a) provides that opinion and reputation evidence of character are admissible to attack or support the credibility of a witness, subject to some limitations. First, the evidence must refer only to character as it relates to truthfulness or untruthfulness of a witness. Although it may be obvious, keep in mind that to be a witness, the person must testify. Thus, a criminal defendant must testify in order to be deemed a witness. Secondly, evidence of the witness's *truthful* character is only admissible after the witness's character has been attacked for untruthfulness. Under FRE 608, testimony must be restricted so as not to invite in any evidence of character for anything other than the witness's truthfulness or lack thereof.

FRE 608 represents a substantial departure from those constraints on the admissibility of character evidence found in FRE 404(a)(1) and (2), which require that the accused introduce character first, or it is inadmissible. Under FRE 608(a), character evidence is admissible to impeach a witness's veracity as long as the witness testifies. These two rules may at first appear contradictory; however, they are not. FRE 404(a)(1) and (2) deal with restraints on the admissibility of character evidence to prove *conduct.* FRE 608(a) allows the introduction of character evidence to prove the absence of veracity. In other words, character evidence is not admissible to show that a defendant committed the crime, but it is admissible to show that the defendant, if he testifies, is a liar.

FRE 404(a)(1) and (2), P. 265

As mentioned earlier, FRE 608 constrains the introduction of evidence supporting a witness's credibility, which is admissible only after the witness's character for truthfulness has been attacked. Consider the following examples.

Jerald is being prosecuted for assault with a deadly weapon. After the prosecution has presented its evidence, Jerald, in his case-in-chief, testifies that he was taking Shila to the movies in his hybrid car the night a smug cloud caused him to run over a North Park Police Officer. On rebuttal, the prosecution might decide to call witnesses to testify that in their opinion Jerald is a habitual liar, but the prosecution has not yet *otherwise* attacked Jerald's character for truthfulness during the defendant's case-in-chief.

Also during the defense case, the defense attorney calls Shila who testifies that she was with Jerald while he was driving the hybrid car, and indeed there was a huge smug cloud which covered the car and prevented both of them from seeing the police officer. The prosecution does not cross-examine Shila. Right after Shila's testimony, Jerald's defense lawyer attempts to call a witness to testify that Shila has an irrefutable reputation for honesty.

The judge would sustain a prosecution objection and preclude the testimony as premature because the prosecution did not

cross-examine Shila and has not otherwise yet attacked Shila's credibility. Shila's credibility cannot be bolstered by a character witness unless Shila's credibility first has been attacked by reputation or opinion testimony for untruthfulness.

The above example provides a framework for understanding the mechanisms of FRE 608(a). Remember, the rule applies to witnesses. Jerald is a criminal defendant. If he chooses not to testify then neither the prosecution nor the defense could call character witnesses to testify about their opinion or Jerald's reputation for truthfulness or untruthfulness. In the example, he did testify, so he became a witness just like Shila. So the same rule applies to him as to a non-defendant witness. He cannot call character witnesses to bolster his credibility, that is his character for truthfulness, until the prosecution attacks his character for truthfulness. Mere cross-examination is not sufficient to constitute an attack. Jerald must wait to see whether the prosecution really will call rebuttal witnesses to attack Jerald's character for untruthfulness. If the prosecution does, only then would the defense be able to rehabilitate Jerald's credibility by calling character witnesses to testify as to opinion or reputation for Jerald's truthfulness. The witnesses would not be allowed to give specific examples of his truthfulness, nor would they be able to testify that Jerald is a great dad, helps little old ladies across the street, or is an avid environmentalist.

FRE 608(a) imposes the methods by which to attack or support a witness's character for truthfulness—"by opinion or reputation evidence *or otherwise*" (emphasis added). As you might expect, the witness must have sufficient knowledge to provide an opinion or reputation testimony. The interview questions suggested in Section 3.6 can be modified to usefully interview the prospective veracity witnesses. The "or otherwise" method is not defined, so the creative paralegal may find a way to implement this part of the rule!

6.4 Evidence of Specific Conduct on Cross-Examination

FRE 608(b), P. 274

FRE 608(b) allows the judge the discretion to permit a witness to be cross-examined about specific past conduct for the purpose of either attacking or supporting the witness's character for truthfulness. To attack the witness's veracity, the opponent may ask the witness about prior misconduct relating to untruthfulness even if the misconduct did not result in a conviction. (FRE 609 controls the use of prior convictions and will be discussed later in this chapter.)

Although pursuant to Rule 608(b), an attorney may inquire into the past misconduct of a witness if the inquiry is probative of the

Extrinsic Evidence
Evidence other than the testimony of the witness who is testifying.

witness's character for truthfulness, after making such an inquiry the attorney must take the answer that the witness gives. The attorney cannot bring in **extrinsic evidence** if the witness lies or refuses to admit the allegations underlying the inquiry. Extrinsic evidence is evidence that comes from any place other than the mouth of the witness testifying. So, the attorney can question the witness but cannot contradict the witness's testimony by calling another witness, or by introducing as evidence a document, a photograph, or any other piece of physical evidence. The rationale in precluding the extrinsic evidence is to keep the parties and the jury focused on the issues in the case. Otherwise they could be endlessly sidetracked in mini-trials trying to prove or disprove the **collateral issue** of the witness's veracity.

Collateral Issues
Questions or issues which are not directly involved in the matter.

In the following case, the prosecution cross-examined the defendant about a prior letter (unrelated to the crime) on which the defendant had forged someone's signature. The defendant did not deny doing so, but had she denied it, or equivocated, or said that she did not remember, the prosecution would have been stuck with the answer. Either way, the prosecutor's ability to ask the damaging questions most certainly obtained the desired impact on the jury.

United States v. Waldrip

981 F.2d 799 (5th Cir. 1993)

Waldrip was indicted for scheming to defraud [banks] AAB and TCB . . . and for knowingly making a false statement for the purpose of influencing the action of [bank] TCB.

*   *   *

Waldrip filed a pre-trial motion to suppress evidence of a separate transaction in which she signed Accountant Steve Hill's name to a letter that was subsequently sent to investors. The district court elected to carry the motion as a motion in limine. At trial, Waldrip elected to testify in her own behalf. The government was allowed to use the Hill letter in cross-examining Waldrip pursuant to Federal Rule of Evidence 608(b) as a matter affecting her character for truthfulness.

*   *   *

Specifically, Waldrip complains of the following exchange that took place during cross-examination:

GOVERNMENT: . . . Your various signatures of Bernice Harrell's name [in the instant case] isn't the first time you've signed somebody's name to a document without their permission, is it?

WALDRIP: To a document?

GOVERNMENT: That's right. To a document, a piece of paper.

WALDRIP: No. I've signed-yeah, I've signed people's names to things before.

GOVERNMENT: In fact, approximately one year before . . . you had a partner in one of your companies, yours and your husband's companies, by the name of Jim Cox, did you not?

WALDRIP: Yes.

GOVERNMENT: And he was an attorney, wasn't he?

WALDRIP: Yes.

GOVERNMENT: And he wanted to get out of the partnership, didn't he?

WALDRIP: He wasn't actually in the partnership. He had a right to exercise an option and he wanted to not do that so he wanted to not be a part of the company.

GOVERNMENT: He wanted an accounting of partnership matters, didn't he?

WALDRIP: Yes.

GOVERNMENT: He wanted a financial statement from you, didn't he?

WALDRIP: He wanted an accounting of four months' worth of activity. Yes.

GOVERNMENT: And you sent him a compiled financial statement or an informal financial statement, didn't you?

WALDRIP: Yes.

GOVERNMENT: And it had a cover letter on it, didn't it?

WALDRIP: Yes.

GOVERNMENT: And it was signed by Steve Hill, CPA, was it not?

WALDRIP: Yes. It was.

GOVERNMENT: And in fact, Mr. Hill never signed it. You signed it, didn't you?

WALDRIP: Yes. I did.

GOVERNMENT: And you signed it without Mr. Hill's permission, didn't you?

WALDRIP: I read it to him first.

GOVERNMENT: Did you sign it without his permission?

WALDRIP: Yes.

*   *   *

Waldrip contends that the district court abused its discretion in admitting the letter because, even if a forgery, it is not probative of her character for truthfulness. However, forgery has been held to be probative evidence of a witnesses' character for truthfulness. In *Leake*, the court stated "Rule 608 authorizes inquiry only into instances of misconduct that are clearly probative of truthfulness or untruthfulness, such as perjury, fraud, swindling, *forgery,* bribery, and embezzlement."

We hold that the district court did not abuse its discretion when it allowed the government to cross-examine Waldrip concerning the letter because such misconduct was probative of Waldrip's character for truthfulness.

The above case is an excellent example of a using a prior act to attack the veracity of the witness. Under FRE 608(b), the forged letter, itself, was not admissible, but the prosecution was able to use the contents of the letter to formulate cross-examination questions in order to effectively impeach the defendant-witness. Thus, as you can see, a paralegal should never assume that a liar will not admit past problematic conduct!

Various tools are available to the attorney to persuade a witness to admit past conduct, and the inquiry has value even if the conduct isn't admitted. There are times when you need as much armor as you can muster to levy assaults against the opponent witnesses, and Rule 608(b) questioning should not be overlooked. If the paralegal sees the potential for impeachment in cross-examining an opposition witness with inquiries as to past conduct, the paralegal should document the past conduct even though it may seem like **collateral evidence.**

FRE 608(b), P. 274

Collateral Evidence
Evidence that is tangential and only marginally probative.

FRE 412, P. 267

FRE 413-415, PP. 269-270

Keep in mind that the victim witness in a rape case may not be impeached with regard to character to the extent that the character relates to the victim's sexual history or predisposition. FRE 412. Also note that the accused in a rape or child molestation case may be questioned about past sex crimes for any purpose pursuant to FRE 413-415. These rules are anomalies and form very distinct exceptions for rape and child molestation cases. They should not be confused with the general rules regarding character evidence and impeachment.

In the following sections, we will discuss other methods of impeachment such as bias, mental capacity, prior inconsistent statements, and other contradictions. Extrinsic evidence offered to impeach a witness in those ways may or may not be admissible to prove the witness's credibility. But its admissibility is not evaluated under FRE 608 because those forms of impeachment do not relate to the witness's *character* for truthfulness. Rather, as we will see, those methods are analyzed under the general relevancy rules FRE 402 and 403.

6.5 Impeachment by Evidence of Conviction of a Crime

In the preceding section, a discussion of FRE 608(b) indicated that extrinsic evidence is generally inadmissible to prove specific instances of misconduct for purposes of character impeachment. However, if the prior misconduct resulted in a criminal conviction, then extrinsic evidence of the conviction may be admissible for impeachment purposes.

FRE 609(a)(1), P. 274

Pursuant to 609(a)(1),

> evidence that a witness other than an accused has been convicted of a crime shall be admitted, subject to Rule 403, if the crime was punishable by death or imprisonment in excess of one year under the law under which the witness was convicted, and evidence that an accused has been convicted of such a crime shall be admitted if the court determines that the probative value of admitting this evidence outweighs its prejudicial effect to the accused.

This rule provides that a witness's "character for truthfulness" is properly attacked by evidence of past felony convictions, subject to

FRE 403, P. 264

FRE 403's prohibition against unfair prejudice. If the *accused* is the witness, however, the court must make an actual determination that the probative value of the evidence of the past crime outweighs its prejudicial effect on the accused, before the evidence can be admitted.

The logic for allowing in evidence of past convictions to impeach a witness seems to be that if a person has broken the law, this indicates a lack of respect for the law and a lack of trustworthiness that can be generalized to cast doubt on his credibility. This policy is reminiscent of the common law policy against allowing felons to testify at all.

FRE 609(a)(2) requires the trial court to admit evidence of prior convictions for dishonesty and false statements no matter how highly prejudicial. The courts had difficulty determining with consistency which crimes directly or indirectly involved deceit and lying. So, recently the rule was amended to help distinguish those two types

FRE 609(a)(2), P. 274

of crimes. FRE 609(a)(2) now states:

> Evidence that any witness has been convicted of a crime shall be admitted, regardless of the punishment, *if it readily can be determined that establishing the elements of the crime required proof or admission of an act of dishonesty or false statement by the witness.* [Emphasis added.]

This recent amendment provides for automatic admissibility if the dishonesty or false statement aspects were central to the prior conviction and necessarily had to be determined by the fact finder or admitted by the defendant.

It doesn't matter whether the past conviction was for a felony or a misdemeanor. It doesn't matter whether the evidence will have a highly prejudicial effect. The evidence is admissible and the trial court has no discretion to exclude it as long as the conviction is less than ten years old, and not the subject of a pardon or other expungement.

You might be lulled into believing that you've finally come across a black-and-white rule that requires no penetrating insight on the part of the paralegal when preparing for trial. At long last, here's something you don't have to worry about when interviewing witnesses, right? Not exactly. As always, the problem has been that the courts were confused as to what constituted a crime of "dishonesty or false statement." The recent Advisory Notes specify such crimes as perjury, subordination of perjury, false statement, criminal fraud, embezzlement, or false pretense. The intent was and is that the prior offense should be of a type which would provide the jury with information to evaluate the witness's ability to provide truthful testimony. The new "readily determined" language allows the court some discretion to look at the supporting documents such as the indictment, the statute, the jury instructions, or the factual basis the defendant admitted if she entered a guilty plea to determine whether the conduct for which the defendant was convicted was for dishonesty or lying. The key, however, is that the inquiry should be an easy one.

For example, child abuse is not considered a crime of dishonesty or false statement. But consider the following hypothetical situation.

Sick Sam hung around near the local school yard. He befriended a kindergarten child, Davie, who walked home alone each day. For several weeks, Sick did nothing more than talk to the young bay, later admitting this befriending was part of his scheme of seduction. Finally, Sick lured Davie to come with him instead of going home after school, by promising Davie treats. Sick took Davie to an abandoned building where he sexually abused him. Sick was captured and convicted of felony sexual abuse of a child.

FRE 609(a)(1) and (2), P. 274

Later, Sick was charged with another unrelated crime. Prosecution attempted to impeach Sick's testimony by bringing in the prior felony conviction of sexual abuse pursuant to Rule 609(a)(2), claiming that in Sick's case, the prior crime involved a great deal of deception, dishonesty, and false statements. In the past, courts were mixed as to whether this type of conviction should come in automatically under 609(a)(2), or whether it should be subject to the determination of fairness pursuant to 609(a)(1). With the recent amendment, the conviction now only could be admitted under 609(a)(1) because the child sexual abuse crime does not require a finding of dishonesty or false statement for a conviction.

As a paralegal, when confronted with an interviewee who admits to prior convictions of crimes, it is important to at least make some inquiry into the nature of those crimes in order to see if the witness will be vulnerable under Rule 609(a)(1) or 609(a)(2). Even if the crimes are misdemeanors, they must be investigated because

609(a)(2) does not require that the prior conviction be a felony. If the crimes do not involve dishonesty, then a FRE 403 motion to exclude the evidence must be considered. If the crimes do involve dishonesty, then no such motion can be entertained.

6.6   Impeachment Based on Religious Beliefs or Opinions

FRE 610, P. 275

Pursuant to Rule 610, "Evidence of the beliefs or opinions of a witness on matters of religion is not admissible for the purpose of showing that by reason of their nature the witness's credibility is impaired or enhanced." Consider the following example.

Assume that a trial is going on in a small midwestern town. The jury is composed primarily of Christian men and women. A witness is called to testify for the defense. The opposing attorney may not impeach this witness by asking, "Isn't it true that you are an atheist?"

The reasons for this are primarily constitutional in nature, and the fact that this rule is not widely litigated seems to indicate that it poses no real problems in the courts, at least not in its direct application.

For the paralegal, a witness's religious belief system should be a "hands-off" area in an interview. You cannot use such information to enhance your witness's credibility, even though you might feel that his or her religious practices might support such an inference. Conversely, you cannot use such information against a witness to impeach credibility. In an interview, you should not inquire into the religious belief system of your witness, unless that belief system is a fundamental issue in the case. The belief system becomes fundamental only when it is the actual basis for the conduct of the parties in the litigation. Consider another example.

Assume your firm is representing a client who is a Christian Scientist and who elects to withhold certain medical treatment from his child. Assume further that Child Protective Services (CPS) is seeking an injunction to compel the parent to allow the child to receive treatment. CPS claims the parent is abusing the child by failing to provide it with proper medical care. Your client's belief system is a fundamental issue in the case and is, of course, an area of inquiry worthy of pursuit. This is considered unrelated to impeachment.

The prohibition against impeachment based on a religious belief system becomes complicated when a witness has affiliations with organizations that have religious overtones. Actually, there is a blurred line as to when an affiliation or membership with any group, even one that is not religious in nature, is admissible to impeach a witness, and this will be discussed more in the section of this chapter about bias. The following example shows where a defendant's association with an organization that has religious overtones is admissible for impeachment purposes.

Mary has been charged with violating a law prohibiting antiabortion demonstrations within close proximity of an abortion clinic. Mary is an active member of the National Right to Life Organization, has signs around her house supporting this cause, and has bumper stickers on her car calling for laws prohibiting abortion. Mary testifies that she was near the clinic praying but not part of the demonstration for which she was arrested. Her active association with the antiabortion organization would be admissible for impeachment on this issue.

6.7   Prior Inconsistent Statements

Hearsay
An out-of-court statement offered to prove the truth contained in the statement.

Perhaps one of the most often used methods to impeach the credibility of a witness with regard to his or her testimony is to show where the witness has previously made contradictory or conflicting statements. A witness who says different things at different times in answer to the same question raises doubts as to the truthfulness of any answer he or she might give, especially to that question.

In order to explain the admissibility of prior inconsistent statements for impeachment purposes, it is necessary to define the word **hearsay** in terms of its evidentiary meaning. In future chapters we will discuss hearsay at length, but a brief introduction here will help the reader gain some perspective on impeachment evidence in general. Hearsay is defined as an out-of-court statement offered into evidence to prove the truth of the matter asserted. Hearsay is generally inadmissible in trial, although the exceptions to the hearsay rule are voluminous, and a substantial amount of hearsay is in fact admissible under the Federal Rules of Evidence. When discussing prior inconsistent statements for impeachment purposes, however, we are not talking about hearsay at all.

When offering a prior inconsistent statement to cast doubts on the truthfulness of a witness, the prior statement is not offered as true. It is offered to show that what the witness has to say *cannot* be relied on to be true. Therefore, the use of a prior inconsistent statement for impeachment purposes is not hearsay because it is not evidence of an out-of-court statement offered to prove *the truth of what is said in the statement itself.* This is important because it means that any number of out-of-court statements, when offered for impeachment purposes, are admissible even when they don't qualify for a hearsay exception.

This is a very large back door through which evidence otherwise inadmissible can come in, and courts carefully weigh the probative value of such evidence against its potential for unfair prejudice.

Under FRE 613, a witness may be interrogated about prior inconsistent statements without advance warning. The witness need not be shown the documentation of the prior inconsistency before being interrogated. This can be a very powerful tool. The witness will not have time to reconcile the contradictions between his or her current testimony and the prior statement, and will frequently appear to be caught directly in a lie.

FRE 613, P. 276

Even when the prior inconsistent statement isn't directly contradictory, it may be admissible for impeachment purposes. A witness who claims he or she cannot remember an event while on the stand can be impeached by his or her prior statements recalling the event. This type of impeachment is equivocal. It may be that the witness really did remember something before that now he has forgotten. It may also be that the witness really does remember the event, but doesn't want to tell the truth. It is generally the jury's job to determine whether the witness is credible, and which inference to draw from the testimony.

FRE 608(b), P. 274

Prove up a Denial
To introduce evidence to prove a fact that a witness has denied.

Unlike FRE 608(b), which precludes the introduction of extrinsic evidence to **prove up a denial** on the part of a witness, FRE 613 allows extrinsic evidence to be brought in to prove the prior inconsistent statement when the witness has denied making the prior statement. This doesn't leave the door as wide open as it seems, however. The admissibility of extrinsic evidence to impeach a witness based on prior inconsistent statements is constrained by common law restrictions on collateral evidence. This is discussed at length in the last section of this chapter

Consider the following case in which the trial court admitted a prior inconsistent statement of the defendant's alibi witness. In concluding that the trial court correctly allowed the statement, the appellate court distinguished FRE 608(b) and FRE 613, and discussed the tension between the two rules.

United States v. Winchenbach

197 F.3d 548 (1st Cir. 1999)

*   *   *

[A jury convicted the defendant Winchenbach for distribution of cocaine resulting from an long-term, undercover investigation by the Maine Drug Enforcement Agency.] At trial, [Winchenbach] called . . . Robbie Flint, as an alibi witness. Flint testified, inter alia, that the [Winchenbach] was not in the trailer when [co-conspirator]

Spinney arrived on September 3. On cross-examination, the following exchange took place:

Q: Do you have any knowledge of [Winchenbach] selling drugs or being involved in drugs on September 3rd 1997?

A: No.

Q: None at all?

A: No.

Q: As far as you know he was not involved in anything?

A: Right.

Q: . . . [I]n that interview with [agent] Dan Bradford, you did talk about [Winchenbach's] drug activity that night, didn't you?

A: No.

Q: You didn't? Well, isn't it true that what you told Dan Bradford was that the night that MDEA searched the house . . . they missed several ounces of cocaine that were buried in jars outside the residence?

A: No.

Q: You did not tell that to Dan Bradford?

A: No I didn't.

On redirect examination, defense counsel ignored this testimony. In rebuttal, however, the prosecutor called Bradford and sought to interrogate him about the conversation. The court overruled [Winchenbach]'s objections, and Bradford testified that he spoke with Flint some months after the fact and that Flint . . . told him that the agents overlooked a quantity of buried cocaine during the search of Winchenbach's trailer. The judge then instructed the jury to consider Bradford's testimony only as it related to Flint's credibility and not for the truth of the matter asserted.

*   *   *

[Winchenbach] . . . maintains that . . . the court should have excluded Bradford's testimony under either Fed. R. Evid. 608(b) or Fed R. Evid. 403. We address both objections.

In this court, as below, the government parries [Winchenbach]'s Rule 608(b) objection by claiming that Rule 613(b), not Rule 608(b), controls. On a superficial level at least, an apparent tension exists between these two rules. Rule 608(b) bars the credibility-related use of some extrinsic evidence, while Rule 613(b), albeit by negative implication, permits the credibility-related use of some extrinsic evidence if the proponent satisfies certain enumerated conditions. In this instance, [Winchenbach] characterizes Bradford's testimony as extrinsic evidence relating to a specific instance of Flint's misconduct, offered by the prosecutor to attack Flint's credibility (and thus prohibited by Rule 608(b)). The government demurs, characterizing the testimony as extrinsic evidence of a prior inconsistent statement made by Flint, offered after Flint had been afforded an opportunity to explain or deny the remark and in circumstances wherein [Winchenbach] had a full opportunity to interrogate both Flint and Bradford on the matter (and thus admissible under Rule 613(b)).

At first blush, neither of these characterizations seems implausible—but they cannot both be right. There are, moreover, two wrinkles. In the first place, the district court, though deeming the evidence admissible, mistakenly relied on Rule 608(b). This bevue need not detain us, for the trial court's use of an improper ground for admission of evidence is harmless if the evidence was admissible for the same purpose on some other ground. Thus, this wrinkle irons itself out.

In the second place, each party presses a theory that fails to fit. [Winchenbach] seems to say that the evidence should be excluded under Rule 608(b) simply because it was offered to impugn Flint's credibility. This is an overbroad generalization which, among its other vices, contradicts the time-honored tenet that prior inconsistent statements ordinarily may be used to impeach a witness's credibility. . . . In the bargain, this interpretation of Rule 608(b) leaves no room at all for the admission of extrinsic impeachment evidence under the auspices of Rule 613(b). Thus, we reject it.

For its part, the government urges us to hold that a strict statement/conduct dichotomy triggers the choice of rule. Under this dichotomy, Rule 613(b) always would apply to statements and Rule 608(b) always would apply to conduct. A glance at the case law unmasks this gross oversimplification. Cases invoking Rule 608(b) in respect to statements, as opposed to conduct, are not uncommon. . . . The commentators likewise abjure the proffered distinction. . . . We, too, reject it.

. . . [W]e think that there is a principled distinction between the types of evidence covered by the two rules. In our view, Rule 613(b) applies when two statements, one made at trial and one made previously, are irreconcilably at odds. In such an event, the cross-examiner is permitted to show the discrepancy by extrinsic evidence if necessary—not to demonstrate which of the two is true but, rather, to show that the two do not jibe (thus calling the declarant's credibility into question). . . . In short, comparison and contradiction are the hallmarks of Rule 613(b). As one treatise puts it:

> The theory of attack by prior inconsistent statements is not based on the assumption that the present testimony is false and the former statement true but rather upon the notion that talking one way on the stand and another way previously is blowing hot and cold, and raises a doubt as to the truthfulness of both statements.

McCormick on Evidence.

In contrast, Rule 608(b) addresses situations in which a witness's prior activity, whether exemplified by conduct or by a statement, in and of itself casts significant doubt upon his veracity. . . . Thus, Rule 608(b) applies to, and bars the introduction of, extrinsic evidence of specific instances of a witness's *misconduct* if offered to impugn his credibility. . . . So viewed, Rule 608(b) applies to a statement, as long as the statement in and of itself stands as an independent means of impeachment without any need to compare it to contradictory trial testimony. . . .

Applying this analysis to the case at hand, Bradford's testimony falls within the compass of Rule 613(b). At trial, Flint denied any knowledge of drug dealing at the premises, of [Winchenbach]'s involvement with drugs, or of having told the agent about jars of cocaine buried in the yard. Bradford's testimony—that Flint had told him that the MDEA, in searching the premises, had overlooked several ounces of buried cocaine—directly contradicted Flint's trial testimony in all three respects and therefore constituted extrinsic evidence of a prior inconsistent statement.

That ends the matter. Inasmuch as Flint was afforded an opportunity to explain or deny the prior inconsistent statement and [Winchenbach] had a chance to interrogate him about it, the conditions for the operation of Rule 613(b) were fully satisfied.

As a paralegal, part of your job may be to scrutinize the police reports, interviews, diaries, affidavits, depositions, court records, prior testimony, and any other statements to see if your witnesses or opposition's witnesses have contradicted themselves at different times. You must have the documentation to back up the impeaching questions the attorney intends to ask at trial, in case the witness denies having made the contradictory statement. If the witness denies having made the statement, extrinsic evidence may be admissible to prove that the prior statement was made.

6.8   Refreshing a Witness's Memory

There are times when a witness develops a case of amnesia during trial and cannot remember things about which she or he may have been clear in the past. Or for whatever reason, the witness may no longer be able to accurately articulate or relate a previous event. Merely impeaching the witness about her or his prior inconsistent statements is insufficient when what you really want is to compel the witness to remember or admit knowledge of the facts and to testify about them in court. Keep in mind that a prior inconsistent statement admitted for impeachment purposes tends only to prove that the witness is a liar. Absent some other basis of admissibility, that prior inconsistent statement is not evidence of the truth of the statement itself.

FRE 612, P. 276

Refresh a Witness's Recollection
To remined a witness of something that the witness once reported or knew to be true.

FRE 803(5), P. 281

Provided proper procedure is followed, pursuant to FRE 612, a past recording or writing such as a diary, business record, signed interview statement, tape recording, or letter may be presented to a witness to **refresh** his or her **recollection.** This may be done either prior to the witness's testifying or while the witness is on the stand. FRE 612 is distinguishable from the hearsay exception dealing with recorded recollections, FRE 803(5), but is often confused with that exception. Unlike the hearsay exception, however, FRE 612 doesn't allow the recorded information to be admitted as evidence. It merely provides a mechanism for the document or recording to be used to assist the witness in remembering the information, so that the witness can testify properly. (Hearsay exceptions dealing with previously written or recorded information will be addressed in a later chapter.) Consider the following example.

In a case brought by P. Owner against D. Walker for trespass, Mr. Walker claimed Ms. Owner verbally gave him license to cross her property as a shortcut to his property. Ms. Owner denied ever having so authorized Mr. Walker and claimed to have no recollection of ever having spoken with Mr. Walker at any time. At trial, Mr. Walker produced Ms. Owner's diary, which he obtained during discovery proceedings. The diary contained an entry dated approximately ten months prior to the filing of the suit, which stated, "This morning I had coffee with my new neighbor Mr. Walker. We had a lovely conversation, and I expect it will be quite pleasant having him as a neighbor." After being asked to review this entry to refresh her recollection, Ms. Owner was then asked about her conversation with Mr. Walker.

The same entry in the diary used to refresh Ms. Owner's recollection in the above hypothetical would be usable to impeach her credibility because it contains a prior inconsistent statement relative to Ms. Owner's claim to have no recollection of having spoken with Mr. Walker before. The diary entry might be admissible under the hearsay exception 803(5) as well. However, when presented to Ms. Owner at trial in the above hypothetical, it was being used to cause Ms. Owner to remember the content of her conversation with Mr. Walker.

6.9   Personal Bias

An inexhaustible area for impeachment and one which the paralegal will want to explore extensively is the potential bias of a witness.

A witness's bias in relation to either party or to issues in the case may taint the witness's testimony and therefore affect his or her credibility. The ways in which a witness might incur a bias are endless, but usual ways include family relationships, business and financial connections, common memberships, educational and governmental party affiliations (remember Monica Goodling!), and beneficial or detrimental consequences of testifying such as cooperation agreements or fear of retribution. Extrinsic evidence is admissible to prove bias where the witness denies the bias exists but evidence suggests the opposite. As you might imagine, this type of back door allows a great deal of evidence to come in for impeachment purposes that otherwise would be inadmissible.

If a witness has a relationship with a party, even if it appears to be a tangential one, it is important to explore the nature of that relationship in order to know if there is bias for or against your client, or if bias is an issue that is likely to be raised by the opponent. It is especially important to explore this area because the courts are generous in allowing extrinsic evidence of bias. There is not a specific federal rule of evidence that governs the admissibility of such evidence. Instead, the evidence is analyzed pursuant to the general rules of relevancy, FRE 401-403.

The following case exemplifies one court's discussion of impeachment techniques and its affirmation of the admissibility of extrinsic evidence to rebut or rehabilitate an attempted bias impeachment.

Unites States v. Lindemann

85 F.3d 1232 (7th Cir. 1996)

"Charisma," a show horse, died in its stall on the night of December 15, 1990. The insurance company that had issued a policy on Charisma's life concluded that the death was the result of natural causes and paid the $250,000 value of the policy. Subsequently, the Federal Bureau of Investigation uncovered an alleged conspiracy between Tommy Burns and Barney Ward to kill horses for pay, allowing the horses' owners to collect insurance proceeds. Burns gave the FBI information indicating that George Lindemann, Jr. ("Lindemann"), a partial owner of Charisma, had arranged the horse's death in order to gain the proceeds of its life insurance policy. Lindemann was tried and convicted of three counts of wire fraud. . . . He appeals that conviction and we affirm.

*   *   *

. . . During Burns' cross-examination, Lindemann attacked the credibility of his testimony by suggesting that he would not have gotten a plea deal if he hadn't come up with the name of a "big fish" like Lindemann. Naturally, the government wanted to offer evidence to rebut Lindemann's assertion. Specifically, it wanted to explain to the jury that Lindemann's indictment and Burns' cooperation were the result of a much larger investigation involving the killing of 15 horses, including Charisma. Thus the government elicited from Burns the following testimony:

Q: Now, Mr. Burns, when the federal agents came down to Florida after you were arrested for killing a horse, Streetwise, they asked you a lot of questions about your crimes; is that right?

A: Yes, they did.

Q: Were those agents focused on George Lindemann?

A: No, they weren't. They basically focused on Helen Brach.

Q: During the course of your cooperation, Mr. Burns, you cooperated against other wealthy people, isn't that right?

A: Oh yeah.

Q: And you've cooperated, have you not, Mr. Burns, with respect to other famous equestrians?

A: Yes, I have.

*   *   *

Q: Is George Lindemann a big part of your cooperation or a small part of your cooperation?

A: They never treated him like he was a big part.

Q: In fact, Mr. Burns, you told the government about many, many people that you killed horses for. To your knowledge, how many people did you discuss with the government, roughly?

A: 30.

Q: And how many of those people have pleaded guilty?

A: 90 percent of them.

*   *   *

Lindemann argues that Burns' testimony was inadmissible because it was essentially "bolstering." "Bolstering" is the practice of offering evidence solely for the purpose of enhancing a witness's credibility before that credibility is attacked. Such evidence is inadmissible because it "has the potential for extending the length of trials enormously, . . . asks the jury to take the witness's testimony on faith, . . . and may . . . reduce the care with which jurors listen for inconsistencies and other signs of falsehood or inaccuracy." Once a witness's credibility has been attacked, however, the non-attacking party is permitted to admit evidence to "rehabilitate" the witness. (citations omitted)

Lindemann's suggestion that Burns falsely implicated him to obtain a plea deal was certainly an attack on the credibility of Burns' testimony. More specifically, it was an attempt to show that Burns had a bias:

> Bias is the relationship between a party and a witness which might lead the witness to slant, unconsciously or otherwise, his testimony in favor of or against a party. Bias may be induced by a witness' like, dislike, or fear of a party, or *by the witness' self-interest.* . . .

Bias is one of the five acceptable methods of attacking the credibility of a witness's testimony: (1) attacking the witness's general character for truthfulness; (2) showing that, prior to trial, the witness has made statements inconsistent with his testimony; (3) showing that the witness is biased; (4) showing that the witness has an impaired capacity to perceive, recall, or relate the event about which he is testifying; and (5) contradicting the substance of the witness's testimony. . . . Thus Lindemann was perfectly entitled to suggest his theory that Burns was lying about Lindemann in order to better the parameters of his plea deal. . . . However, the direct consequence of the attack was that the government was entitled to introduce evidence to rehabilitate Burns on the issue. . . .

The Federal Rules of Evidence specifically address the bolstering/rehabilitation aspect of only two of the five attack methods: Character for truthfulness and prior inconsistent statements. The admissibility of evidence regarding a witness's bias, diminished capacity, and contradictions in his testimony is not specifically addressed by the Rules, and thus admissibility is limited only by the relevance standard of Rule 402. . . . Therefore, because the attack at issue was on Burns' bias, and not on his character for truthfulness in general, Lindemann's contention that the limitations of Rule 608 should have applied is incorrect. Moreover, because bias is not a collateral issue, it was permissible for evidence on this issue to be extrinsic in form.

*   *   *

Here we conclude that the admission of evidence regarding Burns' cooperation in other cases was relevant. The evidence specifically rebutted the allegation that Burns was biased out of self-interest in Lindemann's case: Burns' successful participation in numerous other cases meant that at the time he was negotiating over his plea deal, he had lots of information to use as bargaining chips. That fact was relevant under the standards of Fed. R. Evid. 402 because it made less probable the assertion that Burns was lying in Lindemann's case out of self-interest. . . . Finally, the district court immediately warned the jury that it was not to infer Lindemann's guilt from the fact that other indicted individuals had pleaded guilty. Thus the evidence was used only to assess Burns' credibility, not as evidence of Lindemann's guilt.

In conclusion, because Lindemann attacked the credibility of Burns' testimony by asserting that Burns had a bias in Lindemann's case, the government was permitted to rebut that assertion by introducing evidence of its own. Furthermore, because that evidence was relevant according to Fed. R. Evid. 402, the district court's decision to admit it was not an abuse of discretion.

The parties in the above case were allowed to introduce extrinsic evidence of the cooperation agreement as well as the extent of the investigation and of Burn's cooperation in an effort to impeach and to rehabilitate him. This case was related to bias, but the attack and counterattack impeachment techniques are applicable to all impeachment methods regardless of whether extrinsic evidence is admissible.

6.10   Collateral Extrinsic Evidence

As has been noted, extrinsic evidence is not always admissible to impeach a witness. Rule 608(b) specifically precludes the introduction of extrinsic evidence to prove specific acts of character for truthfulness or untruthfulness. The attorney may be allowed, on cross-examination, to interrogate a witness regarding specific acts of conduct that are probative of the witness's character for untruthfulness, but the attorney may not offer up extrinsic proof if the witness lies.

Even when extrinsic evidence is admissible, however, the trial court may cut off impeachment questioning. Evidence that is tangential or not sufficiently related to the trial issues in a case is called "collateral." It is important for the paralegal to consider when evidence may be collateral.

The following example illustrates a case where extrinsic evidence would be deemed collateral and therefore inadmissible.

J. Sharpeye, witness for the prosecution, testified that he observed the defendant in front of the bank, at 8 P.M. on the night of the robbery. Mr. Sharpeye further testified that he had been driving past the bank at that time on his way home from work.

Mr. Sharpeye was actually on his way home from a poker game when he went past the bank. He denied this on cross-examination.

Defense will not be allowed to introduce extrinsic evidence that Mr. Sharpeye was in fact on his way home from a poker game and not from the office. Mr. Sharpeye's location prior to observing the defendant has no independent relevance to any issue in the case other than impeachment. Therefore, extrinsic evidence of Mr. Sharpeye's poker party detour will not be admitted because it is collateral.

Consider, however, the above hypothetical with the facts altered as follows.

Assume an extrinsic witness will testify that Mr. Sharpeye drove past the bank on his way home from the poker game at 10 P.M. and not at 8 P.M. as he had testified. This would be used to show that Mr. Sharpeye could not have placed the defendant at the scene of the crime at 8 P.M., as well as to impeach Mr. Sharpeye's credibility. This extrinsic evidence therefore has independent relevance to the case other than to merely impeach the witness. It will therefore be admissible.

The following case illustrates a situation where seemingly independently relevant evidence is inadmissible as collateral.

Illinois v. Jones

499 N.E.2d 510 (Ill. 1986)

Defendant Walter Jones was convicted, following trial by jury, of the offenses of rape and indecent liberties with a child. [D]efendant argues that the jury should have been permitted to hear impeachment testimony regarding prior inconsistent statements of one of the defense witnesses.

*   *   *

During the trial, the defense called as a witness Willie Mae Stephenson, the mother's landlady, who lived on the first floor of the family's building. Mrs. Stephenson testified that she was not at home on the day the girls told their mother what had happened, and that she did not hear any argument or shouting coming from their basement apartment on that day. Mrs. Stephenson further testified that the prosecutrix told her that she had been raped by defendant. This testimony was contrary to that which the defense had expected Mrs. Stephenson to give, and the court allowed the defense to question her as an adverse witness. Mrs. Stephenson denied that she had ever had a telephone conversation in which she told Defense Attorney Cohan that she saw the mother repeatedly hit the prosecutrix [victim], who was telling her mother, "He didn't do nothing," until the prosecutrix finally said, "He did it." The trial judge refused to permit the jury to hear testimony from Mr. Cohan or two other witnesses who claim to have heard Mrs. Stephenson say that the prosecutrix was beaten until she implicated defendant.

*   *   *

Defendant now claims that this refusal was error. . . .

[H]owever, the law is well settled that:

[W]hen a witness unexpectedly gives testimony against the party calling him, such party has the right to examine him and by such examination to show that the witness is giving unexpected testimony, and to specifically call the attention of the witness to former statements made by him for the purpose of refreshing his memory or awakening his conscience, and to cause him to relent and speak the truth if he was lying. This, however, is as far as the party may go, and under no circumstances may he show, either by the written statement of the witness or by other witnesses, that the witness did, in fact, make those statements.

If the witness admitted making the previous statement, it would prove nothing except that he, an admittedly unreliable witness, had said so. If the witness denied making the statement, the matter would necessarily end there, because to pursue it further would be trying a collateral issue rather than a fact material under the indictment.

We acknowledge that the law of this state recently was changed to permit either party to challenge the credibility of his own witness:

(a) The credibility of a witness may be attacked by any party, including the party calling him.

(b) If the court determines that a witness is hostile or unwilling, he may be examined by the party calling him as if under cross-examination.

Although this . . . rule permits any party to impeach his own witness, it does not grant permission to try collateral issues in order to prove the unreliability or untruthfulness of the witness. Here, the trial court was asked to try the collateral issue of whether Mrs. Stephenson had made the statements. We find no error in the trial court's refusal to allow Mr. Cohan, Mr. Jones, and Ms. Wardlow to testify on that issue.

AFFIRMED.

The important thing to note in this case is that Mrs. Stephenson's out-of-court statements were hearsay and inadmissible to prove the truth of the matter asserted. (Hearsay we introduce only briefly in this chapter, but it will be the subject of substantial discussion in later chapters.) Mrs. Stephenson's prior inconsistent statement that the prosecutrix (victim) had been beaten into accusing the defendant would have been admissible only to show that Mrs. Stephenson was not credible. It would not have been admissible to prove that the prosecutrix had in fact been beaten into making the accusation. Even had Mrs. Stephenson admitted making the prior inconsistent statement, the jury would not have been allowed to consider that statement as proof of the matter asserted therein. She would have had to testify directly in trial that she observed the prosecutrix being beaten into accusing the defendant of rape. Therefore, calling other witnesses to basically prove that Mrs. Stephenson (the defense's own witness) was not credible would have taken the trial on a tangential trip that would have provided only marginal probative value. The evidence was collateral and therefore excluded.

6.11 Overlapping Rules and Limitations on the Use of Impeachment Evidence

The Federal Rules do not enumerate every permissible method of impeachment. The Rules attempt, by their construction, to be clear and unambiguous, while allowing a great deal of flexibility in order to accommodate the diverse types of situations that the courts encounter. Because of their specificity, there are times when an offer of proof does not fit squarely within any single evidentiary rule. Because of their flexibility, there are times when a single piece of evidence is admissible under several rules. This is especially evident when dealing with evidence that is admissible for impeachment as well as for other purposes. The following example illustrates this point, while reviewing some concepts presented previously.

FRE 404(b), P. 265

FRE 608(b), P. 274

FRE 609, P. 274

Recall Harry, our peeping Tom, who had a history of peeping in the past. Assume in the current case, Harry testified he was hanging around outside the window of the alleged victim's house totally by accident. Evidence of Harry's prior peeps is admissible under Rule 404(b) to show absence of mistake and intent. The prior peeps may also be inquired into pursuant to Rule 608(b), to impeach Harry's credibility and his character for untruthfulness. Finally, if Harry's previous peeping episodes resulted in a felony conviction, evidence of a prior conviction may be admissible under Rule 609.

You may wonder why, if evidence is admissible for one purpose, you should be concerned about whether it is also admissible for other purposes. There are several reasons. One is that when the jury is allowed to hear evidence strictly for impeachment purposes, it is instructed not to consider that evidence as proof of the truth of the matter. It can only consider impeachment evidence as it relates to the credibility of the witness. Introducing the evidence under more than one rule allows the jury to consider the same evidence for more than one reason. Furthermore, there are limitations under certain impeachment rules about bringing in extrinsic evidence. Perhaps extrinsic evidence might be excludable under one impeachment rule but admissible under another.

Although there is often substantial overlap and the rules seem to combine and blur, it is important to approach each evidentiary matter from as many perspectives as you can to optimize the usefulness and admissibility of the material.

6.12   In Summary

- Impeachment evidence serves to attack the credibility of a witness.
- A witness may be impeached by either the proponent or the opponent.
- A witness's credibility may be attacked with character evidence relating to the witness's untruthfulness and rehabilitated with character evidence relating to the witness's truthfulness.
- A witness may be impeached by cross-examination about specific instances of past conduct which exemplify the witness's character for truthfulness or untruthfulness, but the cross-examining party may not use extrinsic evidence to disprove a denial of any such past conduct.
- Prior felony convictions are admissible for impeachment purposes subject to review for unfair prejudice, except that prior convictions for crimes which require proof of dishonesty or false statements are admissible irrespective of any prejudice such evidence might cause.
- A witness may not be impeached, nor can the witness's character for truthfulness be rehabilitated, with evidence based on the religious beliefs of the witness.
- A witness may be impeached with his or her prior inconsistent statements.
- A witness may be impeached based on personal bias, and extrinsic evidence is admissible to prove bias, if bias is denied.
- Extrinsic evidence, the sole purpose of which is to impeach a witness's credibility, is excludable based on being collateral to matters at issue in the case.
- Evidence admissible under the impeachment rules is frequently admissible under other rules as well.

End of Chapter Review Questions

1. What is impeachment?
2. Who may impeach a witness?
3. How does one impeach a person who is reputed to be dishonest?

4. May a witness be impeached based on specific instances of past misconduct?
5. May a witness be impeached based on past felony convictions?
6. May a witness be impeached based on past misdemeanor convictions?
7. May a witness be impeached based on religious beliefs?
8. What is a prior inconsistent statement?
9. What does it mean to refresh a witness's recollection?
10. What is a personal bias, and how might this be used to impeach a witness?
11. What is extrinsic evidence?
12. What is collateral evidence?
13. Is evidence ever admissible under more than one rule?

Applications

Consider the following hypothetical situation.

Mr. Smith testified for the state during the trial of Mr. White, who was charged with gun smuggling. Mr. Smith testified that he observed Mr. White's boat leave the dock just before midnight on May 9th, and return at 6 A.M. on May 10th, the next morning. White claims he never took the boat out that night. The evidence of the boat's departure is a critical part of the state's circumstantial case against Mr. White.

Mr. Smith previously told his sister that Mr. White's boat never left the dock at all during the entire month of May. Mr. Smith's sister had at one time been engaged to Mr. White, but Mr. White had jilted her.

1. Is evidence of Mr. Smith's prior statement to his sister admissible? If yes, how would this testimony be presented? Could Mr. Smith's sister be called? Why or why not?
2. Is evidence of Mr. Smith's sister's prior engagement to Mr. White admissible? Why or why not?
3. If Mr. Smith's sister is allowed to testify to Mr. Smith's prior inconsistent statement regarding Mr. White's boat never having left the dock during the entire month of May, is this testimony usable by defense to prove that in fact Mr. White's boat stayed docked during that time? Why or why not?

Consider the following hypothetical situation.

Sharon is charged with aggravated assault. She claims she didn't intend to actually shoot the gun but was only trying to scare the victim when the gun went off by accident. Sharon was convicted seven years ago of the crime of embezzlement. She took $200 from her employer's petty cash drawer and placed phony receipts in the box to cover her theft.

4. Under what rule would evidence of Sharon's embezzlement conviction be admissible?
5. How is Sharon's embezzlement conviction relevant to this case?
6. Is Sharon's embezzlement conviction excludable on either grounds of irrelevancy, or unfair prejudice pursuant to Rule 403? Why or why not?

Assume for the following question that Sharon's conviction seven years ago was for the crime of felony robbery.

7. Under what rule would evidence of Sharon's felony robbery conviction be admissible?
8. How is Sharon's felony robbery conviction relevant to this case?
9. Is Sharon's robbery conviction excludable on either grounds of irrelevancy, or unfair prejudice pursuant to Rule 403? Why or why not?

During depositions prior to trial in a fender-bender case, defendant's paralegal noticed that Doris Bistander was wearing glasses and a hearing aid. She was questioned about her eyesight and her hearing during the deposition. Defendant then requested discovery of Doris's eye and hearing records which documented that Doris had been newly fitted for both the glasses and the hearing aid the day after the accident. At trial, the defendant asserts that another car had hit the plaintiff's car and that the damage to defendant's car was from a previous accident. Doris, who was the only eyewitness, testified that the defendant's silver Porshe screeched to a halt by slamming into the back of plaintiff's green beemer.

10. Could the defense impeach Doris with the medical records regarding her eyesight and her hearing? Would the extrinsic evidence be admissible?
11. Is there any way that the plaintiff could rehabilitate Doris if the defense does successfully impeach her? Would the extrinsic evidence be admissible?
12. Would the impeachment be regarding her veracity? Discuss.

7

Lay and
Expert Opinions

7.1 Opinion Testimony by Lay Witnesses

FRE 701, P. 277

Pursuant to Rule 701 of the Federal Rules of Evidence,

Opinion
A belief based in part on impression and in part on direct knowledge.

Inference
A conclusion derived from implied as well as direct information.

If the witness is not testifying as an expert, the witness's testimony in the form of **opinions** or **inferences** is limited to those opinions or inferences which are (a) rationally based on the perception of the witness, (b) helpful to a clear understanding of the witness's testimony or the determination of a fact in issue, *and (c) not based on scientific, technical, or other specialized knowledge within the scope of Rule 702.*

The italicized language is the amendment to the rule which became effective December 1, 2000. It clarifies that a witness testifying to an opinion based on scientific, technical, or other specialized knowledge must first meet the requirements set forth in FRE 702 which governs expert testimony. In other words, a party cannot try to sneak in expert testimony under the guise that it is a lay opinion. We will discuss expert testimony later in this chapter.

FRE 602, P. 272

Rule 701 is consistent with FRE 602, which requires that a witness is only competent to testify to those matters about which the witness has personal knowledge. Personal knowledge includes those opinions and inferences formed from the witness's perceptions and observations.

FRE 601, P. 272

You will perhaps recall that under FRE 601, where state law supplies the rule of decision, the competency of a witness is determined in accordance with state law. Rule 701 provides no comparable constraint. Even in diversity cases, where state law provides the rule of decision, opinion evidence of nonexperts is governed by FRE 701.

In order to determine whether an opinion of a **lay** (nonexpert) witness is in fact based on the perception of a witness and not merely speculation, the proffering party must **lay a foundation** showing that the witness has the requisite personal knowledge to formulate the opinion to which he is testifying. The factual basis for nonexpert opinion testimony must appear on the record of the trial proceeding. Unfortunately, it is not easy to predict when a foundation is sufficient to admit opinion testimony. But consider that courts have found lay witnesses competent to testify on a broad range of topics such as the physical appearance of persons or things, identity, age, a person's demeanor or conduct, a person's competency, weights and measures, degrees of light or darkness, sounds, value of a person's property, time, speed, and distances.

Lay Opinion
An opinion of an ordinary person applying to particular expertise in offering testimony.

Laying a Foundation
Providing sufficient preliminary information to allow the evidence to be admitted. Generally, identifying the evidence and tying it to the issue in question

When a lay witness predicates an answer with phrases such as "I think," "I believe," "My impression is," "I'm not sure but to the best of my recollection," the issue is raised as to whether that person is speaking from personal knowledge or whether the witness is merely speculating. Such precursive comments can actually bolster the credibility of a witness's testimony because it appears that the witness is trying not to overstate facts. They can alternatively be indicative of the witness's poor recollection, and although this might make his testimony less credible, it does not cause the evidence to be excluded. Only when such comments are used to indicate that the witness hasn't had sufficient personal observations to support the opinion he offers is the evidence excludable. There is no absolute predictor to determine when there is sufficient personal knowledge. The trial court has wide discretion and the outcomes between courts vary. Clear examples can be given as follows.

A nonexpert witness will be allowed to testify, "He seemed agitated." This is considered a "shorthand" for the various actions and comments observed by the witness. The witness can be questioned about the concrete details of the perception.

On the other hand, a witness who has never smelled marijuana before would not be allowed to testify, "He smelled like he'd been smoking marijuana." This witness lacks sufficient personal knowledge, so there is no foundation for the opinion.

There are many more examples, however, which are less clear. In one case, the testimony of a co-worker as to his belief that the defendant was purchasing products from the plaintiff was based on his observation of "daily telephone calls" between the parties. Nothing more specific than this was placed into the record. Although the court agreed that the evidence was "tenuous," it was admissible within the discretion of the trial court.

In the case below, the appellate court found that the prosecutor was unable to lay sufficient foundation for the witness's lay opinion testimony. This is a brief summary of an otherwise factually and legally complex case. The Sherman brothers, who had a medical clinic, and other conspirators developed fraudulent insurance schemes resulting from staged car accidents. Galkovich, as the attorney of record, also participated in the scheme. Thereafter, the FBI arrested Galkovich for his complicity in the scheme. The Shermans then structured a transaction to make it appear that Galkovich had sold his law practice to the new attorney, Kaplan. Galkovich began cooperating with the FBI. He tape recorded about ten conversations with the conspirators including Kaplan during which they discussed Galkovich's criminal case, and various false stories to explain the sham transfer of Galkovich's law firm to Kaplan.

United States v. Kaplan

490 F.3d 110 (2d Cir. 2007)

[Solomon Kaplan was convicted by a jury in the United States District Court for the Southern District of New York for an insurance fraud scheme and interference with the investigation into that scheme. He appeals]

*   *   *

Galkovich testified that on the way to the closing in October 2001, Kaplan and Galkovich discussed the sale of the Law Office, and Kaplan stated that "he had handled cases like this before," which Galkovich understood to mean that Kaplan had previously handled fake accident cases.

*   *   *

Kaplan principally objects to two colloquies in which [the lawyer] Galkovich recounted a conversation he and Kaplan had as they drove together to the meeting in October 2001 to finalize the sale of the Law Office to Kaplan. After describing the conversation, Galkovich was allowed to offer his lay opinion testimony regarding Kaplan's knowledge of the fraud. First, on direct examination, Galkovich testified as follows:

PROSECUTOR: Did you have any discussions in the car ride on the way to Davis' office?

GALKOVICH: Yes. It was actually the first time we really talked, me and Solomon Kaplan. And I asked him, What do you do? What kind of work do you do? Are you familiar with car accident cases, with the process of settlement and what it takes to settle? And he explained, yes he has handled cases like this before. Yes, he has settled cases before. . . .

He explained that he has experience with these kinds of cases.

PROSECUTOR: What did you understand him to mean when he said "these kinds of cases"?

DEFENSE COUNSEL: Objection.

The Court: I will allow it.

GALKOVICH: That he understood that these were car accident cases where people exaggerated their injuries, where it was crucial to have a narrative report that exaggerated the injuries, that these reports were bought for the best of prices to get the best of reports and that you could settle these cases for very good money in a short period of time. . . .

Then, on redirect, Galkovich elaborated:

PROSECUTOR: What happened in this conversation?

GALKOVICH: I asked him what experience he had with the car accident cases and generally what kind of experience he had, and he told me that he knew about these car accidents, he knew how to handle these cases, he knew how to maximize potential recoveries, and what is supposed to be in the files, how they are supposed to be worked up.

PROSECUTOR: What was your purpose in asking Kaplan this question?

GALKOVICH: I wanted to know how much he knew about the fraudulent office that he is participating in.

PROSECUTOR: And after you got this answer from Mr. Kaplan, what did you think?

GALKOVICH: I think he knew exactly what he was getting into.

*   *   *

The government's evidence failed to demonstrate that Galkovich's lay opinion testimony was "rationally based on the perception of the witness." Fed. R. Evid. 701(a). We note that Rule 701(a) requires that lay opinion testimony be *both* (a) based on the witness's first-hand perceptions *and* (b) rationally derived from those first-hand perceptions.

As to the first of these requirements, Rule 701(a) reflects, in part, the Rules' more general requirement that "[a] witness may not testify to a matter unless evidence is introduced sufficient to support a finding that the witness has personal knowledge of the matter." Fed. R. Evid. 602. . . . When Galkovich was asked to articulate the basis for his opinion, he answered, "I based it on the only thing I could base it on, which is my experience there, what people said about [Kaplan], my conversation with [Kaplan], everything that I [had] been involved in. That's what my opinion could be based on." Although Galkovich asserts that his testimony was based in part on first-hand experience—principally his prior experiences at the Law Office and his conversation with Kaplan–his response was extremely vague. Thus, Galkovich's testimony failed to show that his opinion as to Kaplan's knowledge was rationally based on facts he had observed.

We are therefore unable to conclude, as we must under Rule 701, that the opinion he offered was *rationally based* on his own perceptions. . . . We applied this requirement to similar facts in *Rea*, and observed that lay opinion testimony regarding a defendant's knowledge will, in most cases, only satisfy the rationally-based requirement if the witness has personal knowledge of one or more "objective factual bases from which it is possible to infer with some confidence that a person knows a given fact . . . includ[ing] what the person was told directly, what he was in a position to see or hear, what statements he himself made to others, conduct in which he engaged, and what his background and experience were." Because the Government did not lay an adequate foundation, Galkovich's testimony expressing his opinion as to Kaplan's knowledge was not admissible.

Accordingly, having found that Galkovich's lay opinion testimony does not satisfy Rule 701, we conclude that the district court erred in admitting it.

*   *   *

As a result, and because Kaplan's knowledge of the fraud was the central disputed issue in the case, Galkovich's lay opinion testimony was vitally important—just the sort of evidence that might well sway a jury confronted with a marginal circumstantial case. Our concern is heightened by the Government's trial strategy with respect to the evidence; the Government repeatedly called the jury's attention to Galkovich's lay opinion testimony. In its opening statement, the Government told the jury that "Galkovich will recount for you conversations he had with Kaplan during the sale in which they discussed the fraudulent nature of the law practice." In its closing, the Government reminded the jury that "Galkovich explained to you that that conversation, and Kaplan's comments, satisfied Galkovich that Kaplan understood all about the fraud," and that "[w]e know . . . from the testimony of the witnesses, that Solomon Kaplan knew, undeniably knew, about the fraud at the law firm." In rebuttal, the Government stated that "[Kaplan] essentially admitted to Galkovich that he knew what was going on at this law office. That was how Galkovich understood what he said. It is not his opinion. He was there. He had the conversation." And, finally, we observe that this evidence was unique and thus was not cumulative of properly admitted evidence.

Because we cannot, in light of the foregoing, say with fair assurance that Galkovich's lay opinion testimony did not "substantially sway[ ]" the jury's verdict . . . , we conclude that this error was not harmless and therefore vacate Kaplan's conviction on those counts.

Most any prosecutor would consider the result in this case a disaster because the convictions which were reversed would have to be retried, plea bargained, or dismissed. Perhaps the result might have been different had the prosecutor been able to more artfully question the witness. It may be that the lay witness simply did not have sufficient reason or "a rational basis" to form the opinion that Kaplan knew about the fraudulent scheme, but it also may be that more specific and in-depth questions would have established a satisfactory foundation. After you read the *Hankey* case excerpt in Section 7.3, consider the extensive foundation which the trial court there elicited from the opinion witness in contrast to the prosecutor's questions in the case above.

As we have learned in previous chapters, there are numerous ways to explore whether the witness has the requisite knowledge and capacity to be a competent witness. Thoroughly interviewing the witness as contemporaneously with the event as possible and inquiring about documents such as memos, letters, or journals which might aid the witness's memory and ability to be more concrete may avert imprecise and therefore inadequate answers.

It may not always be obvious that a witness is offering an opinion rather than a statement of fact. Each assertion made during an interview should be followed by the question, "How do you know that?" (if the answer is not obvious). The interviewer might ask the question of the witness a bit more diplomatically, but some type of inquiry should follow any assertion where it is possible that the witness is not speaking entirely from direct observation. Documenting how the witness "knows that" provides a record of the witness's basis of opinion. If she forgets at trial, her recollection can be "refreshed," as discussed in Chapter 6. This type of documentation also assists the attorney in laying a proper foundation when the opinion evidence is offered in court.

Part of trial preparation involves checking for "holes," or finding unanswered questions that need to be answered before the matter is fully ready for trial. In the case of opinion evidence, the holes may not be easy to see, but a lot of evidence can fall through them.

7.2 Expert Opinions

Expert Opinion
The opinion of an expert with specialized knowledge that may assist the trier of fact in understanding evidence or determining an issue.

FRE 702, P. 277

The Federal Rules of Evidence treat the admission of **expert opinions** differently from lay opinions, as one might expect. According to Rule 702, "if scientific, technical, or other specialized knowledge will assist the trier-of-fact to understand the evidence or to determine a fact in issue, a witness qualified as an expert by knowledge, skill, experience, training, or education may testify thereto in the form of an opinion or otherwise . . ."

Because the calling of experts is costly, time-consuming, and may at times be overly influential on a jury, the court must be persuaded that the expert testimony will help the trier-of-fact assess the facts at issue.

The courts were aided in making this determination by the December 1, 2000 amendment to FRE 702. The amendment conforms with the holding in *Daubert v. Merrell Dow Pharmaceuticals, Inc.*, 509 U.S. 579, 588 (1993) wherein the U.S. Supreme Court rejected a longstanding test for determining the admissibility of expert testimony. Accordingly, FRE 702 now provides for expert testimony where "(1) the testimony is based upon sufficient facts or data, (2) the testimony is the product of reliable principles and methods, and (3) the witness has applied the principles and methods reliably to the facts of the case."

Sometimes, the need for expertise is obvious.

In a medical malpractice case, an expert witness would be necessary to testify as to the standard of care in the relevant medical field.

Sometimes, the need for an expert is more subtle.

Assume in an accident case there is a dispute as to who is at fault. An expert reconstructionist might be useful to testify as to what, scientifically, appeared to have happened.

Sometimes, there is no right to use an expert at all.

An expert witness may not be called to offer an opinion as to the credibility of a witness. As a matter of law, that is something strictly for the trier-of-fact to determine and is solely within its province.

Since the decision to call an expert witness incurs substantial expense, it should be made collaboratively by the client and legal team working on the case.

7.3   Laying a Foundation for Expert Testimony, and Demonstrative Evidence

Once the decision has been made to use an expert, the paralegal frequently has an important role working with the expert to prepare for trial. Before the expert will be allowed to testify, a foundation must be laid proving that she is, in fact, an expert. The paralegal is often responsible for documenting the educational and career credentials of the expert, so that the attorney can properly lay a foundation establishing the expertise of the witness at trial.

Questions that should be asked of the expert at this stage of the interview include the following:

- Please provide a detailed description of your educational background.
- Please provide a detailed description of your work experience.
- What special skills do you use in your work?
- Have you performed any research in your field of expertise?
- Have you made any innovations in your field of expertise?
- Do you belong to any professional organizations related to your field of expertise?
- Do you hold any positions of responsibility in any of those organizations (such as chairman of a committee or as an officer)?
- Do you have any other information about your credentials that would be useful in establishing your expertise to a jury?
- Have you ever testified as an expert before?
- Have you ever provided guidance as an expert in any other matter where litigation was involved?
- What, if anything, might the opponent use to discredit your testimony?

As you read the following case, you will see the utility of the above-suggested interview questions. Be mindful that FRE 702 encompasses not only scientific and technical expertise but also "other specialized knowledge" expertise. In the case below, the officer's training and experience qualified him as an "other."

United States v. Hankey

203 F.3d 1160 (9th Cir. 2000)

Lavern Hankey appeals his conviction and sentence for distributing and conspiring to possess with intent to distribute . . . "PCP." At trial, after Hankey's co-defendant [Welch] testified that Hankey was not involved in the transactions, the district court admitted rebuttal testimony from a police gang expert that gang members who testify against one of their own are customarily beaten or killed by other members of their gang.

*   *   *

Hankey first argues that the district court abused its discretion in admitting the opinion testimony of Officer Anderson regarding the gang affiliations of the co-defendants and the consequences Welch would suffer if he were to testify against Hankey. Specifically, he contends that the district court failed to properly discharge its gatekeeping function for the admission of testimony offered under FRE 702 as set forth in *Kumho Tire* and *Daubert*. Hankey further argues that Officer Anderson's testimony ran afoul of FRE 403.

*   *   *

In *Daubert*, the Supreme Court, in addressing admissibility of "scientific expert evidence," held that FRE 702 imposes a "gatekeeping" obligation on the trial judge to "ensure that any and all scientific testimony ... is not only relevant, but reliable." . . . While holding that the trial court has substantial discretion in discharging its gatekeeping obligation, it suggested a number of factors that the court might consider: 1) whether a theory or technique can be tested; 2) whether it has been subjected to peer review and publication; 3) the known or potential error rate of the theory or technique; and 4) whether the theory or technique enjoys general acceptance within the relevant scientific community. . . .

In *Kumho Tire*, the Court clarified that the gatekeeping function is not limited to "scientific" expert testimony, but applies to all expert testimony. . . . The Court stated that "it would prove difficult, if not impossible, for judges to administer evidentiary rules under which a gatekeeping obligation depended upon a distinction between 'scientific' knowledge and 'technical' or 'other specialized' knowledge." . . . "There is no clear line that divides the one from the others." . . .

*   *   *

Thus, admissibility of expert opinion testimony generally turns on the following preliminary question of law determinations by the trial judge under FRE 104(a).

- Whether the opinion is based on scientific, technical, or other specialized knowledge;
- Whether the expert's opinion would assist the trier of fact in understanding the evidence or determining a fact in issue;
- Whether the expert has appropriate qualifications-i.e., some special knowledge, skill, experience, training or education on that subject matter;
- Whether the testimony is relevant and reliable;
- Whether the methodology or technique the expert uses "fits" the conclusions (the expert's credibility is for the jury);
- Whether its probative value is substantially outweighed by the risk of unfair prejudice, confusion of issues, or undue consumption of time.

Here, the district court conducted extensive voir dire to assess the basis for and the relevance and reliability of Officer Anderson's testimony. Anderson stated that he had been with the Compton Police Department for 21 years; he had been working undercover with gang members in the thousands since 1989; he had received formal training in gang structure and organization; and he taught classes about gangs. He stated that he had extensive personal knowledge regarding the two affiliated gangs of which Hankey, Welch and Rogers were members. Further, he testified he personally knew Hankey and Welch for 10 or 11 years each and that in the early 1990's Hankey and Welch told him they were members of these affiliated gangs during the late 1980's and early 1990's. He testified he believed that, because they continued to live in the neighborhood and associate with gang members, they were still members themselves because those who become unaffiliated leave town. Further, he based his opinion about Hankey's current gang membership on the criminal activity and observations he made in the field prior to the arrest for the current offenses. Upon further questioning by the court, Officer Anderson stated that he had personally seen Hankey and Welch together in 1996, but that he had not seen Rogers in several years. On this basis, the court refused to allow Officer Anderson to testify regarding Rogers' gang membership, but allowed testimony regarding the membership of Welch and Hankey, as well as the "code of silence" and retaliation that prevented members of affiliated gangs from testifying against one another. Anderson based his testimony as to the "code of silence" and retaliation upon his current and past communications with gang members and gang officers.

Given the type of expert testimony proffered by the government, it is difficult to imagine that the court could have been more diligent in assessing relevance and reliability. The *Daubert* factors (peer review, publication, potential error rate, etc.) simply are not applicable to this kind of testimony, whose reliability depends heavily on the knowledge and experience of the expert, rather than the methodology or theory behind it.

*   *   *

In sum, the district court did not err in admitting the "gang" related evidence for impeachment purposes.

Because this case is instructive on several evidentiary rules which we have studied thus far, you may want to read it in its entirety. For purposes of this chapter, the excerpts of the case provide a clear discussion and analysis of FRE 702 and the foundational requisites for scientific and non-scientific expert testimony. You can see that the trial court, in deciding whether to admit the testimony, thoroughly tested the officer's expertise about gangs. The officer's testimony regarding his gang-related background, experience, and knowledge unquestionably provided sufficient foundation to qualify him as a non-scientific expert. Likely, an astute paralegal had exhaustively interviewed the officer to discern his expertise! The prosecutor then was able to use the officer as a rebuttal witness to impeach Welch based on his bias for the defendant and fear of retaliation were he to testify against the defendant. As you may expect, the defendant also contested, unsuccessfully, on appeal that the expert testimony was improper impeachment and that it was unfairly prejudicial pursuant to FRE 403. Consequently, parts of the case not included here examine bias as a proper impeachment method as well as its relevance and probative value pursuant to the FRE relevancy rules.

As noted above, FRE 702 does not require that an individual have the highest educational degree in the relevant discipline. To the contrary, anyone who has sufficient skills and experience may be competent to testify as an expert witness. So, don't overlook a witness who could be invaluable to your case—a high school dropout who has excelled in any area such as the plumbing field may be your best expert.

The expert most likely will be testifying about fairly complex matters. Working with the expert to create **demonstrative evidence** to assist the trier-of-fact in understanding the complexities is often the job of the paralegal. Demonstrative evidence is "created" evidence through which the trier-of-fact may get a "picture" of the facts. It includes such things as models, diagrams, photographs, graphs, and charts.

Demonstrative Evidence
Created evidence that illustrates testimony, such as diagrams, charts, and photographs.

The following two examples illustrate the use of demonstrative evidence in conjunction with expert witness testimony.

Assume you are using a criminologist expert to testify as to the probable direction from which a gunshot was fired. A diagram of the crime scene and its surrounding area gives the jury a visual image to attach to the oral testimony of the criminologist.

Forensic Evidence
Scientific evidence in which the sciences are applied to matters in the law.

Assume you are using a "forensic" criminalist expert. Assume that blood typing is to be used to provide an inference that some of the defendant's blood was found at the crime scene. A graphical display showing the statistical likelihood that the blood was in fact that of the defendant would be useful to visually show the trier-of-fact the probability of a blood match. A numerical display could be used to reinforce the expert's testimony regarding the probability that the blood belongs to the defendant.

The paralegal is frequently asked to help "illustrate" information that is especially confusing when presented orally by an expert witness. The paralegal assists in preparing demonstrative exhibits to help illuminate and clarify the information for the trier-of-fact. Since anything that is displayed via demonstrative evidence must reflect admissible evidence, the paralegal must be sufficiently familiar with the rules of evidence to know what legitimately can be included in the display. Although trial practice varies in this regard, generally the idea is that once a foundation is laid supporting the facts illustrated in the demonstrative evidence, the demonstrative evidence is admitted and may be examined by the jury at the time of deliberation. Since Rule 403 is in full force to protect against unfair prejudice in the use of demonstrative evidence, the evidence must not be prepared in such a way as to be particularly inflammatory.

FRE 403, P. 264

Keep in mind that although demonstrative evidence is particularly useful when used in conjunction with expert testimony, it can be used in any situation where a graphical or illustrative display enhances the ability of the jury to understand the oral testimony being presented.

Indeed, today the courtroom has become an "it's show time" presentation. Almost any type of exhibit—a document, a photograph, a chart—can be scanned, created, or otherwise incorporated into a digitized computer presentation. The jurors, even the judges, have become accustomed to obtaining information and being entertained through televisions, computers, and the Internet. Accordingly, many courtrooms are now equipped with electronic podiums, audio systems, and monitors at the witness box, in the jury box, at the judge's bench, on counsel tables, and in the audience section. The paralegal is uniquely advantaged to assist the trial team in preparing for the courtroom "show" because other automated litigation support people are not necessarily knowledgeable about the evidentiary and procedural rules and because many "seasoned" attorneys are not adept with computerized presentations.

7.4   The Use of Lay Testimony in Lieu of Expert Testimony

Sometimes, the lines between expert opinion testimony and lay testimony overlap. One should not overlook the possibility that a lay witness, in a position to observe and analyze, may well be an excellent witness in lieu of an expensive expert. The following case which was decided subsequent to the changes to FRE 701 and FRE 702 provides an illuminating discussion regarding the congressional intent for the amendments. The trial testimony excerpt demonstrates the use of lay opinion in lieu of expert opinion.

Tampa Bay Shipbuilding & Repair Co., v. Cedar Shipping Co., Ltd.

320 F.3d 1213 (11th Cir. 2003)

[Ship repairer brought a claim in admiralty to recover payment for repair services rendered upon an ocean-going bulk carrier, and owner counterclaimed for return of escrowed funds and for revenue it lost during the prolonged repairs. . . . The Court of Appeals . . . held that testimony offered by ship repairer's employees and/or officers as to whether charges were fair and reasonable or in line with similar services provided by similar operations was admissible under amended Rule of Evidence on lay opinion testimony.]

*   *   *

As stated previously, Cedar filed a motion *in limine* to exclude certain opinion testimony by Mr. Mikolay, Mr. Hillis, Mr. Jenkins and Mr. Hartley. The district judge denied that motion without prejudice to reassert it should the objected-to testimony be presented at trial. At trial, the judge formally took that motion up for the first time during the following testimony by Mr. Mikolay:

Q: Can you confirm for us that the figure shown on the spreadsheet here is the total amount of the bill on the job?
A: Yes. . . .
Q: Was there ever any point in this whole process where [Cedar] communicated . . . with you . . . that [it] had any particular specific problem with the means and manner by which the shipyard was going about the job?

A: No. . . . The only thing I did hear from [them was] some gruntle [*sic*] about time frames for different tasks of the job.

Q: Did [they] ever instruct you to do any work on this job that you failed to do?

A: No. I done everything [they] requested us to do.

Q: Did you carry out all the work that you did in accordance with [their] instructions?

A: Yes, we did.

Q: In the light of 20/20 hindsight sitting here in the court, do you know of anything that you could have done that would have sped this job up if you would have done it differently?

A: The only thing I would—I would say is probably we should have cut the rudder. But the other work, I couldn't see how else to do it. Maybe I could have built a stronger jack on day one of the tiller. That might be the only thing I can say.

Q: Well, was it your decision as to whether to cut the rudder or to do the this weldment and rebore this hole?

A: No, it's not my decision. We suggested options and [certification class representatives and Cedar] chose which way—which methods.

Q: Did the yard complete all the work that they were asked to do?

A: Yes we did.

Q: And was all of it tested, inspected and accepted by the owner and the class surveyor?

A: Yes it was.

Q: And did it all work properly during these tests?

A: Yes, it did.

Q: Were the charges that you put on these condition reports that we've offered into evidence, Exhibits 5 to 37, all reasonable charges?

At this point, Cedar's counsel objected to what they termed expert evidence being offered by a lay witness without proper expert disclosure. . . .

*   *   *

In denying Cedar's motion *in limine*, the district judge stated that: "I've read the rule and I've looked at the amendments and obviously the commentary . . . [a]nd . . . it says, for example, most courts have permitted the owner or officer of a business to testify to the value or projected profits of the business without the necessity of qualifying the witness as an accountant, appraiser or similar expert."

*   *   *

[The appellate court stated] The Advisory Committee Notes to amended Rule 701 explain that the addition of subsection (c) was an attempt "to eliminate the risk that the reliability requirements set forth in Rule 702 will be evaded through the simple expedient of proffering an expert in lay witness clothing." The notes further explain, however, that the amendment was:

> not intended to affect the "prototypical example[s] of the type of evidence contemplated by the adoption of Rule 701 relat[ing] to the appearance of persons or things, identity, the manner of conduct, competency of a person, degrees of light or darkness, sound, size, weight, distance, and an endless number of items that cannot be described factually in words apart from inferences." (Citations)

Further, the Committee notes specifically discuss testimony by business owners or officers and explain that

> most courts have permitted [owners and officers] to testify . . . without the necessity of qualifying the witness as an . . . expert. Such opinion testimony is admitted not because of experience, training or specialized knowledge within the realm of an expert, but because of *the particularized knowledge that the witness has by virtue of his or her position in the business. The amendment does not purport to change this analysis.* (Citations)

Reading these two comments together, it would appear that opinion testimony by business owners and officers is one of the prototypical areas intended to remain undisturbed.

*   *   *

We have considered both pre-amendment and post-amendment cases and have determined that the testimony offered by Tampa Bay employees and/or officers was of a type traditionally and properly considered lay witness testimony, as it was not based on specialized knowledge subject to Rule 702.

*   *   *

Tampa Bay's witnesses testified based upon their particularized knowledge garnered from years of experience within the field. Their testimony was helpful to the district judge and relevant to the issues presented in the case.

*   *   *

AFFIRMED

When assembling evidence, it is clearly important to consider the use of experts. It is equally important to consider the use of lay witnesses when they can be used in lieu of experts, especially in civil litigation, when the client is footing the bill for the expense of using experts. In the above case, a lay witness was properly permitted to testify. This case serves to remind us that pursuant to Rules 602 and 701, a witness can testify as to his or her personal knowledge and as to his or her opinions rationally based on that knowledge. As you work on a case in which it is appropriate to consider the use of accountants, securities experts, or financial analysts, keep in mind that there are secretaries, bookkeepers, or other employees who may be able to give testimony that could be as useful as lay or expert testimony and perhaps be even more persuasive.

FRE 602, P. 272

FRE 701, P. 277

7.5   The Bases of Opinion Testimony by Experts, and Refreshing the Expert's Recollection

FRE 703, P. 277   Pursuant to FRE 703,

> The facts or data in the particular case upon which an expert bases an opinion or inference may be those perceived by or made known to the expert at or before the hearing. If of a type reasonably relied upon by experts in the particular field in forming opinions or inferences upon the subject, the facts or data need not be admissible in evidence *in order for the opinion or inference to be admitted. Facts or data that are otherwise inadmissible shall not be disclosed to the jury by the proponent of the opinion or inference unless the court determines that their probative value in assisting the jury to evaluate the expert's opinion substantially outweighs their prejudicial effect.*

This very liberal rule allows the expert to give an opinion based on facts and data even when the facts and data would be inadmissible, if they are the type reasonably and ordinarily relied on by experts in the field. The amendment effective December 1, 2000, is intended to allow experts to base their opinions on reliable opinions of other experts and to permit experts to opine on hypothetical facts supported by the evidence. For example,

A physician/expert diagnosed a child as having multiple sclerosis. He based his diagnosis on a variety of data:

- **Information that the child's mother had given him;**
- **Symptoms described to him by the child herself;**
- **A series of neurological tests performed by technicians and reviewed by the physician himself;**
- **Laboratory results of blood work and urinalysis. The blood was drawn by phlebotomists and analyzed by technicians in the laboratory;**

■ **A tissue sample taken by the physician himself, but then analyzed by a pathologist, whose report the physician reviewed.**

Much of what the physician used to make his diagnosis in this case would be inadmissible as hearsay. However, this physician may testify as to his diagnosis anyway, because these data are reasonably relied on, as provided under FRE 703. As pointed out in the Advisory Notes, physicians make life and death decisions based on this type of data. Therefore, the physician's diagnosis, "expertly performed and subject to cross-examination, ought to suffice for judicial purposes."

FRE 705, P. 277

Furthermore, pursuant to FRE 705, the physician may give his opinion prior to the introduction of any underlying facts or data, unless the court requires otherwise. The Federal Rules of Evidence leave it to the cross-examiner to query as to the specific bases of a diagnosis if this information is not offered on direct.

When interviewing an expert, it is appropriate to ask for as much specificity as possible about the bases of his opinion even though this evidence is not required for the expert opinion to be admissible. Counsel needs this information to be prepared to rehabilitate the expert if he is impeached on cross-examination at trial.

FRE 612, P. 276

It is also important to aggregate all the documents on which your expert has relied. In Chapter 6, FRE 612 was briefly discussed regarding the use of a writing to refresh memory. (Additional rules under the hearsay exceptions relate to this topic but are the subject of future discussion.) It is to be anticipated that your expert will not remember all the data underlying his opinion. Having all the documents the expert used to formulate his opinion is very important, even though those documents may not be admissible. The expert will need those documents to refresh his recollection regarding the bases for his opinion.

Consider the hypothetical case involving the physician's diagnosis above. If asked about the data underlying his diagnosis, the physician will undoubtedly wish to look at his notes, the laboratory records, the results of the neurological tests, and other data to refresh his recollection as to the basis of his diagnosis. Documents containing this data, although not admissible per se, are usable in court to refresh the physician's recollection. If the physician is going to use these documents to refresh his recollection, copies must be provided to opposing counsel, who must be given the opportunity to inspect the documents, and be allowed to cross-examine the witness on the contents.

Part of trial preparation is to get the expert to provide all the relevant documentation he has used in preparing for the case, and then to reproduce these documents and have copies available for opposing counsel. This is frequently the job of a paralegal.

7.6   Opinion as to the Ultimate Issue

Ultimate Issue
An issue upon which a finding must be made for the case to be decided.

Testamentary Capacity
The legally required mental ability to make a will.

FRE 704(a), P. 278

FRE 403, P. 264

Elements
Specific components that must be proven for a cause of action to be proved.

The **ultimate issue** in the case is that question which, when answered, determines the outcome of the litigation. In a criminal proceeding, the ultimate issue would generally be the guilt or innocence of the defendant. In civil litigation, the ultimate issue is determined by the type and substance of the pending action. For example, in a probate matter involving a will contest, the ultimate issue might be whether the testator (person writing the will) had **testamentary capacity** to make a will at the time of the will's signing (i.e., did the testator meet that jurisdiction's standards for the competence to make a will).

At common law, it was not unusual to prohibit an opinion if it addressed the ultimate issue of the case. Consequently, a mental health expert witness could not, at common law, offer an opinion as to the competence of a testator if the will was being contested on the basis of the alleged lack of the testator's capacity. Under modern rules of evidence, and pursuant to FRE 704(a), the general rule is "testimony in the form of an opinion or inference otherwise admissible is not objectionable because it embraces an ultimate issue to be decided by the trier-of-fact."

This doesn't mean that an expert witness can simply testify, "in my opinion, the testator didn't have testamentary capacity."

Such testimony would be objectionable as potentially misleading (under the Federal Rules the objection would be made pursuant to Rule 403). This is because the witness has not yet shown he has knowledge of the legal criteria involved in establishing testamentary capacity. The witness must show that he knows what the legal criteria or **elements** of the claim are before such testimony is admissible.

Elements are what must be proved or disproved to make your point. For almost every legal claim, there is law (from cases or statutes) that identifies the elements that must be proved to resolve the issue. These elements are like pieces of a jigsaw puzzle, all of which must be addressed before the issue can be resolved. If you intend to use an expert to testify as to an ultimate issue in your case, then you or others working on the case must first complete the requisite legal research to ascertain the elements that make up the issue. The opinion testimony can then be shown to be based on the proper legal criteria involved. Consider the next example.

Suppose under State X's statutes, testamentary capacity was defined as the testator "knowing the extent of his property, and having a

rational understanding of his distribution scheme." Expert testimony would be proper as follows:

"In my opinion, the testator did not know the extent of his bounty. The testator did not have a rational understanding of his distribution scheme."

In this example, each of the elements of testamentary capacity was addressed to properly bring in expert opinion regarding the ultimate issue (testamentary capacity) in the case.

There is one common exception where expert opinion testimony is inadmissible to prove an ultimate issue, and this is in a criminal action in which the defendant's state of mind is an element in the case. FRE 704(b) specifically prohibits an expert witness from stating an "opinion or inference as to whether the defendant did or did not have the mental state or condition constituting an element of the crime charged or of a defense thereto. Such ultimate issues are matters for the trier-of-fact alone." Therefore an expert cannot be asked to give an opinion about whether or not the defendant in a case had the requisite state of mind to be found guilty. In a first degree murder case, the expert cannot be asked, "Did the defendant premeditate this crime?" In such cases, expert opinion testimony must generally be indirect. The expert may offer opinions about the defendant's mental disorders and the characteristics of such disorders, but not about the defendant's actual mental condition at the time of the crime.

FRE 704(b), P. 278

7.7 Court Appointed Experts

FRE 706, P. 278

The court has the authority to appoint its own experts. Under FRE 706, any party can ask the court to appoint an expert, or the court can do so on its own motion. In a civil action, the court even has the authority to require the parties to pay for the expert it appoints. As you might expect, the court does not avail itself of this authority with great frequency. When it does appoint an expert, the jury may be informed that the expert is court appointed. The result is that the testimony of a court appointed expert usually has a high degree of credibility. An expert who is retained and paid by one of the parties is generally impeachable based on self-interest. Court appointed experts are not assailable in that manner.

In fact, when a jury is aware that an expert is court appointed, the testimony given by the expert can be too persuasive. Because court appointed experts have no obvious bias or prejudice, juries sometimes ascribe to them an air of infallibility. If such an expert intends to testify adversely, the paralegal may be asked to draft a motion requesting that the court not inform the jury that the expert is court appointed. Pursuant to FRE 706(c), disclosure of the fact that the court has appointed the expert is discretionary, and therefore this information may be withheld.

When preparing a case, there are times it is appropriate to consider asking the court to appoint a witness rather than to attempt to procure an expert independently.

For example, assume that your firm is appointed by the court to represent the child in a custody dispute (frequently lawyers are appointed to protect the child's best interest in custody cases). You might consider asking the court to appoint an expert psychologist to testify as to the child's emotional needs and each parent's ability to meet those needs. Experts hired by either parent will be retained to pursue that parent's interest. A court-appointed expert is a more credible witness, who is likely to testify without bias about the child's best interests.

When an expert witness is appointed by the court, in most jurisdictions as well as in the federal system, both parties are entitled to be informed of the witness's findings, if any. Both parties may depose the witness, either party may call the witness to testify, and either party may cross-examine the witness. Nothing stops either party from calling their own experts in addition to the court-appointed experts if either wishes to do so.

7.8   In Summary

- Lay witnesses must testify based on personal knowledge or on those opinions or inferences that are based on personal knowledge.
- Experts may testify as to their opinion based on specialized knowledge, without direct personal knowledge of the case.
- Demonstrative evidence is very valuable in the presentation of highly technical, scientific, or specialized information to the jury.
- Lay and expert opinions sometimes may overlap. If a lay individual is able to offer an opinion that is rationally based on personal knowledge, the opinion is admissible and may be a valid substitute for an expert opinion.
- Expert opinions are admissible even though they may be and usually are based on hearsay.
- Expert opinions are generally admissible even though they embrace an ultimate issue in the case, so long as a proper foundation is laid and the expert opinion will be of value to the jury. However, in any criminal proceeding in which the defendant's state of mind is an issue, the expert may not state an opinion as to

whether or not the defendant did or did not have the mental state of mind at issue.

■ The court may appoint an expert on its own motion, or on the motion of either party.

End of Chapter Review Questions

1. What is a lay witness?
2. When may a lay witness offer an opinion?
3. What is an expert witness?
4. On what may an expert base an opinion?
5. Do all experts need to have advanced college degrees?
6. How might the use of a lay witness replace using an expert?
7. What problem(s) might one face with a court appointed expert?

Applications

Consider the following hypothetical situation.

In a civil claim against a home builder for breach of contract, the homebuyer/plaintiff called a master carpenter to testify as an expert witness. The master carpenter testified that he had been in the homebuilding business for 20 years. He was not a contractor or builder, but he had 20 years' experience in carpentry and was thoroughly familiar with all commonly used building materials. He further testified that the house in question was built in a negligent matter, that the materials used were substandard, and that the house did not meet the specifications in the contract. He testified specifically as to each contractual specification and the manner in which the home failed to meet each specification. He used the bill of materials, provided by the builder through the discovery process, to base his opinion as to the types of materials that had been used in building the home.

1. Did the master carpenter qualify as an expert? Why or why not?
2. Did the master carpenter testify as to the "ultimate question" in the case? If so, was this proper? Why or why not?
3. Did the master carpenter improperly rely on hearsay (the bill of materials) in formulating his expert opinion? Why or why not?

Assume that in the same lawsuit, defendant called his office manager to testify about the bill of materials she prepared, related to plaintiff's house. The office manager had no experience in the actual building of houses; however, she was thoroughly familiar with all the materials that had been ordered to build plaintiff's house and with the materials that the defendant used in all his homebuilding projects. Defendant wanted the office manager to be allowed to testify as to which materials were ordinarily used by defendant as comparable substitutes, based on the availability of product in the market.

4. Does this office manager qualify as an expert?
5. Will this office manager be allowed to testify? Why, or why not?
6. May the office manager testify as to her opinion of the comparability of the substitutes used in building plaintiff's house? Why or why not?
7. May the office manager testify as to her opinion that the materials used in plaintiff's house and those materials specified in the contract were of the same price, and consistently interchanged by defendant based solely on availability? Why or why not?
8. Does testimony of the office manager carry the same weight as testimony of an expert? Why or why not?

CHAPTER 8

Settlement, Negotiation, and Remedial Measures

8.1 The Role of Paralegals in Settlement and Negotiation

Negotiation
Discussion and exchange of information between parties to reach a settlement.

Settlement
Resolution of a dispute by the parties.

Paralegals now have a significant role in the **negotiation** and **settlement** of civil law suits. Many plaintiff and defense attorneys have their paralegals brief the case to ascertain the negotiation merits for settlement purposes. For instance, the paralegal may be asked to review the case file and then to prepare memorandum summarizing the nature and extent of the plaintiff's injuries or of the property damages, the compensatory damages, the mitigation efforts, and the liability and defense theories. Additionally, the paralegal may assist in drafting negotiation and settlement documents as well as assist in actual communications regarding the negotiations. But paralegal beware . . . you must be vigilant that your participation in the settlement process conforms with the paralegal's code of ethics as defined by statutes and case law governing the paralegal's conduct in your particular state. A common ethical canon prohibits the paralegal from engaging in the unauthorized practice of law including but not limited to giving legal advice. Practically, what this means is that the paralegal must refrain from making an independent legal judgment which could affect any aspect of the client's case. The attorney may well instruct the paralegal to formulate such opinions and judgments but only for the purpose of informing the attorney. It is then the attorney who must decide upon the settlement options. Nevertheless, the paralegal can prove to be indispensable to the attorney and to the client in the settlement process.

The paralegal also must be aware of the evidentiary issues surrounding the compromising of claims in order to avoid pitfalls that might jeopardize the client's rights later on should the settlement fall through. The beginning segments of this chapter will focus on rules relating to settlement and compromise. The paralegal should keep in mind, however, that knowledge of evidentiary rules in general is important to properly negotiate the case. In addition to the rules relating to settlement matters, the paralegal should be able to understand:

■ Which evidence is problematic;
■ Which evidence is persuasive;
■ Which evidence is likely to be admissible;
■ Which evidence is likely to be excludable;
■ Whether the amount of evidence available is sufficient;
■ Whether the opponent has any problems from their side.

These topics are addressed throughout this book and are legal principles worthy of study for a variety of paralegal applications. They are useful in settlement negotiations because understanding the strengths and weaknesses of a case is key to negotiating a reasonable outcome. After studying the rules of evidence generally, and studying the rules regarding settlement and compromise specifically, the paralegal will be able to enter into negotiations with more confidence and competence.

8.2   Compromise and Offers to Compromise

Compromise
A settlement based on concessions made by each side.

In the Federal Rules of Evidence, an offer of settlement is referred to as an offer to **compromise**. The term "compromise" means the same thing in "legalese" as it does in ordinary English: a resolution of conflict based on concessions made by each side. In other words, the parties each agree to give up something, meet at some middle ground, and stop fighting.

FRE 408 was promulgated, in part, to promote the public concern of encouraging parties to settle disputes in order to avoid lengthy and expensive litigation and to expedite compensation to the wronged party. To that end, FRE 408 prohibits the admissibility of statements and offers made during compromise negotiations and settlements when offered to prove the validity or the amount of the claim. The rule was extensively revamped by an amendment effective December 2006 to clarify the constraints and scope of the rule, and to resolve conflicts among the courts. Although the rule was basically gutted and rewritten to make it easier to read, the import of the rule still comports with public policy to encourage expeditious non-trial litigation.

The general rule regarding negotiations and offers to compromise is that evidence of settlement offers and of statements made during settlement negotiations is not admissible to prove liability. One party's willingness to settle cannot be used against him later to create an inference of guilt. This is quite liberating. It enables a party's negotiator to discuss the merits of the case with some candor and to try to work out a settlement without fear that later an offer to compromise will be construed as an admission of guilt. Federal Rule of Evidence 408 prohibits the admission into evidence of offers or acceptances of settlements, statements made in negotiations, and conduct during negotiations. The policy reasons for this rule are well documented in the Advisory Notes and are summarized below.

FRE 408, P. 266

The first policy reason behind excluding evidence relating to settlements is the philosophy that such evidence should be viewed as irrelevant. This is because settlement offers may in reality be attempts to purchase peace rather than admissions of guilt. Therefore, admitting such evidence to prove liability would be misleading.

The second and more compelling reason to exclude evidence related to settlements and settlement offers is that compromises are favored by public policy, and compromises would be discouraged if the parties could not negotiate without fear of later reprisal. The system functions more appropriately when parties resolve their own disputes, and evidentiary rules should encourage rather than discourage dispute resolution.

Even at common law, compromises and offers to compromise were inadmissible to prove liability. However, the modern rule adopted by most states has a significant advantage over its common law ancestor. FRE 408 excludes all statements of fact made during the negotiations, if such statements are offered to prove liability. At common law, factual statements during settlement talks were admissible, unless they were couched in language such as "for discussion only," or "hypothetically speaking." Requiring the facts to be discussed in such abstract terms was ultimately found to be unnecessarily restrictive. The modern rule allows for free discussion without all the "waffle words." Consider the following hypothetical.

Assume you are attempting to settle an accident case, and the adjuster insists that your client was also negligent in the accident. You do not disagree with this assertion. Instead you say, "Let's apportion the negligence as follows: Let's say my client was 25 percent responsible, and your client was 75 percent responsible. The damages can be adjusted in accordance with that formula." This "apportionment" is not admissible at trial, if the matter does not settle under the modern rule.

Historically, with regard to the above example, you would have had to couch your suggested apportionment with words indicating the hypothetical nature of your proposal. Instead of saying "Let's apportion," you would have had to say something like "Hypothetically speaking, suppose we were to apportion." The modern rule allows a much freer settlement negotiation.

Although, for the most part, the components of settlement negotiations and agreements are inadmissible in court proceedings, there are very important exceptions to the rule that must be noted and considered when negotiating a case. These exceptions including the December 2006 amendment to the rule are discussed in the next section.

8.3   When Settlement Negotiations and Agreements Are Admissible

Although statements made in the course of civil negotiations are not admissible to prove civil liability, such statements and other information presented during negotiations both may be admissible if otherwise discoverable and may alert the opponent to the need to investigate for the new information. This must be considered when negotiating a settlement. Prior to the December 2006 amendment, FRE 408 specified that the rule did not require ". . . the exclusion of any evidence otherwise discoverable merely because it is presented in the course of compromise negotiations." The intent was to prevent a party from strategizing the exclusion of information in a subsequent proceeding by offering it during negotiations. The amended rule omits that language as unnecessary because evidence which is otherwise discoverable cannot be excluded simply because it is presented during negotiations. Thus, if you "tip your hand" and provide information otherwise unknown to your opposition, your opponent can use the discovery process to acquire other evidence related to your disclosure, and use that evidence against your client in court. Consider the following example.

Assume that you represent a plaintiff who was injured in a car accident. An eyewitness told police that she observed the defendant run a red light prior to hitting your client. You have since determined, however, that the eyewitness was viewing the light from the wrong direction, and that she couldn't be certain the light was actually red for the defendant at the time of the accident. Your opponent has no knowledge of this fact. If you reveal it during settlement negotiations, *your* statements will not be admissible. However, if the matter doesn't settle, nothing stops your opponent from eliciting testimony from the eyewitness on this subject during discovery and at trial.

This is initially a cause of concern for many students. How "free" are negotiations if a lawyer must be secretive about her client's case? It is important to keep in mind, however, that the need for open negotiation must be balanced against the need to preserve the rights of the parties in the event that the matter continues on to trial. Barring evidence because it had been alluded to in settlement negotiations would yield silly results. Opponents would manipulate early settlement negotiations to reveal case weaknesses for the sole purpose of keeping evidence of those weaknesses out of the courtroom. The rules don't allow this outcome.

Keeping in mind the limitations of the protective rules regarding settlement negotiations, the following rule of thumb is useful. The lawyer or paralegal needs to negotiate within the ambit of already shared knowledge. One simply shouldn't reveal more than is advantageous to one's client, unless the other side already knows or will clearly find out the information.

Perhaps the most noteworthy change made by the December 2006 amendment to FRE 408 relates to the subsequent use of negotiation statements and conduct in criminal cases. The amendment not only resolves years of conflict among courts but it ends years of troubled discussions between the Advisory Committee for the Rules of Evidence, the public, and the Department of Justice which oversees federal prosecutions. The new rule provides in FRE 408(a)(2) that "conduct or statements made in compromise negotiations regarding the claim, [are prohibited] except when offered in a criminal case and the negotiations related to a claim by a public office or agency in the exercise of regulatory, investigative, or enforcement authority." Now the distinctions are clear. First, conduct and statements from civil negotiations with a governmental agent are admissible in a subsequent criminal prosecution. Considering the following hypothetical.

During a negotiation of Ida Lie's tax audit, she admitted that she had fibbed about her work-related deductions and that was why she could not provide the supporting documents to IRS Agent Bet Erstop. Ida admitted that she had fibbed. She then offered to settle her tax liability by offering two-thirds of what she owed. In a subsequent criminal prosecution, the prosecutor called IRS Agent Bet Erstop to testify that Ida fibbed and that she was unable to produce the supporting documents. The court ruled that both the statement and the failure to produce the records were admissible. But the court would not allow Ida's settlement offer.

Under the new provisions of FRE 408, the court correctly ruled on the three issues. The Advisory Committee Notes explain that anyone who makes statements in front of government agent should not be surprised when the statements are used in a criminal prosecution. Note, that FRE 408 refers to both "statements and conduct." The rule, however, does not include "offers or acceptance." This is not a surprise because an offer or an acceptance does not necessarily reflect the person's guilt but rather the person's willingness to settle the case—which makes the public happy!

Conversely and in accord with public policy, the rule does not permit statements and conduct made during compromise negotiations between private parties to be admitted in subsequent criminal proceedings. No one would be likely to fess up and settle the dispute knowing that prison might be looming! Thus, the paralegal should be careful to determine whether the negotiations are between private parties or between a private party and a governmental agency. The distinction could be more critical than losing money. It could mean a loss of liberty.

Another point to consider—a more subtle one—is that statements and conduct made to a government agent during civil negotiations under FRE 408(b) would still be admissible in a criminal proceeding even if the a criminal case had not yet been charged by a formal complaint. However, if the civil settlement offer occurs between private parties but prior to a "claim that was disputed as to validity or amount," FRE would not apply at all. This is more easily described by example than by description.

Darlene, a 48-year-old supervisor, was laid off during cutbacks at her place of employment. The day of the layoff, Darlene was brought to the company's department of human resources to speak with a manager. The manager informed her that she was to be laid off. He then presented her with an agreement whereby, in exchange for six weeks of severance pay, she would waive any rights under "federal, state, or local laws prohibiting age or other forms of discrimination." Darlene refused to sign the waiver and was not paid any severance benefits. She thereafter sued the company for age and sex discrimination. Evidence of the "termination agreement" was admissible pursuant to FRE 408.

The rationale for admitting evidence in this situation is that Darlene had never even asserted any claim prior to the employer asking for a release. This type of "waiver," requested at the time of termination, in exchange for severance benefits, is viewed by the courts as coercive in nature. Such proposed "agreements" are admissible and are considered probative of the ultimate issue in the case (i.e., discrimination).

In Darlene's hypothetical above, the employer was anticipating and trying to foreclose a prospective lawsuit. If the employer had made the settlement offer during a lawsuit but Darlene rejected it, the employer could not try to introduce that offer at a jury trial. You might wonder—what is the problem if the employer does not mind the jury knowing about the offer? The problem is that the jury would know that Darlene had been willing to enter into negotiations, but then hold it against Darlene for not settling the case. FRE 408 is meant to help both parties so that their negotiation attempts are not subsequently used to unfavorably affect either party.

The December 2006 amendment also bars the use of evidence from negotiations "to impeach through a prior inconsistent statement or contradiction." This differs from the general use of prior inconsistent statements as we discussed in Chapter 6. Usually, if a witness testifies differently from a previous statement, the opponent is permitted to explore the witness's credibility for the jury by cross-examining on the prior inconsistent statement. The reason for the prohibition under FRE 408, however, makes sense because we, the public, want the parties to speak freely during negotiations.

Finally, evidence of settlement negotiations or agreements is potentially admissible when such evidence is being offered for reasons other than to prove or disprove liability in the civil claim. FRE 408 specifically enumerates some instances when such evidence is potentially admissible. These are:

- To prove a witness's bias or prejudice;
- To negate a contention of undue delay;
- To prove an effort to obstruct a criminal investigation or prosecution.

Notwithstanding the "list" provided in FRE 408, it is extremely rare for the court to admit evidence of settlement negotiations or agreements for any "limited" purpose. This is because, where evidence is admissible for only a limited purpose, the court must evaluate the evidence for potential unfair prejudice. The court must weigh the probative value of the evidence as compared to its prejudicial effect. The court must also consider the probable effectiveness of any limiting instruction. More often than not, the probative value of such evidence is insufficient to overcome the problems.

In the case below, the trial court admitted evidence from settlement negotiations pursuant to the "other purposes" exception in FRE 408. The appellate court found error and reversed. The dissenting judge dissented because he reasoned that the settlement evidence was admissible pursuant not only to long-standing precedent but also to the newly amended FRE 408.

Stockman v. Oakcrest Dental Center, P.C.

480 F.3d 791 (6th Cir. 2007)

Defendants Oakcrest Dental Center ("Oakcrest") and Dr. Louis Leonor appeal a judgment of $479,491.63 in favor of Plaintiff Dr. Samuel Stockman. Defendants allege several trial errors including the erroneous admission of a settlement offer in violation of FED. R. EVID. 408. Because we agree that the district court abused its discretion in admitting the settlement offer and the record demonstrates substantial prejudice, we REVERSE the judgment and REMAND to the district court for a new trial.

*   *   *

In late 1999, Dr. Stockman agreed to sell his dental practice of over forty years to Dr. Leonor and Oakcrest. The sale was completed in January 2000. Pursuant to a side agreement, Dr. Leonor hired Dr. Stockman to work as a dentist at Oakcrest. Dr. Leonor's goal was to use this as an opportunity to attract and retain Dr. Stockman's patients. The parties set no time limit or date of termination. Dr. Stockman began working at Oakcrest four days per week in December 1999, and Oakcrest sent out mailers announcing the move and invited his old patients to remain with him at his new location. Few ever came.

*   *   *

In October 2001, because of his low revenue production, Dr. Stockman's work week was scaled back from four days to three. Dr. Leonor wanted to give the chair occupied by Dr. Stockman to a higher revenue-producing dentist. He hired two other dentists, Drs. Lavasseur and Long, who were both in their thirties. However, neither lasted at Oakcrest very long.

By early June 2002, Dr. Leonor reduced Dr. Stockman's days from three to two, citing Dr. Stockman's continued low production. Dr. Stockman went home that day claiming he was ill. Dr. Leonor called his home and spoke to Mrs. Stockman who informed Dr. Leonor that Dr. Stockman was in bed with flu-like symptoms. Dr. Leonor expressed his relief that Dr. Stockman had not suffered a heart attack.

At the time, Drs. Mac and Bailey had produced between 50 per cent and almost 200 per cent more revenue over the same period, even adjusting for the reduced hours. Based upon this information, Dr. Leonor concluded that Dr. Stockman ought to be terminated. Dr. Leonor claimed that he did not have the heart to terminate Dr. Stockman himself because he "liked the guy a lot," and had someone else inform Dr. Stockman upon his return to the office. Dr. Leonor hired Dr. Don Bui, 33, to replace Dr. Stockman.

Dr. Stockman filed suit in the Eastern District of Michigan in February 2003, alleging violation of the Age Discrimination and Employment Act (the "ADEA") . . . and the Michigan Elliott-Larsen Civil Rights Act (the "ELCRA"). . . . He alleged that he was 73 years old at the time and was subject to disparate treatment because of his age. He alleged he was afforded fewer operatories (rooms in which to do dental work); he was not given a dedicated and competent dental assistant; and new patients who required more expensive treatments were steered away from him, thus reducing his potential to generate more revenue per patient-hour. He also alleged that on three occasions, culminating in a Christmas party in 1999 right after he joined Oakcrest, Dr. Leonor asked whether Dr. Stockman realized he "[was] the oldest dentist" at Oakcrest. Dr. Stockman also cited Dr. Leonor's criticism of certain of his dental practices because they were older methods.

Two years later and a few weeks before trial, attorneys for Dr. Leonor and Oakcrest sent the following letter to Dr. Stockman's attorneys:

Dear Ms. Adams:

I have been authorized by my client to extend an offer of reinstatement of employment to Dr. Stockman.

The specifics of the offer are as follows: Dr. Stockman would be rehired as an associate dentist under the terms of his prior employment. His responsibilities would be identical to those of his prior employment as would be his benefits. Based upon Dr. Stockman's testimony in his deposition (see page 96 of the transcript) we will compensate him on a percentage-based pay plan.

Further, my client is amenable to conducting whatever meetings may be necessary between Dr. Stockman and office staff to address any concerns that Dr. Stockman may have a smooth transition to his return to his employment. My client wishes to convey that, despite its respectful disagreement with Dr. Stockman's claims of age discrimination, there is no animosity toward Dr. Stockman and that every effort will be made to assure professional and hospitable working conditions in the future. . . .

Two days later, Dr. Stockman's attorneys responded:

Dear Mr. Chiasson:

This letter is for settlement purposes only and is in response to the offer of reinstatement set forth in your letter of June 9, 2004.

Dr. Stockman accepts the offer of reinstatement . . . However, your letter then modifies the prior terms of Dr. Stockman's employment. . . . As you know, we have contended that the reduction of Dr. Stockman's hours and/or days was discriminatory. Hence, the offer is accepted based on the presumption that Dr. Stockman will be guaranteed his original terms of employment, except for the hourly rate of pay.

Next, your letter does not address other conditions of Dr. Stockman's employment which we have contended were discriminatory. . . .

Next, as you know, the offer of reinstatement does not resolve all claims in the case. Among other things, Dr. Stockman is still eligible for back-pay, emotional anguish damages, liquidated damages and attorneys' fees and costs. Of course, we will remain open to discussing settlement of all claims at any time. . . .

*   *   *

Believing that Dr. Stockman's reply was a rejection and counter-offer, Defendants withdrew their offer of reinstatement and Dr. Stockman sought to enforce the contract. The district court refused to enforce the contract because (1) the offer was clearly an offer of reinstatement in exchange for settlement of the entire action, and (2) Dr. Stockman's letter was a rejection and counteroffer. However, the district court denied Defendants' motion to have the document precluded from being admitted into evidence at trial under Fed. R. Evid. 408. The district court ruled that the Letters were admissible under Rule 408's "another purpose" exception, and that they could be read into evidence if Defendants presented evidence that Dr. Stockman failed to mitigate his damages.

At trial, Defendants cross-examined Dr. Stockman about job offers he received and refused in the months following his termination. The Letters were then read into the record over defense counsel's renewed objection. . . .

The jury found Dr. Leonor and Oakcrest liable for age discrimination and awarded back pay, front pay, and other damages totaling $479,491.63. . . .

*   *   *

Clay, Circuit Judge, dissenting.

The jury's verdict should be upheld, inasmuch as the majority's view of Federal Rule of Evidence 408 rests on an implausible reading of the Rule which cannot be reconciled with the intent of the Rule or the case law that was approved by the advisory committee's note to Rule 408's recent amendment. I would hold that the district court did not abuse its discretion, under the unique circumstances of this case, in admitting the evidence of settlement negotiations. Furthermore, there was substantial evidence admitted at trial to support the jury's verdict. Accordingly, I would affirm the judgment of the district court.

At trial, Defendants put the issue of mitigation into play by arguing that Plaintiff refused to accept employment offers that were available to him for reasons that were pretextual or unreasonable. Defendants' theory of mitigation rested in part on convincing the jury that Plaintiff was not disposed to continue working as a dentist. As Defendants summarized the evidence at closing, Plaintiff made "excuses" for not finding employment, and did not have "the attitude of a man who wants to get back to work."

The district court did not abuse its discretion when it held that, pursuant to Rule 408, Defendants opened the door by offering mitigation evidence, and hence Plaintiff could offer evidence that he was willing to accept what he interpreted to be an unconditional offer of employment. Although Rule 408 bars the admission of "[e]vidence of . . . offering . . . a valuable consideration in . . . attempting to compromise a claim . . . to prove . . . [the claim's] amount," the Rule "does not require exclusion when the evidence is offered for another purpose." When a party seeks to admit evidence of a settlement offer made by an opposing party to rebut the opposing party's claim that the party seeking admission of the settlement offer failed to mitigate damages, that evidence is offered for "another purpose" under Rule 408. The evidence that Plaintiff was immediately ready to resume employment with Defendants was unquestionably relevant to the issue of mitigation. This evidence was properly admitted under Rule 408 to demonstrate that Plaintiff was willing to mitigate damages, and the district court gave an instruction limiting the use of the evidence to that purpose.

. . . [T]he district court's holding—that evidence of the Letters was admissible if and only if Defendants opened the door by arguing that Plaintiff failed to mitigate damages—is also consistent with the examples of "other purposes" set forth in the text of Rule 408. Specifically, this holding accords with Rule 408's allowance of settlement evidence offered to "negat[e] a contention of undue delay." The fact that Rule 408 uses the word "negate" suggests that, while evidence of a settlement may be relevant to *rebut* evidence that a party engaged in undue delay, this evidence cannot be admitted unless the door is first opened by a party raising the issue of undue delay. . . . Evidence that a party failed to mitigate damages is analogous to evidence that a party's claim is invalid because of undue delay. Although both types of evidence ultimately go to the "validity" or the "amount" of the claim, neither type of evidence "does [ ] so via any inference as to the belief [on the part of the offeror] in [the claim's] validity arising from the offer to compromise." Since using the evidence for this purpose does not ask the factfinder to engage in impermissible reasoning—"because the defendant made the offer to settle, he must be liable"—using settlement evidence to negate a contention that the plaintiff failed to mitigate damages constitutes "another purpose" for which evidence is permissible.

Likewise, the majority's reading of Rule 408 is inconsistent with most or all of the formidable body of case law defining other permissible purposes. This body of law has developed in the thirty-plus years that Rule 408 has been in effect, and these purposes were recently approved by the advisory committee's note to the 2006 amendment. See Fed. R. Evid. 408 advisory committee's note (2006 amendment). . . . The district court did not abuse its discretion in concluding that evidence offered to rebut a claim that Plaintiff failed to mitigate damages was offered for "another purpose."

When truly considering the evidence with the maximum reasonable view of the probative value and the minimum reasonable view of the potential prejudice—rather than ignoring sources of probative value and factors that decrease the potential prejudice—it cannot be said that the district court abused its "broad discretion," even if other jurists would have reached a different outcome if faced with the issue *de novo*. Accordingly, the evidence was not inadmissible under Rule 403.

As you can see, reasonable minds can differ! The district court's analysis was in conformance with the intent of the "other purposes" exception in FRE 408 even before the recent elucidation of the rule.

8.4   Excludability of Evidence of Remedial Measures

Remedial Measures
Measures taken to change a produce after an accident to "remedy" or fix the problem.

One of the more complex rules of evidence relates to the introduction of evidence regarding changes made to a product or a situation after the product or situation has caused injury or harm. The words **remedial measure** describe an action taken to remedy or fix a problem that has caused or contributed to the injury. The general rule is that if a manufacturer takes remedial measures to fix a product after it has caused injury, evidence of such remedial measures is not

FRE 407, P. 266

admissible to prove liability. FRE 407. This rule applies to owners of real property and to employers, as well as to manufacturers. If a landlord remedies an unsafe condition on real property that allegedly caused an injury, evidence of the repair is not admissible to prove negligence. If an employer institutes an affirmative action policy to remedy a racial or gender imbalance in the workplace, this is not admissible to prove prior discrimination.

The policy reasons given by the Advisory Committee to generally exclude evidence of remedial measures are similar to those related to excluding evidence of settlement offers and compromises. Taking remedial measures is not necessarily an admission of guilt, any more than is offering to settle a case. Therefore, admission of such evidence to prove guilt is potentially misleading. The more compelling reason to exclude such evidence, however, is that public policy encourages people to take remedial measures, and admitting such evidence might deter them from doing so.

In 1997, FRE 407 was amended to formally provide protection in products liability cases. The rule now specifically protects manufacturers who remedy a "defect in a product" or its design or who insert a "warning or instruction" subsequent to an injury. The majority view in most circuits was consistent with this extension even prior to the amendment.

As you might have assumed, there are exceptions to this rule, and therein lie the complexities. FRE 407 allows the admission of evidence of remedial measures when offered for purposes other than to prove liability, such as "proving ownership, control, feasibility of precautionary measures, if controverted, or impeachment." For example, if ownership is an issue, proving that a party took remedial measures to correct a defect would be good circumstantial evidence that the party owned the product.

The following example illustrates the exception regarding "feasibility of **precautionary measures**, if controverted." This exception applies when the manufacturer disputes whether a precautionary measure (a design change to the product that would have prevented the injury in the first place) was feasible. Evidence of remedial measures is allowable to refute the manufacturer's claim that precautionary measures were not feasible. Frequently, evidence of remedial measures is admitted under this exception.

Nicket, Inc., manufactures electronic testing devices. One of the users of a Nicket device inadvertently reversed the lead wires when attaching the device to another unit. The user suffered from a severe electric shock. After Nicket learned of the incident, it redesigned the leads so that only the correct lead would fit into the correct socket. If Nicket later claimed that there was no feasible design alteration that could have prevented or reduced the risk of the incident, evidence of

Precautionary Measure
A design change that could have prevented an accident from occurring.

the redesigned leads and socket would be admissible to show that precautionary measures were, in fact, feasible.

Allowing evidence for limited purposes always subjects that evidence to scrutiny for unfair prejudice or potential jury confusion. However, the courts have been mixed in their use of discretion in relation to evidence of remedial measures, and the cases seem to contain inconsistent outcomes.

The following case excerpt illustrates how the court used a very technical analysis to determine which evidence was excludable, which evidence was admissible, and for what purposes. The outcome appears to follow the letter of the law without ever trying to reconcile its spirit.

Chase v. General Motors Corp.

856 F.2d 17 (4th Cir. 1988)

[Plaintiffs suffered injuries as a result of a car accident caused when the brakes in their Chevrolet Citation failed. Plaintiffs brought a suit against defendant General Motors (GM), alleging negligence in design, strict liability, and breach of implied warranty. Plaintiffs won, and GM appealed.]

*   *   *

[T]his accident occurred in 1982; the car had been purchased by the Chases in April 1980. In July 1980, GM made a design change in the braking system of Citations of the type purchased by the plaintiffs. This change involved the lining material of the rear brakes. As a result of complaints of rear brake lock involving 1980 model Citations of the type owned by the plaintiffs, GM, in February 1983 in response to the NHTSA [National Highway Transportation Safety Administration], recalled plaintiffs' vehicle to make the change it had made in July 1980 on Citations assembled subsequent to that time.

The recall letter recited that the Chases' car under certain operating conditions and braking situations might experience premature rear wheel skid, most likely on a wet or slick surface, and authorized the Chases to bring their car in to their dealer for the July 1980 modification to be made to the braking system. Only a few days after the wreck, however, Chase had sold his car for scrap and the same had been crushed, so the Chase vehicle was not available either for modification or inspection.

The district court excluded the February 1983 recall letter on the ground that it had been required by the government and was not any voluntary act on the part of GM, but it allowed testimony during the trial of the fact of recall. This fact was used powerfully by plaintiffs' attorneys in closing argument. . . .

Exclusion of the letter is not the issue on appeal; it is admitting the evidence of recall. GM argues that it should be excluded under F.R. Evid. 407, which is, in pertinent part:

> When, after an event, measures are taken which, if taken previously, would have made the event less likely to occur, evidence of subsequent measures is not admissible to prove negligence or culpable conduct in connection with the event.

The "event" spoken of in that rule in our case is the date of the accident, which was in January 1982. That the evidence of the recall was used "to prove negligence or culpable conduct," is undoubted. . . . That the February 1983 recall was taken "after [the] event" is also undoubted. That the plaintiffs take the position that the changes occasioning the recall "would have made the event less likely to occur" is also beyond question. Therefore, we are of opinion that evidence of the fact of recall was improperly admitted under Rule 407. This is not a new principle and has been the rule in the courts of the United States at least since 1982. . . .

[I]t is now settled, upon much consideration, by the decisions of the highest courts of most of the states in which the question has arisen, that the evidence is incompetent, because the taking of such precautions against the future is not to be construed as an admission of responsibility for the past, has no legitimate tendency to prove that the defendant had been negligent before the accident happened, and is calculated to distract the minds of the jury from the real issue, and to create prejudice against the defendant.

Our decision here is in accord with our opinion in *Werner v. Upjohn Co.*, in which we held that Rule 407 applied not only to a theory of negligence but also to a theory of strict liability in products liability cases, and we adhere to that opinion.

But that is not the end of the matter. The change in the brake design of the Citation occurred in July 1980, some two or three months after the plaintiffs' car was manufactured and sold to them. That was a "measure" which was "taken" before the "event" mentioned in Rule 407. So Rule 407 does not exclude evidence with respect to that change. On retrial, the plaintiffs are perfectly free to explore the July 1980 change in the braking system and the reasons for it if such change might tend to be evidence of negligence, or if such evidence is otherwise admissible under the law of strict liability as it exists in West Virginia.

REVERSED.

FRE 407, P. 266

This case used the technical language of Rule 407 to exclude evidence of a post-accident recall, while allowing evidence of a preaccident voluntary design change to come in. The rule of evidence was followed scrupulously, but the policy behind it was ignored. If the policy is to encourage manufacturers to repair defects without fear of added liability for "doing the right thing," then allowing a voluntary design change into evidence to prove negligence or strict liability goes against that policy, even though the design change predated the incident at issue. A different court may well have excluded the pre-accident design change as being unfairly prejudicial, even though it didn't fall under the specific criteria of Rule 407.

Some courts have questioned the policy underlying Rule 407. In their opinion, whether or not the remedial measures taken by the manufacturer are admissible as evidence of liability for the past incident, the manufacturer will fix the problem because the continuing liability would otherwise be too great. Therefore, they would argue, the exclusion of such evidence is unnecessary for public policy purposes. Courts that follow this reasoning are inclined to allow evidence of remedial measures over objections of unfair prejudice, and to be extremely narrow in applying Rule 407 exclusions. This appears to be what occurred in the GM case excerpted above.

Because of the uncertainty in this area, it is best not to assume that a certain outcome is predictable. If the case on which you are working involves a manufacturer who has taken remedial measures, it is best to consider a strategy for both possibilities: the evidence coming in or staying out. A pretrial motion is often made to resolve this issue in advance of trial.

8.5   Payment of Medical and Similar Expenses

FRE 409, P. 266

Another corollary to evidentiary exclusions for policy reasons is the rule that payment of medical expenses by an opposing party is not admissible to prove liability. Pursuant to FRE 409, "Evidence of furnishing or offering or promising to pay medical, hospital, or similar expenses occasioned by an injury is not admissible to prove liability for the injury."

The policy reasons behind this are clear. This rule allows a victim to receive assistance for medical care prior to any assignment of blame. Otherwise, the opposing party would be disinclined to offer assistance to the injured party for fear that such an offer would be construed as an admission of guilt. This frees the hands of insurance companies who might genuinely dispute the extent of their insured's liability, but who are willing to assist with medical expenses when it appears that the victim has at least some legitimate claim.

8.6   Exclusion of Evidence of Liability Insurance

FRE 411, P. 267

Evidence of the existence or nonexistence of insurance coverage is uniformly inadmissible, both in the state and federal systems, to prove fault or lack of fault. FRE 411 states in part:

> Evidence that a person was or was not insured against liability is not admissible upon the issue whether the person acted negligently or otherwise wrongfully.

According to the Advisory Committee,

> At best the inference of fault from the fact of insurance coverage is a tenuous one, as is its converse. It is therefore of only marginal relevance.

The most important reason for excluding evidence of insurance coverage is that the jury might alter a judgment based on the presence or absence of insurance, and this is improper. A jury might well be more inclined to award a victim damages when the defendant isn't going to have to pay out of his own money. The presence of an insurance company's deep pocket gives the jury an emotional push to provide the sympathetic victim compensation, even when the victim is not entitled to recovery under the law.

Likewise, a jury might be inclined to be sympathetic to a defendant who is known to be uninsured, and might render a verdict out of sympathy.

Consistent with the other rules discussed in this chapter, FRE 411 allows evidence of insurance to come in for "other purposes" than establishment of liability. The rule provides that evidence of insurance is admissible when it is offered for a purpose such as to prove agency, ownership, control, bias, or prejudice.

8.7   Exclusion of Evidence of Unaccepted Plea Bargains, Withdrawn Pleas, and No Contest Pleas

Plea Bargains
A negotiated agreement between the prosecution and the defendant in which charges or penalties are reduced in exchange for a guilty or no contest plea.

The rules regarding the inadmissibility of settlement offers and settlements in the civil domain have a parallel in the criminal courts dealing with compromises and offers to compromise, the criminal courts deal with **plea bargains**. A plea bargain is a negotiated agreement whereby the prosecutor agrees either to reduce the charges or penalty to a predetermined lesser charge or penalty, in exchange for

Nolo Contender
A plea of *nolo contendere* is the same as a plea of no contest.

No Contest Plea
A plea that leads to a conviction, without an admission of guilt.

FRE 410, P. 267

FRE 410, P. 267

which the defendant agrees to enter either a guilty or ***nolo contendere*** (no contest) plea. A plea of **no contest** essentially avoids the issue of admitting guilt. The defendant doesn't admit guilt, but says instead that he isn't going to fight about it. The defendant is convicted without having to go through a trial or admit his guilt. Under the Federal Rules of Evidence, plea bargaining discussions and related statements, as well as evidence of pleas of nolo contendere (no contest), are inadmissible pursuant to FRE 410.

Plea negotiation is currently done by attorneys, so some of the logistics of plea bargaining may not seem relevant to paralegal practice today. However, evidence of a plea or plea bargain can be extremely important to the paralegal who is working on related civil cases.

It is important to note that many state jurisdictions do not acknowledge a "no contest" plea exclusion and treat such pleas exactly as guilty pleas. However, in jurisdictions having rules equivalent to FRE 410, a *nolo contendere* plea is inadmissible against the defendant in any other proceeding. Consider the following example in a jurisdiction that follows the Federal Rule.

Randall is being sued by Warren for malicious assault and battery. Randall had fired a gun into a crowd of teenagers who had been standing on the corner near his home, yelling threatening comments. A bullet from Randall's gun hit Warren, seriously wounding him. Randall was charged criminally for this conduct and entered a plea of *nolo contendere*. This plea cannot be used against him in the civil action brought by Warren. A pretrial motion excluding such evidence would be appropriate.

Had Randall been convicted of the related criminal charges, or plead guilty instead of *nolo contendere*, or been in a jurisdiction that doesn't exclude evidence of *nolo contendere* pleas, the opposite outcome would have resulted. Randall would have been unable to defend himself in the civil trial on the issue of his culpability. The issue, under those circumstances, wouldn't have been whether Randall had to pay damages to Warren; the issue would have been how much he would have to pay. Consider the next example.

Officers Smith and Jones were convicted in a jury trial of using excessive force and brutality against a suspect in a tumultuous arrest. After this conviction, the officers (and their department) were sued. The officers were unable to present evidence showing they should not be held liable because the issue of their guilt had been determined beyond a reasonable doubt during their criminal trial. The only triable issue at the civil trial was the amount of damages to which the suspect was entitled.

In a criminal trial, the standard for a guilty verdict is that the evidence must prove guilt "beyond a reasonable doubt." In a civil trial, generally speaking, the burden is that the plaintiff must prove liability with a "preponderance of the evidence." This is a much lower standard to meet than "beyond a reasonable doubt." In other words, if the defendant in the criminal trial is already guilty beyond a reasonable doubt, he is guiltier than necessary to be found liable in the civil trial. The legal doctrine that applies here is called "collateral estoppel." This simply means that the same issue has been tried and fully resolved in another proceeding. The defendant is stopped from retrying the same matter.

Of course, being found liable in a civil trial would not collaterally estop a defendant from asserting innocence in a criminal trial. This is because the civil plaintiff had to prove liability only with a preponderance of the evidence. In the criminal setting, the defendant is entitled to a finding of guilt beyond a reasonable doubt, and this is not ascertained in a civil trial. In other words, the defendant isn't proven as guilty as he needs to be to establish criminal liability.

The rule prohibiting the plea of no contest from being used as evidence in a "collateral setting" accomplishes an important purpose. It allows the defendant to resolve the criminal matter without trial, but without the inevitable incurrence of civil liability as a result. Such civil liability might deter a defendant from entering or negotiating a plea, and this is not always in the best interests of the public.

The rule prohibiting the introduction into evidence of statements made during plea negotiations is applicable only when no guilty plea is entered or when a guilty plea has been **withdrawn**. If a guilty plea is entered, then all statements are admissible. This is because once a guilty plea is entered, the charges are deemed admitted.

The rule prohibiting introduction of evidence of a *nolo contendere* plea does not affect the right of an opponent to use the conviction for impeachment purposes as discussed in earlier chapters.

Whenever a case involves both criminal and civil actions, evidence in the civil action will be impacted by the criminal proceeding.

Withdrawn Plea
A plea that has been entered but then, for either technical or constitutional reasons, withdrawn with the court's permission.

8.8   In Summary

- The role of the paralegal in the settlement process is growing, and knowledge of the rules of evidence is essential to properly negotiate a compromise.
- The paralegal must be mindful of the ethical canons governing the paralegal's role in the legal process.
- Offers, acceptances, and other statements made during negotiations between private parties are generally inadmissible as evidence in subsequent court proceedings.

- An inconsistent or contrary statement made during negotiations cannot be used in a later proceeding to impeach the party-declarant.
- Conduct and statements from civil negotiations with a governmental agent are admissible in subsequent criminal proceedings.
- Evidence from settlement negotiations and agreements may be admissible for "other purpose," but are subject to the balancing analysis pursuant to FRE 403.
- Evidence of remedial measures taken after a product has caused injury is inadmissible to prove negligence.
- Payment of medical or related expenses by the opposing party in a civil suit is inadmissible to prove liability.
- Evidence regarding insurance coverage is inadmissible to prove liability.
- Evidence of unaccepted plea bargains or withdrawn pleas, and of no contest pleas, is generally inadmissible in any civil or criminal proceeding.

End of Chapter Review Questions

1. What is a legal compromise?
2. What is the role of the paralegal in settlement negotiations today?
3. Are settlement negotiations admissible? If so, for what purpose?
4. What is a remedial measure?
5. If a remedial measure is taken *prior* to an injury or accident, is evidence of the remedial measure admissible?
6. Is evidence that a victim's insurance company has already paid for the damage admissible?
7. Is evidence of an offer for a plea bargain admissible?
8. Is evidence of a guilty plea based on a plea bargain admissible?

Applications

Consider the following hypothetical situation.

Jessie drank a six-pack of beer and decided to drive to the store to purchase another. En route, he ran a red light and collided with another vehicle, owned and driven by Marvin. Jessie presented Marvin with his insurance card indicating that he was covered by Risk Management, Inc. When the police arrived at the scene, Jessie was asked and agreed to take a breath analyzer test. His blood alcohol level was recorded at 1.6 percent, which is .6 percent above the legal limit in that jurisdiction. Jessie entered a no contest plea to a charge of driving under the influence of alcohol. Marvin sued Jessie for negligence and extreme recklessness.

1. Is evidence of Jessie's no contest plea admissible against him in the civil case against him? Why or why not?
2. Is evidence of the results of Jessie's breath analysis admissible in the civil trial? Why or why not?
3. Is evidence of Jessie's insurance coverage with Risk Management, Inc., admissible? Why or why not?

Suppose at the scene of the accident Jessie had asked Marvin to take a check for $1,000 and forget the incident. Marvin declined.

4. Is evidence of Jessie's offer admissible? Why or why not?

9

Hearsay

9.1 Introduction to Hearsay

Hearsay
Statements made out of court, offered into evidence to prove the truth of the statement.

`FRE 801, P. 279`

Hearsay rules deal with statements made out of court. The Federal Rules of Evidence define hearsay as, "A statement, other than one made by the declarant while testifying at the trial or hearing, offered in evidence to prove the truth of the matter asserted." FRE 801. The "declarant" is defined as the person who makes the statement. A "statement" is defined as "(1) an oral or written assertion or (2) nonverbal conduct of a person, if it is intended by the person as an assertion." These definitions mirror those used in most states, although there are some differences between the Federal Rules and some state rules. These differences will be discussed where relevant throughout this chapter as the hearsay definition is more thoroughly explored.

FRE 802, P. 280

The general rule is that hearsay is inadmissible in a court of law unless a specific exception allows the hearsay to be admitted. FRE 802. However, the law regarding what constitutes hearsay is confusing and complex. Even armed with a firm understanding of what constitutes hearsay, the law carves out so many exceptions, they overshadow the general rule.

It is important to recognize that the Rules approach hearsay in three ways. First, the Rules say what hearsay is. Not every out-of-court statement constitutes hearsay. A statement is hearsay only if it is offered to prove the truth of the matter asserted.

Suppose a police officer testifies that a witness at the crime scene said, "The defendant hit the victim." This is hearsay if the statement is offered to prove that the defendant did, in fact, hit the victim.

After identifying what hearsay is, the Rules say what hearsay is not.

Suppose a declarant says, "I am the King of the world." If offered to prove that the declarant was not mentally competent at the time he made the statement, the statement would not be hearsay. The statement is clearly not being offered to prove that the declarant is, in fact, the King of the world, so it is not being offered to prove the truth of the matter asserted.

Finally, the Rules identify exceptions and allow certain types of hearsay to be admitted into evidence. The effect of identifying evidence as nonhearsay is often the same as the effect of finding an exception to the hearsay rules that applies to specific evidence and allows it to come in. Although the outcome may be the same, it is important to understand the difference between nonhearsay and hearsay admissible under an exception, in order to properly formulate legal arguments in support of admitting or excluding the evidence. This chapter will deal with evidence that is admissible because it is defined as nonhearsay. The next chapter will identify evidence that is hearsay, but admissible because of an exception in the rules.

In spite of its complexity (or maybe because of it), hearsay is probably the most interesting body of evidence law to study. If you like intellectual jigsaw puzzles, you'll love this.

9.2 Purpose of Hearsay Rules

The fundamental purpose behind the hearsay rules is to limit the admission of inaccurate testimony. Testimony based on what was said out of court is generally considered to be unreliable because out-of-court statements are usually not under oath, and are not subject to scrutiny or cross-examination at the time they are made. The evidentiary rules encourage admitting evidence obtained directly "from the horse's mouth," in order to avoid inaccuracies. It is generally desirable to have the witness who makes the statement available in court to be cross-examined or impeached, so the trier-of-fact can assess the witness's perceptions and credibility. The following example is illustrative.

Assume there has been a fire, and the police suspect arson. Ms. Listner says that Mr. Looker told her that he saw George Jones out walking near the fire at the time the fire started. Ms. Listner can provide no other information about Mr. Jones or about what Mr. Looker saw. However Mr. Looker, who made the statement, could be examined further. He could be asked, "At what time did you see George Jones? How do you know when the fire started? Describe what Mr. Jones was wearing. Was he carrying anything at the time you saw him? How do you know Mr. Jones? Have you had any difficulty with him in the past?"

The answers to these questions provide more than information. They provide a gauge by which the reliability of Mr. Looker's perception can be measured. Ms. Listner's testimony is inadmissible hearsay. Mr. Looker's testimony is not.

It is important to differentiate between the reliability of the witness who is repeating the hearsay and the reliability of the hearsay statement itself. In developing hearsay policy, the legislatures and courts have looked at the probability that the statement itself is reliable. Whether the witness on the stand reporting the statement is reporting it accurately, or honestly, or just making it up is for the trier-of-fact to assess.

9.3 An Introduction to Nonhearsay

Understanding what is excluded from the definition of hearsay involves using both logic and a good memory. Some exclusions are intuitively obvious, and others are the products of legal evolution that may not be entirely logical. The logical exclusions can be reasoned out. The others need to be learned.

Hearsay does not include all out-of-court statements. First, it includes only those statements offered to prove the truth of the matter asserted. Impeachment evidence is nonhearsay because it is not offered to prove the truth of the matter asserted. It is offered to prove that the witness is not credible. The rules we have studied with regard to impeachment, then, are not directly relevant to this chapter because the evidence they address is, by definition, nonhearsay. Similarly, out-of-court statements offered to prove state of mind or motive are nonhearsay because they are not offered to prove the truth. The following example illustrates this point.

> Jack robbed a bank. In the course of the robbery, he pointed a gun at a patron and said, "Put your jewelry in this bag or I'll shoot you." Jack's statement is *nonhearsay* if it is offered to show that the patron was under duress when she placed the jewelry in Jack's bag. To show duress, it doesn't matter whether Jack's statement was true or not. It only matters that the patron believed he might shoot her and for that reason put the jewelry in the bag. Jack's statement is hearsay only if it is offered to prove he would have in fact shot the patron had she not done what she was told.

Students often ask, "What if the patron just made up the statement? What if Jack never threatened the patron at all? What do the hearsay rules say about that?" The hearsay rules don't address that issue. The rules address the reliability of out-of-court statements and the declarant who allegedly made them, rather than the witness who recounts them. The witness who is repeating the statements is there for the jury to evaluate.

9.4 Nonverbal Assertions

Nonverbal Assertion
Gestures, such as a nod of the head meaning "yes," constitute nonverbal assertions.

The Federal Rules provide that **nonverbal** conduct, if intended as an **assertion,** constitutes hearsay. When the assertion is direct as opposed to implied, the state and federal courts are consistent in their assessments. The following example illustrates direct nonverbal conduct that constitutes hearsay.

> Assume you are having a conversation with someone who becomes agitated. She puts her hands over her ears clearly communicating that she does not wish to hear any more on the subject. This is nonverbal conduct intended to be an assertion. It is hearsay in both federal and state courts.

The problem arises when nonverbal conduct implicitly asserts something, but the assertion is not intentional. In this situation, under the Federal Rules the conduct is admissible because it does not constitute hearsay. Many state courts, however, take an opposing view. Consider the following example.

> Assume that you are in the lobby of a building when you observe someone putting on an overcoat and heavy gloves prior to exiting. Implied in this conduct (putting on the overcoat and gloves) is the assertion that it is cold outside. However, under the Federal Rules,

this nonverbal conduct is nonhearsay because there is no intent on the part of the declarant to assert that it is cold outside. He just happens to be putting on a coat and gloves, which creates that inference. In many states, the opposite conclusion would be reached, and the conduct would be considered hearsay.

Had the person directly stated, "Gee, it's cold outside," prior to putting on the overcoat, that statement would be hearsay in any jurisdiction. Although the inference to be drawn from the nonverbal conduct of putting on the overcoat and gloves is the same as the direct assertion of its being cold, the nonverbal indirect assertion is non-hearsay under the Federal Rules.

This dividing line isn't always rational. The actor (who put on the gloves and overcoat) is not in court to be cross-examined as to the accuracy of his perception, or the possibility of mistake. This conduct has the "feel" of hearsay, and many states define it as such. In such jurisdictions, the conduct of putting on the gloves and overcoat would be hearsay if offered to prove it was cold outside because the trier-of-fact would need to assess the credibility of the man putting on the overcoat to determine the value of the evidence.

9.5   Evidence That Is Not Hearsay Because the Rules Say It Is Not

Hearsay does not include out-of-court statements offered to prove the truth if the statements are defined as nonhearsay by the Rules of Evidence. The authors of this textbook are unable to rationalize why certain items are considered nonhearsay under the Rules and others are considered hearsay but admissible under exceptions to the Rules. The student is welcome to speculate and hypothesize about the reasons for the different identifications.

FRE 801, P. 279

FRE 801 specifically identifies as nonhearsay prior inconsistent statements of a witness when the statements were given under oath at a previous hearing, trial, or deposition. Keep in mind that this is not the same thing as FRE 613, under which a witness may be cross-examined about prior inconsistent statements for impeachment purposes. Rule 801 allows the prior inconsistent statement to be considered as direct evidence for its truthfulness.

FRE 613, P. 276

Also under Rule 801, evidence of a prior consistent statement is admissible to prove the truth when offered to rebut an inference that the witness is fabricating testimony. This is nonhearsay according to the Rule.

Finally under Rule 801, evidence of an admission by a party, agent of the party, or co-conspirator of the party, offered against that party, is admissible to prove the admitted conduct. The admission

FRE 801(d)(2), P. 279

need not have been made under oath (unlike prior inconsistent statements). It is not hearsay. FRE 801(d)(2) has been amended however, consistent with case law, to provide that an admission made by an agent or co-conspirator is not alone sufficient to prove the existence of the agency or conspiracy, nor is it sufficient to show the participation of party against whom the statement is offered. In other words, although admissions by co-conspirators are not hearsay under the Rules, the amended FRE 801(d)(2)(E) recognizes the potential for unreliability in such statements and requires that there be corroboration to prove the agency or conspiracy.

FRE 801(d)(2)(E), P. 280

You may well ask why these types of statements are nonhearsay. The answer is because the rule says so. One can logically understand why prior statements admissible for impeachment purposes are nonhearsay; they are not offered to prove the truth of the statement. Prior statements offered to prove the truth are nonhearsay only because the rule says they are not. Some states allow such statements under hearsay exceptions. The Federal Rules simply exclude such statements from the definition of hearsay.

9.6 Evidence That Is Not Hearsay Because the Court Says It Is Not

A long history of case law lingers in the states and even the federal system invoking the logic that certain evidence offered as circumstantial evidence is not hearsay because it is used to create inferences and not to prove the truth of the matter asserted. This argument has not been used frequently and is not easy to explain. In fact, according to Michael Graham, *Handbook of Federal Evidence,* 3rd ed. (1991) 727, the use of this logic is "theoretically unsound." Graham writes:

> The reason for such inaccuracy may be attributed primarily to the fact that in most instances, while the evidence under consideration was highly probative, highly necessary, and highly trustworthy, no applicable hearsay exception existed.

FRE 807, P. 286

Under the Federal Rules of Evidence as currently drafted, there is arguably no need for the circumstantial evidence analysis. According to Rule 807, hearsay statements not specifically covered under any exception may still be admissible if they have "equivalent guarantees of trustworthiness" and are essential to the case. This "catch-all" provision might appear to eliminate the need for the questionable circumstantial evidence argument, at least in the federal system; however, the courts are not all in agreement on that point. In a 1990 case, *United States v. Ashby,* 864 F.2d 690 (10th Cir. 1990), the federal court of appeals upheld a lower court ruling that certain evidence was nonhearsay because it was circumstantial evidence. In this case, a car title found in the glove box showing that defendant was the owner of the seized vehicle was admitted over defendant's hearsay objection. The appellate court affirmed the trial court's ruling, stating,

> [T]he car title was used circumstantially to tie appellant to the car, not to prove that she was the owner. Since these documents were used to tie appellant to the car, they were not hearsay . . . and were relevant for the purpose for which they were introduced.

It is difficult to comprehend how a car title that is introduced to "tie" a party to a car is not being used to show ownership. This appears to be an instance where the title isn't hearsay because the court said it isn't.

9.7 Identifying Nonhearsay Uses of Evidence Offered for Purposes Other Than to Prove the Truth, and Understanding Their Limitations

Most of the time, it is not too difficult to identify statements that are nonhearsay because they are offered to prove matters other than the truth of the assertion. A general category of out-of-court statements that are nonhearsay are those offered to prove a declarant's state of mind or motive. The following hypothetical illustrates this situation.

Mary and Jim were walking down a street when they heard a woman scream, "Stop that—you're really hurting that child!" They walked quickly to the alley from which they heard the scream (which took only seconds) and saw a child, bleeding badly, lying on the ground. A man was standing near the child when Mary and Jim arrived but started to run away when Mary and Jim approached. Mary reached down to help the child, while Jim followed the man, who ran into an apartment building. Jim then called the police and an ambulance. The child was taken to the hospital, and the man who had been observed by Mary and Jim was found by the police with Jim's help in one of the apartments in the building Jim had seen him enter. The man, Rudy, was charged with assault and battery. The woman who had originally screamed, "Stop that—you're really hurting that child!" was not found for questioning.

In this case, the unknown declarant's scream is admissible into evidence to show Mary's and Jim's states of mind when they went to the alley to investigate, and to explain Jim's motive in following Rudy to the apartment building. When offered to prove the state of mind of Jim or Mary, the statement is not hearsay.

Since the statement is not admissible to prove that the defendant was, in fact, hurting the child, the court may issue a limiting instruction ordering the jury to consider the statement only for its non-hearsay purpose. Notwithstanding such a limiting instruction, the jury will most likely be influenced by the statement in the above hypothetical, even if only unconsciously. Attorneys will consequently often object to the use of out-of-court statements introduced allegedly for nonhearsay purposes, if those statements are likely to mislead the jury or cause unfair prejudice against a party (FRE 403). Recent United States Supreme Court cases have added some wrinkles to statements such as the one here. We will discuss the nature and admissibility of similar out-of-court statements in Section 10.2.

FRE 403, P. 264

In the following criminal case, the government argued that out-of-court statements made by an informant were admissible to provide "background" information. Since the out-of-court statements were not used to prove the truth, these statements were technically non-hearsay. The court agreed that the statements were not hearsay, especially in light of the limiting instructions repeatedly given by the judge. However, the appellate court analyzed the testimony for its overall effect and found it should have been excluded for unfair prejudice. The argument was valid that the evidence technically had a nonhearsay purpose, but the court still must consider the evidence for its potential effect on the jury and the harm it might do.

United States v. Mazza and DeCologero

792 F.2d 1210 (1st Cir. 1986)

*   *   *

Antonio Mazza and Anthony DeCologero appeal their convictions for conspiracy to possess cocaine with an intent to distribute it. They primarily attack the way in which the government first presented its case to the jury, namely, by having two government agents describe what an informer had previously told them about what the appellants said and did in a series of meetings with the informer. We agree with the appellants that the admission of the descriptive testimony was erroneous. . . .

I

Our analysis of the appellants' main argument depends heavily on the specific facts of the case. We shall first summarize these facts, then discuss the basic error of law. . . .

A

The government's evidence, much of which was on tape, shows the following series of events, all of which took place in late summer of 1984.

August 3: Agents of the Federal Drug Enforcement Administration lawfully searched the home of Armand Barrasso. They found about a pound of cocaine. In return for a promise to recommend leniency to his eventual sentencing judge, Barrasso promised to help the DEA by becoming an informer. His actions during the ensuing investigation of the appellants were closely supervised by two DEA agents, Peter Vinton and Daniel Doherty.

[Several meetings between Barrasso were monitored, and Barrasso reported back to the DEA agents after each meeting, until the time of arrest.]

*   *   *

The appellants' major claim on this appeal is that the way in which government presented its case to the jury was unfair. Before calling Barrasso to describe what happened during the August and September meetings, the government called DEA agents Doherty and Vinton, who supervised the investigation of Mazza and DeCologero. On direct examination, the agents were permitted to describe what Barrasso had told them outside the courtroom about what he and the appellants had said and done in these conversations, at which the agents were not present. Indeed, in at least one instance, one of the agents testified about what Barrasso had told the other agent (outside the courtroom) about one of his conversations with the appellants. The agents' testimony contained many statements by Barrasso that if taken as true, would strongly incriminate the appellants. Indeed, the jury initially heard much of the story that we have presented . . . through the government agents' descriptions of what Barrasso had told them out of court. This way of presenting the evidence, the appellants claim, led the jury to hear the government's case three times—twice out of the mouths of the government agents, in the form of inadmissible hearsay testimony, and only later in the form of admissible testimony by Barrasso himself. Barrasso, they add, was a highly untrustworthy witness whose credibility was unfairly enhanced by the government's manner of proof.

In our opinion, both reason and authority indicate the appellants are right about the inadmissibility of the challenged testimony of the government agents. Technically speaking, the agents' testimony was nonhearsay, for the court repeatedly cautioned the jury not to consider the out-of-court statements for their truth, but, rather, to consider them as "background," or as showing "the basis for the actions taken by the government." The court apparently meant for the jury to take the agents' accounts of what Barrasso told them as showing only the fact that Barrasso said certain words to the agents, not as evidence of the truth of Barrasso's out-of-court words. Nevertheless, as we shall explain, the risk that the jury would consider those words for their truth was great, and the government's need to present them to the jury—throughout the agents' testimony—was virtually nonexistent. Because the "probative value" of the agents' testimony was "substantially outweighed by the danger of unfair prejudice," it should have been excluded under Rule 403 of the Federal Rules of Evidence.

We fully recognize that out-of-court statements are often admissible for nonhearsay purposes and that a district court has considerable leeway in applying Rule 403. Nonetheless, in this instance, the testimony should have been excluded for three reasons.

First, the amount of out-of-court statement evidence was large. Barrasso's out-of-court statements pervaded the direct examination of both agents. The agents related so many of these statements that the government effectively managed to have the jury hear a second-hand account of Barrasso's entire story through witnesses whose credibility the jury was less apt to question.

Second, when the out-of-court statements were admitted, the risk that they could improperly sway the jury was high. The testimony might have shown facts not later corroborated; it would also likely bolster the credibility of the informer Barrasso before he took the stand. The jury was particularly likely to consider these out-of-court declarations for their truth, for they directly implicated the defendants in the specific criminal acts at issue.

Third, the agents' testimony about Barrasso's out-of-court statements had almost no probative value.

*   *   *

In context, the government could simply have asked the agents to testify that they debriefed Barrasso after his conversations with the appellants. The government could—and should—have left Barrasso to testify about the substance of those conversations.

In sum, the amount of potentially prejudicial testimony admitted, combined with the lack of need, convinces us that its admission was erroneous.

FRE 801, P. 279

Please note in this case that informant Barrasso's accounts of the defendants' out-of-court statements are not hearsay under 801(d)(2) because they constitute admissions of a co-conspirator. (Admissions of a party or co-conspirator are not hearsay because the rule says so.)

This case illustrates that using subterfuge to get in otherwise inadmissible evidence generally will not work. The stated purpose for admitting the hearsay in this case was not persuasive. Prosecution created a technical argument whereby the evidence could come in, but on close scrutiny, when admitted for the argued purpose, the evidence was essentially nonprobative. If an argument is a pretense through which one hopes to get the evidence in front of the jury, there is a good chance the court will see through the sham.

It is incumbent on the person analyzing prospective testimony to evaluate both the legitimate purpose for which the evidence is to be used, and the probative value of the evidence in that context.

9.8   Verbal Acts

Verbal Acts
Words that create a legal relationship or give legal context to an accompanying physical act.

The legal concept of **verbal acts** is not a logical one to many of us. Speaking is a verbal act to most ordinary mortals. When the law refers to verbal acts in the hearsay sense, however, the reference is to words that generally accompany other conduct, or create legal relationships, and that help define the context of a transaction. Words used in this context are also frequently referred to as an "operative legal fact" and are excluded from the definition of hearsay as a matter of developed law. They are nonhearsay.

For example, suppose Grandpa Bucks says to his grandson, "Take this thousand dollars as a gift." His statement is nonhearsay because characterizing the money as a gift is a verbal act. The act of giving money without accompanying words can have a lot of different meanings. The money could be a loan, a gift, a partial payment on a debt or contract, or even an unlawful payoff of a bribe. Out-of-court statements that characterize a transaction are considered verbal acts because without them the transaction would have no specific meaning.

A common place for the concept of verbal acts to apply is in the area of contract law. Words that create contracts, such as offers, acceptances, and rejections, are considered verbal acts. The case law presents various "logical" arguments for this type of exclusion; however, none of them are terribly compelling. It is simply established law that words that create legal relationships are excluded from the hearsay rules as verbal acts, and are therefore nonhearsay.

The concept of verbal acts applies in both the civil and criminal domains. The following case illustrates admissible testimony of a verbal act in a criminal case.

United States v. Jackson

588 F.2d 1046 (5th Cir. 1979)

[Defendant in this case is charged with various crimes related to narcotics sales. The defendant attempted to transport heroin in the suitcases of Miss Johnson, an unsuspecting friend.]

Miss Johnson testified that she was unaware that the canvas bag she transported from Los Angeles to Birmingham contained heroin, and the prosecutor stated in court that the government considered her to be an innocent participant in the criminal scheme. She testified that she met Porter in Los Angeles in June 1977 and that he invited her to his family reunion in Birmingham. On July 6 a woman Miss Johnson did not know came by her apartment and gave her $130 as air fare to Birmingham. She also handed her a small canvas bag and requested that she pack it with the things she was carrying on her trip. The stranger told Miss Johnson that Porter would pick her up at the Birmingham airport. Appellants contend that the witness's testimony as to what the unidentified woman said when she brought the money and canvas bag to the witness at her Los Angeles apartment violated the hearsay rule and the Confrontation Clause of the Sixth Amendment. We disagree. The Federal Rules of Evidence exclude from the operation of the hearsay rule any oral statement not intended as an assertion. F. Rule Evid. 801(a). Furthermore, an out-of-court statement that is not offered as proof of the matter asserted therein is not hearsay. F. Rule Evid. 801(c). We think that the out-of-court statements fall within that class of "cases in which the utterance is contemporaneous with a nonverbal act, independently admissible, relating to that act and throwing some light upon it." Since the unidentified woman in Los Angeles was not a witness against the appellants, there was no Confrontation Clause violation in this case.

The woman who dropped off the money and canvas bag in the above case clearly made an out-of-court statement when she said that Porter would pick up Miss Johnson at the Birmingham airport. This statement was allowed into evidence as nonhearsay because it was not offered to prove whether Porter would actually pick up Miss Johnson. It was offered as a "verbal act," which is a statement that explains conduct as the conduct occurs. It defines the concurrent physical act.

Verbal acts are confusing. They are consistently excluded from the definition of hearsay in the states as well as the federal system. They are difficult to identify. The two main considerations when assessing this type of nonhearsay are:

1. If words create a legal relationship between the parties, they will be considered verbal acts.
2. If the words accompany physical conduct and serve to shed light on the physical conduct, they are likely to be considered verbal acts.

Some examples of verbal acts which have been recognized as nonhearsay include, but are not limited to, a marriage offer, a promise, or a vow; a solicitation of a bribe; solicitation for prostitution; and an ownership declaration.

9.9 Implied Assertions

For there to be hearsay, there must be an out-of-court statement that makes an assertion. Some statements, however, are made in a non-assertive form or indirectly. A question, for instance, is not an assertion and technically, therefore, should not constitute hearsay. However, there are times when questions must be viewed as statements subject to the hearsay rules, or inappropriate outcomes would result.

Suppose a man named Bypasser observed an incident of a victim's being shoved by an assailant who then ran away. Suppose Bypasser went up to the victim and queried, "Can you believe the nerve of that guy, coming up and pushing you like that?" Bypasser technically didn't make a "statement"—he asked a question. Using rigid application of the rules, Bypasser's question isn't hearsay because it is a question and not an assertion. Looking at the "substance" of Bypasser's comment, however, it is clear that Bypasser did make an assertion. He simply put it in the form of a rhetorical question. He wasn't really inquiring about the "nerve" of the assailant. He was asserting his disapproval of what he saw. In this case, Bypasser's comment would constitute hearsay.

Notwithstanding the above example, under the Federal Rules of Evidence, most of the time indirect assertions are not considered hearsay. The Advisory Committee speaks of "verbal conduct which is assertive but offered as a basis for inferring something other than the matter asserted." The Advisory Notes state that such verbal conduct is excluded from the definition of hearsay. The following example illustrates this point.

Enjoin
To cause an action to stop through a court ordered injunction.

On July 1, Nephew Jimmy states, "I always defer to Uncle Harry on financial matters—he is the best." On July 2, Harry tries to give a large financial gift to a University, and his family files an action to enjoin the gift by asserting Harry's mental incompetence. Jimmy's statement is offered into evidence by Harry's attorney to show that Jimmy perceived Harry to be mentally competent near the time of the attempted gift. Jimmy's statement is not a direct assertion regarding Harry's competence. If it were, it would definitely be hearsay. Since, however, the statement isn't being offered to prove the truth of the assertion that Harry handled all of Jimmy's financial matters, or that Harry is "the best," then under the Federal Rules, the comment is not hearsay and is admissible.

The Advisory Committee defends the depiction of Jimmy's comment as nonhearsay because it believes the likelihood of fabrication in such situations is small, and the jury can assess an appropriate weight to give this evidence. Many state courts, however, would not reach the same conclusion. Their logic is as follows.

Had Nephew Jimmy said, "Uncle Harry is mentally competent," his statement would unequivocally be considered hearsay. Since there is no substantive difference between Jimmy's direct statement of Harry's competence and his indirect implication of Harry's competence in his assertion that he used Harry for financial advice, to treat those two statements differently would be placing "form over substance." (Lawyers often argue that applying the law in certain ways puts "form over substance." They mean by this that in applying a rule strictly by its terms without looking at its purpose, the outcome can be the opposite of the one intended.)

For the paralegal, it is important to know that statements implying an assertion (as opposed to statements directly making that assertion) may be treated differently from each other, especially in the federal system. The rules in the relevant jurisdiction must be researched to adequately assess an outcome in this situation.

9.10   In Summary

The theories surrounding hearsay are complicated and not necessarily logically cohesive. To simplify, the following checklist should be used when evaluating out-of-court statements to determine if they are hearsay or nonhearsay.

■ Is there a written or oral statement, or nonverbal conduct, that makes an assertion? (If not, there is no hearsay.)
■ Is the assertion direct or indirect? (If indirect, the statement may be nonhearsay.)
■ Is the assertion offered to prove the truth of the matter asserted? (If not, it is nonhearsay.)
■ Does the assertion serve to explain a concurrent physical act? (If yes, it may be considered a verbal act and nonhearsay.)
■ Does the assertion create a legal relationship between the parties? (If yes, it is nonhearsay.)
■ Is the assertion excluded from the legal definition of hearsay, either by the Rules of Evidence or according to case law? (If yes, it is nonhearsay.)

If, after examining the evidence in light of all the questions above, you determine that you have a hearsay statement, you then must analyze whether the assertion is admissible under one of the many hearsay exceptions to be discussed in the next chapter.

End of Chapter Review Questions

1. What is hearsay?
2. What is nonhearsay?
3. What is the purpose of the hearsay rules?
4. What is a nonverbal assertion?
5. Identify some nonhearsay uses of out-of-court statements.
6. What is a verbal act?
7. What is an implied assertion?

Applications

Consider the following hypothetical situation.

Marissa, who lived with her mother, was a next-door neighbor of Randall, who lived alone. One day Randall asked Marissa if she would take care of his plants over the summer because he was going to be out of town a lot. Marissa agreed, and Randall gave her a key to his house, with his thanks.

Before Randall left, Marissa asked him if it was OK if she used his house while he was gone. She explained that at times she needed to have privacy away from her mother. Randall said,

Statement #1: "Of course, you can use the house any time."

After approximately six weeks of absence, Randall came home unexpectedly. When he entered his house, he found a party going on. Many of his personal things were lying broken, and the house was in a shambles. He began to tell people to leave. One party participant said,

Statement #2: "Look, Marissa said we could party here all we want. She said it didn't matter if anything broke or not—it ain't even her house, man!"

Randall called the police, and the party participants, one of whom turned out to be Marissa, were arrested. They were each charged with criminal trespass and criminal damage to property.

1. With regard to Statement #1, is there a nonhearsay use of this evidence? Discuss.
2. With regard to Statement # 2, is there a nonhearsay use for this evidence? Discuss.

Assume that the proponent of the evidence is attempting to introduce the following at trial. Will the judge rule that it is one of the following (a) not a statement so not hearsay; (b) a statement which might be hearsay; (c) a statement but not hearsay because the rule says so; or (d) a statement but not hearsay because the courts say so?

3. A prescription for bifocal lenses.
4. Professor Smart's selection of Mary to be his teaching assistant.
5. Defendant Alberto's email approving Monica's decision to fire people.
6. Monica's prior statement under oath to Congress now offered because her present testimony differs from that statement.
7. Mr. Comey's exclamation "That's the guy who entered the hospital room!"
8. Defendant Curd's statement to Alberto: "Don't tell anyone that we tried to get his signature."
9. The statement: "You can have this for your twenty-first birthday."
10. Mr. President said: "Don't question my authority to do this for I am divined by god to do this."

CHAPTER

Hearsay Exceptions

10.1 Introduction to Hearsay Exceptions

As you've probably realized, identifying a statement as hearsay does not end the analytical adventure of hearsay exploration. An out-of-court statement determined to be hearsay may still be admissible under one or more of the many hearsay exceptions. In other words, even though the statements are acknowledged to be hearsay, if they

FRE 802, P. 280

qualify under one of the exceptions, they may be admissible anyway. FRE 802 states:

> Hearsay is not admissible except as provided by these rules or by other rules prescribed by the Supreme Court pursuant to statutory authority or by Act of Congress.

FRE 803 & 804, PP. 280 and 284

FRE 807, P. 286

There are 27 specific hearsay exceptions in Rules 803 and 804 of the Federal Rules of Evidence (23 found in FRE 803, and 4 additional exceptions in FRE 804). In addition, a "catch-all" provision found in FRE 807 allows for the possible admission of compelling hearsay evidence that does not fit into any of the 27 specific exceptions. To add to the options, as FRE 802 indicates, exceptions to the hearsay exclusionary rule are not limited to those in the Rules of Evidence.

For example, in the Federal Rules of Civil Procedure (FRCP), there are a variety of hearsay exceptions providing for the use of affidavits in lieu of direct testimony in nontrial settings. An affidavit is a written declaration, signed by the declarant (affiant), who attests to the truthfulness of the affidavit under penalty of perjury. An affidavit is ordinarily considered unreliable hearsay since it consists of out-of-court statements, made without the opportunity for cross-examination, offered to prove the truth of the matters asserted. However, the FRCP allows the use of affidavits when applying for restraining orders, filing proofs of service, and submitting motions. State rules of civil procedure have similar counterparts.

Additional hearsay exceptions are also found in the rules of criminal procedure, both in the state and federal systems. In the criminal realm, however, the Sixth Amendment's confrontation clause puts a limitation on the scope of hearsay exceptions available. The confrontation clause gives the accused the right to be confronted with the witnesses against him. Although the Federal Rules of Evidence were drafted to avoid conflict with the Sixth Amendment, a 2004 United States Supreme Court case has altered the way we traditionally have evaluated whether an out-of-court statement fits within a hearsay exception. Pursuant to *Crawford v. Washington*, 541 U.S. 36 (2004), a hearsay statement made by a non-testifying witness, which previously might have been admitted under a hearsay exception, will no longer be admissible under a hearsay exception if the statement is "testimonial." We will discuss *Crawford* and ensuing cases more thoroughly in the next section. But for now, be forewarned that "testimonial" under *Crawford* is not in the "I promise to tell the truth" sense. Rather, "testimonial" refers to a statement or statements made by a person being questioned by police for the primary purpose of establishing the facts of a past event which may be relevant to a future criminal prosecution. In short, even if a hearsay exception is applicable, the statement if determined to be made during a "testimonial" stage in an investigation may be precluded in order to guarantee a criminal defendant's right to confront the witnesses. Keep this new caveat in mind as you progress through the hearsay exceptions.

As noted above, FRE 803 and FRE 804 delineate the two sets of hearsay exceptions. The first set, found in FRE 803, deals with hearsay exceptions where the declarant's availability is irrelevant to whether the hearsay is admissible. The second set of hearsay exceptions, found in FRE 804, are much fewer in number than those in FRE 803. These exceptions deal exclusively with situations where the declarant is unavailable, such as when the declarant is dead, or otherwise beyond the subpoena power of the court.

The next several sections of this chapter will deal with the first set of hearsay exceptions—those that apply whether or not the declarant is available to testify. FRE 803. Out-of-court statements falling under this rule may be admissible whether the declarant is present, absent, known, or unknown. Most states are in accord with the Federal Rules with regard to these hearsay exceptions.

10.2   The *Crawford* Confrontation Wrinkle

As you study the hearsay exceptions in FRE 803 and FRE 804, you will notice that the excepted statements are inherently reliable because of the conditions under which they were made. That rationale previously had been extended to the admissibility of excepted hearsay statements even against criminal defendants. As noted in the previous section, the Supreme Court in *Crawford v. Washington*, 541 U.S. 36 (2004), held that if a hearsay statement is "testimonial," the criminal defendant must be able to confront the declarant either at trial or before otherwise the statement is barred.

Thus, pursuant to *Crawford*, the Sixth Amendment constitutional guarantee to confront one's accusers precludes the admission of "testimonial hearsay" when the witness is unavailable to testify at trial unless the defendant had a previous opportunity to cross-examine the declarant. In that case, Crawford's wife was interviewed by the police at the police station after someone had tried to rape her. During her statement, she identified her husband, Crawford, as assaulting the rapist. At Crawford's trial for assaulting the rapist, (can you believe they would try the husband for assaulting the rapist!), Crawford invoked the marital privilege thereby rendering his wife unavailable to testify. The trial court decided that the wife's statements to the police were reliable hearsay and admitted the statements. The Supreme Court reversed the conviction finding that the wife's statements were "testimonial" and therefore the admission of them at trial violated the defendant/husband's constitutional right to confront or cross-examine the witness against him. The Supreme Court did not define "testimonial."

Then, on June 19, 2006, the United States Supreme Court, in one opinion, *Davis v. Washington,* 126 S. Ct. 2266 (2006), decided two separate cases in which hearsay statements by unavailable witnesses had been admitted at the trials of two defendants.

In *Davis v. Washington,* the Court considered whether the victim's statements, made during her 911 call while her ex-boyfriend was assaulting her, were testimonial within the meaning of *Crawford.* The victim telephoned in a 911 emergency call and identified by name her ex-boyfriend as he was assaulting her. She did not appear at the trial to testify. Over the defendant's objection, the trial court allowed the government to play the 911 tape-recorded call. The Supreme Court concluded that the statements made by the victim in the emergency phase of the 911 call were not testimonial and therefore were properly admitted.

In *Hammon v. Indiana,* the Court considered whether the wife's statements during "initial inquiries" by the police at her home were testimonial. In that case, the police responded to the home of Amy and Hershel Hammon in response to a domestic disturbance report. There, the police found a "somewhat frightened" Amy on the front porch. She denied that anything was wrong. But an officer saw a fire flaming out of a gas heating unit in the living room. There was broken glass in front of the unit. Hershel admitted to an argument with Amy but contended that all was well. After learning more from Amy, the officer had her hand write and sign a battery affidavit in which she wrote the following: "Broke our Furnace & shoved me down on the floor into the broken glass. Hit me in the chest and threw me down. Broke our lamps & phone. Tore up my van where I couldn't leave the house. Attacked my daughter." Amy did not appear at the bench trial despite being subpoenaed. Over the defendant's objection for his inability to cross-examine Amy, the judge allowed the police officer to recount Amy's statement under the "excited utterance" hearsay exception and allowed the admission of the affidavit as a "presence sense impression." The Supreme Court thought otherwise and found that the victim's statements were testimonial because the statements were made after the event and during part of the police investigation.

In the joint opinion for both *Davis* and *Hammon,* the United States Supreme Court summarized its holdings in the two cases thus providing guidance for distinguishing "testimonial" statements.

> Statements are nontestimonial when made in the course of police interrogation under circumstances objectively indicating that the **primary purpose** of the interrogation is to enable police assistance to meet an ongoing emergency. They are testimonial when the circumstances objectively indicate that there is no such ongoing emergency, and that the **primary purpose** of the interrogation is to establish or prove past events potentially relevant to later criminal prosecution.

The decisions in the above cases make sense and actually are consistent with the hearsay rationale of precluding or permitting some out-of-court statements. The nontestimonial statements are statements made during circumstances likely to evoke reliable statements such as the excited utterances during an emergency situation. The testimonial statements are similar to statements for which there are no hearsay exceptions because they were made at a time or in a situation that make them less reliable. Consider the following two situations.

Right before dinner, Lily's mom finds Lily in the kitchen next to the cookie jar. Lily has a cookie in her hand. Lily, who is five, says "Mom, my bad brother threw this cookie at me. I had to catch it before it hit granny's photo."

Right before dinner, Lily's mom hears Lily screaming "You bad brother. That cookie you threw is about to hit granny's photo." Mom walks in the kitchen and finds Lily with a cookie in her hand.

Before *Crawford*, both statements might have been admissible. The first statement would constitute a presence sense impression, and the second statement would be an excited utterance, both of which are discussed in Section 10.3. Now, if Lily were unavailable and bad brother was a defendant in a criminal trial for assaulting granny's photo, the first statement would not be admissible because it was made during an investigative phase. Bad brother would not be able to cross-examine Lily and therefore would not be able to impeach the reliability of her statement. The second statement likely would be considered nontestimonial and admissible as an excited utterance. Be mindful that if the trial court analyzes the hearsay statement as "testimonial" but the declarant is available for trial or the defendant had the prior opportunity to confront the declarant, such as at a preliminary hearing, then the statement should be admissible.

As you can see, determining whether a statement is nontestimonial or testimonial will depend on the specific facts of each case. Thus, during case preparation, you will want to interview and otherwise search for all out-of-court statements relating to the case. Your initial assessment may be that the statement may be precluded as testimonial, but as our study of the Rules of Evidence has demonstrated, the statement may be useful or admissible in other ways. Concomitantly with your study of the following hearsay exceptions, think about in what way each exception might fall within the confrontation exclusion discussed above.

10.3 Present Sense Impression and Excited Utterance

Present Sense Impression
Statements made about an experience during the experience.

Excited Utterances
Statements made during or shortly after an occurrence while the declarant is agitated or excited.

FRE 803(1) and (2), P. 280

Two related hearsay exceptions are referred to as statements based on **present sense impression** and **excited utterances**. FRE 803(1) and 803(2). These exceptions refer to statements made while or shortly after the declarant has perceived an event or condition. The rationale behind the exceptions is that statements made contemporaneous with (at the same time as) an event are not likely to be deliberate misrepresentations.

The difference between these two exceptions is very small. A present sense impression must describe the event or condition being perceived, while the excited utterance need only relate to the event. The present sense impression need not be of a "startling" event, while the excited utterance must be related to an event by which the declarant is startled. The following example illustrates these exceptions.

Jeannie called for emergency police protection by dialing 911 at 5:00 A.M. on February 4, 1994. She made the following statements to the dispatcher:

Statement #1: "I hear some noises outside of my house."

Statement #2: "Could you send a patrol car by to take a look around? Sometimes I just get nervous."

As the dispatcher asked some questions, Jeannie interrupted with the following statement:

Statement #3: "My ex-boyfriend Aladdin is pounding on my back door. I'm afraid he's going to break down the door. He's acting crazy. Please send someone."

The dispatcher stayed on the line while she dispatched a patrol car to the area. While on the line, the dispatcher heard Jeannie make the following statements in a loud, agitated voice:

Statement #4: "Go away—the police are coming. I don't want you in here. Stop—don't do that!"

When the police arrived, Jeannie was unconscious. Aladdin was not there.

Statement #1 is a present sense impression of what Jeannie hears outside her house. It is not an excited utterance because Jeannie is not startled at this point.

Statement #2 is inadmissible under both exceptions. There is no present sense impression because Jeannie is not describing anything related to the event. There is no excited utterance because Jeannie is not startled into making the comments.

Statement #3 constitutes both an excited utterance and a present sense impression. Jeannie is describing what Aladdin is doing and her state of mind, as the events occur.

Statement #4 is only an excited utterance. It is not a present sense impression because Jeannie is not describing what is going on; however, she is clearly startled, and her comments relate to the event, so they are admissible under the excited utterance exception.

These hearsay exceptions are frequently used in criminal proceedings where there may not be eyewitnesses to the event, but there are "ear" witnesses who can recount hearing comments made by the victim of a crime as the crime occurred. Keep in mind that the above statements would require the *Crawford* "testimonial" and confrontation analysis just mentioned in Section 10.2. The above example is very similar to the facts in the *Davis v. Washington* case.

10.4 *Res Gestae*

Res Gestae
Statements made in conjunction with gestures, so that the words and the acts are interwined.

When researching cases to support the use of either the present sense impression or excited utterance exceptions to the hearsay rule, you may see the term ***res gestae*** appear in the analysis of the case. This term literally means "things" or "things happened." *Res gestae analysis* was used when statements or gestures were intertwined (were contemporaneous and connected) with the "thing" that happened. Statements that were part of the *res gestae* were admissible as excepted from the hearsay rule.

This common law term has fallen into disfavor in modern times because it is so vague and was often abused in the courts. It has essentially been replaced by the present sense impression and excited utterance exceptions. However, it hasn't disappeared from the literature, so you should recognize it when you see it.

10.5 Then Existing Mental, Emotional, or Physical Condition

FRE 803(3), P. 280

Statements made by a declarant describing the declarant's feelings or state of mind at the time the statements were made are admissible as hearsay exceptions. FRE 803(3). The statement "I have a headache," would be admissible under this exception to prove that the declarant had a headache at the time the declarant said so. The rationale for this exception is that when people say how they feel about something at the time they feel it, they are giving an account of their own perceptions, and the accuracy or reliability of the statements is generally not a problem.

Although statements admitted under this exception are limited to proving the feelings or state of mind of the declarant, they can provide inferences about conduct. A declarant's motive or intent, for example, can be circumstantial evidence of the declarant's subsequent conduct. However, statements under this exception cannot be used to prove conduct directly. Consider the following examples.

If Marie said, "I gave all the pictures to Lenny," this statement would be hearsay and inadmissible to prove that Marie gave the pictures to Lenny.

If Marie said, "I'm going to give all the pictures to Lenny," this statement would be admissible under FRE 803(3) and its comparable state counterparts. The statement is admissible to show Marie's intent to give the pictures to Lenny at the time she said she would and is circumstantial evidence that she later acted on her feelings and in fact gave the pictures to Lenny.

The "then existing mental, emotional, or physical condition" exception is similar but not identical to the nonhearsay analysis provided in Chapter 9, section 9.7, regarding the state of mind of the declarant. Evidence is not hearsay when it is offered to prove the declarant's state of mind, rather than the truth of the matter asserted.

The statement, "Jack should kill Uncle Fred for this," would be nonhearsay if offered to prove the declarant's state of mind (i.e., the declarant was really angry with Uncle Fred), but it would be hearsay to prove that Jack actually killed Uncle Fred. The jury would be given a limiting instruction to consider the testimony only for the purpose offered and not to determine Jack's guilt.

FRE 803(3), P. 280

This exception is not without limits. FRE 803(3) limits admissibility in that it specifically does not allow the admission of statements of memory or belief to prove the fact remembered or believed. In other words, hearsay statements as to why a declarant held a certain belief would not be admissible to prove the belief. The following example is illustrative.

Jim said, "I believed that Jackie was capable of physical violence, so I took a gun with me to our meeting." This statement is not admissible to prove that Jackie was capable of physical violence.

Evidence must be analyzed carefully for admissibility under this exception. Because the exception is broad, the hearsay will be assessed not only for whether it technically fits within the exception, but also for whether its probative value outweighs its prejudicial effect. FRE 403. The courts are cognizant that whenever an exception encompasses as many possibilities as this one does, it is subject to potential abuse.

FRE 403, P. 264

10.6 Statements for Purposes of Medical Diagnosis or Treatment

FRE 803(3) and (4), P. 280

Statements made by a declarant for purposes of medical diagnosis or treatment are excepted from the hearsay rule. FRE 803(4). This exception is related but not identical to the previous exception, FRE 803(3), which allows admissibility of statements of the declarant's then existing physical, mental, or emotional condition. Rule 803(4), however, is not limited to the immediate (current) perceptions of the declarant. For example, if a patient recounts his or her medical history to a medical provider in order to assist the provider in diagnosis or treatment, this would be admissible under FRE 803(4), as would be descriptions of past pain, sensations, or symptoms.

The rationale for this exception is that there is a high degree of reliability in this type of situation. The declarant would be likely to be extremely careful in recounting correct information to a treating nurse or physician, in order to ensure proper medical treatment.

Subsequent to *Crawford*, however, courts already have begun to limit the admissibility of statements under this exception depending on the medical purpose for the statement. For instance, investigating agencies such as child protection services, adult sexual and physical abuse protection agencies, or law enforcement agencies will refer a victim for a forensic examination for purposes of determining whether a criminal investigation is warranted. Over the years, doctors, nurses, and other medical personnel have become more skilled in detecting the symptoms and behaviors of a sexual assault victim. Accordingly, they have developed interview techniques to elicit the pertinent information from the victim. Until *Crawford* such statements generally have been admissible under FRE 803(4) because the statements ostensibly were made for the medical personnel to determine the appropriate medical treatment. Now, however, the victim's statements will require the "primary purpose" analysis to determine whether the statement might fall within the "testimonial" exclusion or whether the statement was made to deal with an ongoing emergency.

10.7   Recorded Recollection

Recorded Recollection
A dirary or other record of information recorded during the time that the person making the record had clear knowledge or recollection of the information

FRE 803(5), P. 281

FRE 612, P. 276

FRE 803(5) P. 281

A written record, made when information was fresh in the mind of a witness, concerning matters the witness is now unable to remember, is admissible as an exception to the hearsay exclusion. FRE 803(5). If such a written record is offered on direct examination, it may be read into the record but not received as an exhibit. Such a recorded recollection is admissible only as an *exhibit*, when offered by the adverse party.

In a previous portion of this textbook relating to witnesses, the use of documents to refresh a witness's recollection was discussed. FRE 612. A witness is allowed to refresh his or her recollection with a writing made previously. After the witness looks at the writing, if the witness's recollection is indeed refreshed, the witness then testifies about the matter. FRE 803(5) is related to the use of documents to refresh the recollection of a witness, but it is not the same thing. FRE 803(5) provides for the admission of the information in the recorded document itself when the witness is unable to recall the matters recorded even after being shown the written record.

10.8   Records

FRE 803(6), P. 281

FRE 803(8), P. 281

FRE 803(9), P. 282

FRE 803(11), P. 282

FRE 803(12), P. 282

FRE 803(13), P. 282

FRE 803(14), P. 282

FRE 803(16), P. 283

FRE 803(17), P. 283

Hearsay within Hearsay
Out-of-court statements that contain other out-of-court statements.

Ten separate exceptions under Rule 803 relate to the admissibility of various types of (out-of-court) written records. These are:

- recorded recollections (discussed above), FRE 803(5);
- records of regularly conducted activity, FRE 803(6);
- public records and reports, FRE 803(8);
- records of vital statistics, FRE 803(9);
- records of religious organizations, FRE 803(11);
- marriage, baptismal, and similar certificates, FRE 803(12);
- family records, FRE 803(13);
- records of documents affecting an interest in property, FRE 803(14);
- ancient documents, FRE 803(16);
- market reports and commercial publications, FRE 803(17).

The paralegal must be cautious when reviewing these exceptions. Because these records are excepted from the hearsay exclusionary rule does not mean they are not excludable on other grounds. Also, many records contain **hearsay within hearsay** or statements of other individuals incorporated into the statements of the declarant who made the record. Hearsay within hearsay is admissible pursuant to Rule 805, but only if each part of the combined statements conforms to a hearsay exception. In other words, each hearsay declaration in a record must be analyzed to determine whether it falls under an exception. The records exceptions are logically grouped and discussed below. As we discuss specific types of records exceptions more thoroughly, examples will illuminate the potential problems and solutions.

FRE 805, P. 285

Business records. The most frequently used records exception in litigation, when one or more of the parties is a business, is the "business records exception." Records kept in the course of regularly conducted business activity fall under this exception to the hearsay exclusion, unless the records are shown to lack trustworthiness. FRE 803(6). Examples of records that are admissible under this exception would include such things as patient medical records, business accounting records, bank records, and employment records. These records are admissible to prove the truth of the information contained within them. They are also admissible to prove the non-occurrence or nonexistence of a matter, if the matter would ordinarily have been recorded in such a record, but is not recorded therein.

FRE 803(7), P. 281

FRE 803(7). In other words, the records can be used to prove either that something occurred or didn't occur, based on the presence or absence of recorded information. Furthermore, business records are admissible even though they contain hearsay based on other hearsay, as long as all the hearsay is kept in the course of regularly conducted business activity. Consider the following example.

John is the Controller for TicTech, Inc. He makes all entries into the corporate general ledger. John gets his information from Fred, the assistant controller, who gives John the information on journal entry forms. Fred gets his information from the accounts receivable and accounts payable clerks. Each of these multiple layers of hearsay is independently admissible under the business records exception, and therefore, the general ledger is admissible.

However, for hearsay to be admissible as a business records exception, the entries to be admitted must be kept in the ordinary course of business. When there are other types of hearsay within the admissible business record, those portions of the business record are not admissible. In other words, the mere presence of hearsay in a business record does not make otherwise inadmissible hearsay admissible. Consider the following case.

United States v. Bortnovsky and Braz

879 F.2d 30 (2d Cir. 1989)

[Defendants were convicted on various charges of racketeering and mail fraud, related to fraudulent insurance claims for fire loss and theft. Defendant Braz made the fraudulent theft claim.]

*   *   *

The indictment alleged as the third predicate act that Braz's insurance claim of February 1980 for the theft of sheepskin coats from the store was fraudulent because the coats were not delivered until September 1980. In response to evidence introduced by the government in support of its argument, Braz sought to introduce defendant's exhibit G, the report of the insurance adjuster. The report stated in relevant part: "We questioned a Mr. David Belsky of the firm Damer Sheepskin Fashions [the supplier] who advised that the goods were delivered to the assured on January 19, 1980, but to date they had not been paid for by the assured." The district court held that the document was not admissible under either Fed. R. Evid. 803(6) as a business record, Fed. R. Evid. 803(8) as a public record, or Fed. R. Evid. 803(24) or 804(b)(5), which provide generally for admission of documents not covered by other exceptions "but having equivalent circumstantial guarantees of trustworthiness." We conclude that this exclusion was not, as Braz argues, an abuse of discretion. Nor was the decision denying Braz's Rule 33 motion—for a new trial based on the document's exclusion or, in the alternative, for a hearing as to its reliability—reversible error.

Although Braz speaks of the entire document, the real issue is the admissibility not of exhibit G itself, but of the statement of Belsky it contains. Therefore, to prevail on his argument, Braz must establish not only that the report falls within an exception to the hearsay rule, but also that Belsky's statement is covered by such an exception. Braz has failed to do the latter.

Although the adjuster's report might otherwise qualify as a business record within the meaning of Rule 803(6), Belsky's statement does not satisfy the rule's requirements because there was no showing that he had a duty to report the information he was quoted as having given. The admissibility of Belsky's statement within the exception for reports of public agencies or the catch-all exceptions depends upon its "trustworthiness." Judge Mukasey did not abuse his discretion when ruling that there was insufficient evidence of the statement's reliability to provide the requisite circumstantial guarantees of trustworthiness. Not only did Belsky have no duty to report the date on which the goods were delivered, there was no evidence that, as an accountant, he would have had personal knowledge of the date on which the coats were delivered. In addition, the statement was supported only by the testimony of Braz and contradicted by the evidence of the government.

Finally, the post-trial decision denying Braz's motion for a new trial because of the exclusion of the statement or a hearing as to the document's reliability was not reversible error. In support of that motion, Braz submitted the results of the polygraph examination that supported his testimony that the coats were delivered before the robbery. In response the government submitted an affidavit of

Belsky dated August 8, 1988, in which he stated that he did not recall making the statement at issue nor did he think it likely that he made such a statement because, as an outside accountant, he "was usually not in a position to know when merchandise was delivered by [the supplier]."

The district court properly held that Belsky's affidavit indicated that the statement in exhibit G lacked the reliability to be admissible as an exception to the hearsay rule, because Belsky did not have personal knowledge of the facts reported.

* * *

In the preceding case, there is no question that the report of the insurance adjuster was, generally speaking, admissible as a business record. The adjuster's personal observations, recorded during his investigation, are part of his ordinary work conduct and would constitute admissible hearsay. The problem is the business record included information from Mr. Belsky. Mr. Belsky did not provide this information in the ordinary course of business. Mr. Belsky didn't have knowledge of the information from the ordinary course of his business. Mr. Belsky didn't remember giving the information and indicated it wasn't likely he ever had personal knowledge of such information.

The expression "You can't make a silk purse out of a sow's ear" applies in this situation. Mr. Belsky wouldn't have qualified as a witness with personal knowledge to give the testimony at issue directly. Therefore the evidence cannot come in as hearsay, even though it is memorialized in a document that is subject to a hearsay exception.

Prior to the December 1, 2000 amendment, the proponent of the business record was required to lay the foundation for the record through the testimony of the custodian of the record or by another qualified witness. FRE 803(6) did require and still requires the custodian of the record or other qualified witness to establish that the business record was made at or near the time of the act, event, condition, opinion, or diagnosis, that the record was made by a person with knowledge or from information transmitted by a person with knowledge, and that the record was kept in the ordinary course of the regularly conducted business activity.

FRE 902(11) and (12), P. 289

Effective December 1, 2000, however, FRE 902(11) and FRE 902(12) were added to simplify and streamline the foundational requirements for business records, domestic and foreign. The proponent of the business record can now lay the foundation for the record by offering a certified copy of it providing that the certification complies with FRE 902(11), FRE 902(12), or with a statute permitting certification. Thus, the need for testimony of the custodian or any witness is eliminated. We will discuss this foundational method more fully in Section 11.5, Authenticating Business Records.

Public records. Records of births, deaths, marriages, or other vital statistics are admissible, and the absence of a record of a birth, death, or marriage is admissible to show that none occurred. FRE 803(9), (10).

FRE 803(9) and (10), P. 282

Records of real estate transactions, title, and ownership (such as deeds, deeds of trusts, mortgages, and liens), that have been properly recorded are admissible as excepted from the hearsay rule. Statements in real property documents, if relevant to the purpose of the document, are admissible as well. 803(14).

More interestingly, records made or maintained in a public office or agency regarding either the activities of the agency itself, or matters observed pursuant to a duty imposed by law upon the agency, are generally admissible. FRE 803(8). This is a very important exception.

FRE 803(8), P. 281

Suppose the investigators from the Environmental Protection Agency (EPA) observe various types of waste disposal activity by a company and record this information in the ordinary course of their duties as EPA investigators. This report is admissible, even without the presence of the investigator who made the observations.

FRE 803(8) was originally proposed in a manner that would have allowed all police records, including the subjective observations of police officers in the field, to be admissible in criminal proceedings. Such a broad hearsay exception was (not unexpectedly) met with a great deal of congressional debate. The result is that in criminal cases, recorded information concerning matters observed by police officers and other law enforcement personnel is not admissible pursuant to FRE 803(8)(B). If evidence of police observations is required under the current rules, the officers must be brought into court to testify. Keep in mind that the officers will be allowed to refresh their recollections with their previously written reports, and that their recorded recollections under 803(5) may be read into the record if they cannot remember. However, the officers must at least testify and be subject to cross-examination.

Religious and family records. Statements of birth, death, marriage, divorce, or other facts regarding personal or family history are admissible if they are contained in regularly kept records of a religious organization. FRE 803(11). Certificates of marriage, birth, baptism, and other religious ceremonies are admissible if they purport to have been issued at the time of the ceremony. FRE 803(12).

FRE 803(11) and (12), P. 282

Statements of fact contained in family bibles or other family documents regularly maintained, such as genealogies, engravings on rings,

FRE 803(13), P. 282

FRE 803 (17), P. 283

Ancient Documents
Documents more than 20
years old.

FRE 803(16), P. 283

FRE 403, P. 264

FRE 608, P. 273

FRE 404(a)(1), P. 265

or even inscriptions on portraits, are admissible as exceptions to the hearsay exclusion. FRE 803(13).

Market reports and commercial publications. Excepted from the hearsay exclusionary rule are certain records or reports that are published for general use. FRE 803(17). For example, quotations from stock or other financial markets found in reliable compilations, if of the sort generally relied on by the public or normal users of such data, are excepted from the hearsay exclusion. So are such things as telephone directories, mortality tables, and the consumer price index. In other words, to prove a stock price, a party can bring in the *Wall Street Journal.* To prove a telephone number, a party can bring in a phone directory. This type of hearsay is generally considered highly reliable. Although any report is subject to inadvertent mistakes, the likelihood that statements in these types of publications are intentionally misleading is small.

Statements in ancient documents. Statements made in documents over 20 years old are admissible, if the authenticity of the document can be firmly established. FRE 803(16). This exception is one of the most interesting found in the Rules of Evidence. Under this exception, 50-year-old diaries, 20 year-old letters, or even notes written on cocktail napkins in 1986 are all potentially admissible. The rationale behind this exception is that the document most probably existed long before the current litigation, and therefore falsification is unlikely. The biggest obstacle in gaining admissibility for documents under this exception is that the proponent of the document must prove its authenticity.

If such a document, although authentic, is suspect for reasons unrelated to the current litigation, the judge is empowered to exclude the document for its lack of trustworthiness.

Suppose a young girl recorded certain "events" in a diary. Twenty-five years later, this diary was found. If the person who wrote the diary now claims that she was simply writing her fantasies 25 years before, the court can rule that the document lacks trustworthiness and is therefore inadmissible hearsay. The court can also consider whether the contents of the document are unfairly prejudicial. FRE 403.

10.9   Reputation

We have portrayed in previous sections circumstances in which "reputation" evidence may be required to prove such things as character for truthfulness, FRE 608, or the character of the accused, FRE 404(a)(1), or of the victim, FRE 404(a)(2) and 405.

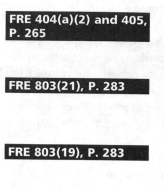

FRE 404(a)(2) and 405, P. 265

Reputation evidence is basically hearsay evidence in that it is based on what other people say about an individual. FRE 803(21) therefore specifically excepts character reputation evidence from the hearsay rule. In other words, where the rules studied in the previous chapters indicate that character may be proved by reputation evidence, FRE 803(21) makes it possible to bring the evidence in, by excepting character reputation evidence from hearsay exclusion.

FRE 803(21), P. 283

FRE 803(19), P. 283

There are several other "reputation" exceptions under FRE 803. There is an exception for reputation concerning personal or family history. FRE 803(19). Under this exception, reputation regarding marriage, divorce, death, relationship by blood, ancestry, or other similar personal or family facts is all admissible. For example, testimony that an individual is reputed to be adopted would be admissible.

FRE 803(20), P. 283

Reputation about land boundaries or community customs is also excepted from the hearsay rule, pursuant to FRE 803(20).

10.10 Learned Treatises

FRE 703, P. 277

In a previous chapter covering the subject of expert witnesses, we noted that pursuant to FRE 703, an expert may base his or her opinion on any facts reasonably relied on by experts in that field.

FRE 803(18), P. 283

FRE 803(18) allows the admissibility of statements contained in published materials that are either relied on by an expert or brought up in the cross-examination of an expert, so long as the materials are established as reliable authority. The publication itself cannot be made an exhibit, but statements made within the publication may be read into the record. This allows an expert to use a published expert to bolster his testimony. It also allows opposition to use a publication to impeach the opponent's expert.

10.11 Judgments

FRE 609, P. 274

Judgment
Written record of the final court decision in a legal proceeding.

In previous chapters, the issue of the admissibility of prior convictions for impeachment purposes was discussed (FRE 609). The **judgment** of the prior conviction, however, is hearsay because it is a statement made outside the current proceeding.

FRE 803(22), P. 283

Therefore, FRE 803(22) provides that judgments of previous convictions are excepted from the hearsay rule if evidence of the prior conviction is allowed under another rule. This means that to prove the prior conviction, the judgment of that conviction is admissible. The rationale for this exception is that judgments are considered to be totally reliable. (Also, it would be plain silly to force the judge who entered the judgment to come and testify.)

FRE 803(23), P. 283

Rule 803(23) provides that civil judgments as they may relate to personal, family, or general history are also admissible.

During the portion of this textbook relating to authentication of documents, the requirements for actually getting documents admitted into evidence will be discussed. As you can see, the Rules of Evidence build on each other. The substantive rules indicate how certain things may be proven. Hearsay exceptions allow the evidence to come in. The rules on authentication provide the standards for the authenticity of the documents offered. One piece of evidence may be governed by several rules.

10.12   "Catch-All" Hearsay Exceptions

As mentioned earlier, if none of the 23 specific exceptions enumerated in Rule 803 or the 4 additional exceptions found in 804 applies to hearsay testimony that is critical to a case, this does not mean that the hearsay is inadmissible. There is a "just in case" provision found in

FRE 807, P. 286

FRE 807(24) saying that hearsay rule does not exclude

A statement not specifically covered by Rule 803 or 804 but having equivalent circumstantial guarantees of trustworthiness, if the court determines that (A) the statement is offered as evidence of a material fact; (B) the statement is more probative on the point for which it is offered than any other evidence which the proponent can procure through reasonable efforts; and (C) the general purposes of these rules and the interests of justice will best be served by admission of the statement into evidence.

FRE 804, P. 284

FRE 807, P. 286

The adverse party must be given notice in advance if the proponent intends to make use of this provision. Rule 804, which provides for those hearsay exceptions applying only when the declarant is unavailable to testify is also covered under FRE 807.

10.13   Availability of the Declarant

FRE 804, P. 284

As previously indicated, certain hearsay rules apply only if the declarant who made the out-of-court statement is unavailable to testify. Under the Federal Rules, the hearsay exceptions restricted to those situations when the declarant is unavailable are found under Rule 804. If a declarant is available within the meaning of the rule, then the hearsay exceptions under FRE 804 do not apply. FRE 804 is reserved for those cases when, absent the use of the hearsay, the evidence would not be available at all to present to the trier-of-fact. Hearsay testimony admissible only when the declarant is unavailable will be discussed in the next sections of this chapter.

The definition of unavailability includes more than mere physical unavailability. A declarant is unavailable if:

1. The declarant refuses or is not allowed to testify due to a legal privilege;
2. The declarant refuses to testify about his or her own prior statement despite the court's order to do so;
3. The declarant testifies that she or he can't remember the subject matter of the out-of-court declaration;
4. The declarant is unable to be present because of death or other physical or mental infirmity;
5. The declarant is beyond the court's jurisdictional powers.

If the proponent is the *reason* the witness is unavailable, the exceptions under FRE 804 would not apply. For example, if a declarant is comatose because the proponent of the hearsay statements took action to keep the declarant from testifying, the declarant is not "unavailable" under FRE 804. (The drafters of the rules obviously felt the need to provide a disincentive to create "unavailability.")

These definitions of unavailability are supported in the rules and case law in the states as well as in the federal system. Merely stating that a declarant is unavailable under one of these definitions, however, is insufficient. The proponent of the evidence must make an affirmative showing that the witness is unavailable, and indicate the steps taken to make the witness available, where possible.

For example, if the unavailability of the witness is based on that witness's refusal to testify, the court must be given the opportunity to warn the witness that continued refusal will result in a citation for contempt. If the witness's refusal is based on legal privilege, the witness must assert the privilege—it cannot be assumed. (The issue of legal privilege is discussed at length in Chapter 13.) The following case illustrates the extent to which the proponent and the court must go to show unavailability based on a refusal to testify.

United States v. Fernandez-Roque

703 F.2d 808 (5th Cir. 1983)

[The defendant was convicted of obstructing justice, as both a principal and conspirator. His co-conspirators were acquitted in a separate trial.]

*   *   *

Roque sought to [introduce] testimony regarding the conspiracy
... by introducing testimony of a co-conspirator, Resende, from a
trial in this same case in which Resende, Goodrich, and Bonvillain
were acquitted. Resende was the only defendant who had testified in
that trial. Urging that Resende, as well as Goodrich and Bonvillain,
would take the Fifth Amendment if called to testify in Roque's
subsequent trial, Roque attempted to examine a government agent
to ask if he had been present at the prior trial where Resende had
taken the stand and denied similar allegations. ... The trial court
ruled that this was an improper attempt to introduce the trial testimony of a witness who was not called to testify in the present case and
that the agent's testimony regarding Resende's statements did not
constitute an exception to the hearsay rule contained in Fed. R.
Evid. 804(b)(1).

Roque's defense counsel did not satisfy the requirements of Rule
804(b)(1), which provides that if the declarant is "unavailable" as a
witness, there is an exception to the hearsay rule for "[t]estimony
given as a witness at another hearing of the same or a different proceeding" of the party against whom the testimony is now offered—in
this case, the government. For purposes of the rule, "unavailability"
encompasses, inter alia, a situation, which the defendant urges is
implicated here, where the witness is "exempted by ruling of the
court on the ground of privilege" or "persists in refusing to testify
... despite an order of the court to do so." Fed. R. Evid. 804(a).
Roque, the proponent of the hearsay evidence, has the burden of
proving the unavailability of the witness from the prior trial.

Roque did not make a record of his efforts to produce Resende as a
witness. He did not subpoena him or ask the judge for a ruling as to the
unavailability on account of privilege or for an order to testify. There
was thus no opportunity for the trial court to evaluate Resende's alleged
refusal to testify and propensity to invoke the Fifth Amendment, or to
ascertain whether some type of immunity was available to Resende from
the effects of his possible incrimination by his testimony.

*   *   *

In the above case, it not unreasonable to assume that Mr. Resende
would have refused to testify in Roque's trial. This assumption,
however, is insufficient to support a finding of unavailability. The
court must be given an opportunity to use its power to try to compel
the testimony of the witness, in all instances where the witness's
unavailability is based on an unwillingness to testify. (Obviously, if
the witness is dead, the court's "clout" would have no utility, and the
mere showing of unavailability on that basis would be sufficient.)

10.14 Hearsay Exceptions When the Declarant Is Unavailable

FRE 804(b)(1), P. 284

If the declarant is unavailable for one of the reasons discussed in the preceding section of this chapter, there are five hearsay exceptions that allow statements to be admitted.

1. *Former testimony.* FRE 804(b)(1). Testimony given under oath at another hearing, or at a deposition, is not excluded by the hearsay rule as long as the opposing party had an opportunity to examine or cross-examine the witness. The reason for this exception is that such testimony has a strong basis for reliability. The witness has been interrogated under oath, subject to cross-examination, and would be likely to testify in the same manner in the current proceeding.

Dying Declaration
Statement made by a declarant who is either dying, or thinks he is dying.

FRE 804(b)(2), P. 284

2. *Dying declaration.* Pursuant to FRE 804(b)(2), if a declarant makes a statement as he is dying about the cause or circumstances of his impending death, that statement is admissible in both a criminal prosecution for homicide, and in a civil proceeding.

If a declarant believes he is dying but is not, any statement made while the declarant believed his death was impending is admissible in a *civil* proceeding. Although the declarant must be unavailable to testify for the civil portion of the exception to apply, he doesn't have to be dead, nor does his unavailability need to be related to the incident that caused him to believe he was dying. The rationale behind this exception is that a person who believes he is dying would not be likely to fabricate or lie.

Dying declarations are available only in a criminal setting in a prosecution for homicide. The declarant must therefore be dead (or there would be no homicide), and the declaration must be related to the charged homicide, for this exception to apply. The rationale for this exception in the criminal context is a practical one. If a victim is murdered, his dying declaration might be the most critical available evidence linking the perpetrator to the crime.

In some states whose rules do not follow the Federal Rules of Evidence, the dying declaration may be inadmissible in civil proceedings.

FRE 804(b)(3), P. 284

3. *Statements against interest.* FRE 804(b)(3). Excluded from the hearsay rule are those statements that at the time made were contrary to the declarant's financial interests, or significantly exposed the declarant to civil or criminal liability. The rationale for this exclusion is that a reasonable person in the position of the declarant wouldn't have made such a statement unless the declarant believed it to be true. For example, the statement "I owe John a lot of money" would ordinarily not be made by an individual who didn't owe John money.

There are some limitations on this type of hearsay exception in the criminal system. Under the Federal Rules, a statement tending to expose the declarant to criminal liability, when offered to exculpate the accused, is not admissible if it isn't corroborated. The reason for this limitation is a practical one. There is concern that a criminal defendant might get a friend to confess to the crime for which the defendant is charged, figuring that the likelihood of the friend actually being prosecuted for the crime would be small. Or, in a case where an individual is already facing the death sentence, or life imprisonment, the individual might confess to a crime for which his friend is charged, because the individual would have nothing to lose even if he were convicted. Because the "reasonable doubt" standard is such a high one, a confession by an out-of-court declarant, even if suspect, might be sufficient to cause an acquittal or a **hung jury.** Consequently, the rules require that any such confession offered to prove the innocence of the defendant must be corroborated.

Hung Jury
When the jurors are unable to reach a verdict.

FRE 804(b)(4), P. 285

4. ***Statements of personal or family history.*** FRE 804(b)(4). Statements made by a declarant about himself or about other members of his family, concerning personal or family history, are excluded from the hearsay rule. Statements made about births, deaths, marriages, adoptions, and other matters of a family or personal nature are included in this exception. These types of statements are considered reliable since a person would generally have information about his own family, and would ordinarily not fabricate such matters. For example, a person who says "I've been divorced twice" would ordinarily not be fabricating this information.

FRE 807, P. 286

5. ***Other exceptions.*** As we discussed in section 10.11, FRE 807 has a "catch all" provision to cover other hearsay which may be admissible if sufficiently reliable.

10.15   In Summary

- The hearsay rules are voluminous and complex. Once you have ascertained that evidence is hearsay, you must research the possible exceptions to the hearsay rule to see if one or more apply.
- Even knowing that the hearsay is admissible under the exclusion doesn't end the query. Any limitations on the exclusion must be researched.
- The probative value of the evidence must be weighed against its prejudicial effect, FRE 403, and the trustworthiness and reliability of the hearsay must be assessed. The court has discretion to exclude evidence that might be admissible under the hearsay exceptions, but which is either unduly inflammatory, or inherently lacks trustworthiness.

- For those hearsay exceptions applying only when a declarant is unavailable, the unavailability of the witness must be proved, and not merely asserted.
- A hearsay statement for which there is an exception may be inadmissible at a criminal trial as infringing on the criminal defendant's Sixth Amendment confrontation rights if the declarant is not available to be cross-examined, the statement is considered to be "testimonial," and the defendant did not have a prior opportunity to cross-examine the declarant.

End of Chapter Review Questions

1. What is a hearsay exception?
2. What is the "primary purpose" analysis?
3. What is the difference between a present sense impression and an excited utterance?
4. What hearsay exception applies to statements made by a declarant that describe the declarant's feeling or state of mind at the time the statements were made?
5. Is a statement made to a doctor about declarant's medical history admissible? When might it not be admissible?
6. What is the difference between a recorded recollection admissible under the hearsay rules and a document used to refresh a witness's recollection?
7. Under which hearsay exception are a patient's medical records admissible? What is the traditional method and the recent method of admitting such records?
8. Name the different types of records that are admissible under the hearsay exceptions of FRE 803.
9. What is an ancient document?
10. How might a witness who is physically available be considered unavailable for purposes of FRE 804?

Applications

Rachel was assaulted by Jim, a wealthy entrepreneur. She suffered skin abrasions, bruises, and a black eye. Rachel has filed suit against Jim for both general and punitive damages. To be awarded punitive damages, Rachel must show that Jim's conduct was intentional and malicious. Jim has claimed that he went into a rage upon seeing Rachel with another man, and that he lost control and assaulted her without ever forming an intent to hurt her. Rachel wants to introduce the following evidence to support her claim that Jim acted premeditatedly, intentionally, and maliciously. The District Attorney's office also has filed criminal assault charges against Jim.

(a) Jim's diary, in which he recorded Rachel's whereabouts several times each week for the previous three months.

(b) A note written by Jim to his secretary telling her to send flowers to Rachel with the message, "I'll be watching you."

(c) A note written by Jim's secretary to the company operator saying, "Jim says to make sure that any calls from Rachel are put directly through to him."

(d) Testimony from Rachel's friend that Rachel repeatedly told her that she was frightened of Jim.

(e) Rachel's statements during a phone call to her mother during which Rachel was sobbing and asking whether she should go to the hospital for her injuries from the assault.

(f) Medical records containing Rachel's statements to the admitting nurse at the emergency room several hours after the assault.

Analyze each of the items of evidence listed above for their admissibility in the civil case and in the criminal case.

11

Authentication, Identification, and Exhibits

11.1 Introduction

Authenticity
Genuineness.

Identification
Evidence that the offer of proof is what it purports to be.

FRE 901. P. 286

Prior to evidence being admitted, the **authenticity** and/or **identity** of the evidence must be established. FRE 901. In other words, a proper foundation must be laid before evidence is introduced, showing that the evidence is what it is said to be. This does not mean that a final ruling on the authenticity of the evidence is made prior to its admission. A preliminary showing that the evidence is authentic is all that is required to get the evidence in front of the trier-of-fact,

209

who will then make a final determination of its authenticity. Consider the following hypothetical.

> Paris, the proponent, wishes to introduce a letter he claims was written by Ophelia, the opposing party. Paris must first introduce evidence that the letter was in fact written by Ophelia before he can move for the letter's admission into evidence.
>
> Paris testifies that he knows what Ophelia's handwriting looks like, having observed her write several letters during the time they were in business together. He then identifies the handwriting in the proffered letter as that of Ophelia. This is sufficient foundational evidence to support a finding that the letter was indeed written by Ophelia, and the letter is admissible.
>
> Ophelia argues in opposition that someone else wrote the letter and provides handwriting experts to testify that the proffered letter is a forgery. Such conflicting testimony doesn't cause the evidence to be excluded. It is for the trier-of-fact to decide which side to believe and how much weight to give to each witness's testimony. The letter is admissible since Paris introduced sufficient facts to support a finding of authenticity, even though the trier-of-fact may ultimately find the letter to be a forgery.

The next several sections of this chapter will address various methods of authenticating or identifying evidence.

11.2 Testimony of a Witness with Personal Knowledge

FRE 901(b)(1), P. 286

FRE 602, P. 272

The first method by which evidence may be identified or authenticated is through the testimony of a witness who has personal knowledge of the matter. FRE 901(b)(1). Recall that a witness may not testify to a matter unless evidence is introduced sufficient to support a finding that the witness has personal knowledge of the matter. FRE 602. This standard applies to testimony given by a witness to authenticate evidence. The witness must be able to show how he or she knows that the evidence is what he or she says it is.

Consider the illustration above where Paris identified Ophelia's letter by testifying as to his personal knowledge of Ophelia's handwriting. His testimony is sufficient to authenticate the letter because he has personal knowledge based on his prior observations of Ophelia's writing.

There are numerous other ways by which a witness may testify as to his personal knowledge of the authenticity of evidence. FRE 901(b) provides illustrations but is not an exhaustive list.

A witness may identify a murder weapon by testifying that he saw the weapon when it was used to commit the crime and noticed distinguishing characteristics about it. If the witness is a police officer, the witness may testify that she marked the weapon at the crime scene and now recognizes her mark.

When interviewing a witness about the authenticity of evidence, the paralegal must always remember to ask, "How do you know that?"

11.3   Chain of Custody

Chain of Custody
A chronology of the custody of the evidence to show it was not tampered with between the time of seizure and the time of analysis or presentation in court.

Sometimes, when evidence is visually indistinguishable from other evidence of the same type, it is impossible for a witness to look at the evidence in court and identify it. For example, blood and urine samples are visually the same. A witness would not be able to look at a vial of blood and say, "That's John Jones's blood." These types of evidence must be traceable from the time they are taken into custody to the time they are brought to the courtroom in order to show that the evidence is what it claims to be and has not been altered. In such circumstances, proper authentication requires that the proffering party show the **chain of custody** of the evidence.

The chain of custody is the route the evidence took, from person to person and place to place, from the time the evidence was taken into custody, to the time of its appearance in the courtroom. However, not every person in the chain need be brought in to testify. The court must be persuaded only that it is likely that the evidence has been adequately safeguarded and that there is a reasonable probability that the evidence has not been tampered with or changed in any important respect from its original condition. It would be an overwhelming burden on the system to require that each and every custodian testify specifically about his or her custodial interlude with the evidence. Consider the following hypothetical.

Heidi is pulled over for a traffic stop and the police observe a bundle being thrown out the car window as they approach Heidi's vehicle. One officer retrieves the bundle and finds it to be a large bag filled with smaller plastic bags, each of which contains a leafy substance that appears to be marijuana. The officer who retrieved the large bag is the first custodian in the chain of custody.

The officer brings the bag to the police station, tags the evidence, and sends it to the laboratory via messenger for analysis.

The messenger who brings the evidence to the laboratory now has custody.

The laboratory clerk takes custody next as he checks the evidence in and places it on a shelf marked "to be tested."

The technician in charge of testing leafy substances takes custody of the evidence next, and she performs tests on the substance in each small plastic bag.

After she determines that the substance in each bag is marijuana, she then forwards the evidence and laboratory results to the evidence locker via a messenger who takes custody.

The evidence is cataloged and checked into the evidence locker by a police officer who takes custody. The evidence locker is guarded by different officers three shifts each day, each of whom has custody over the evidence while it remains in the locker.

The evidence is retrieved by the arresting officer who takes custody of it just prior to trial and transports it to the courtroom.

As you can see, there have been many custodians of Heidi's bundle and its contents. In this type of situation, only the arresting officer who first took custody of the evidence and the laboratory technician who tested the evidence would usually need to testify. Documentary evidence such as laboratory records and evidence locker records (admissible under public records and business records exceptions to the hearsay rule, FRE 803), and evidence of the routine practice of the police department and its handling of evidence (admissible under organizational habit evidence, FRE 406) are admissible to show changes in custody and would ordinarily be used to fill in the gaps.

| FRE 803, P. 280 |
| FRE 406, P. 266 |

As a paralegal, you may be required to assemble the evidence that would support a finding that certain evidence was safeguarded throughout its time in custody. Pulling together the right documents and witnesses to paint the entire picture requires an understanding of the hearsay exceptions and other Rules of Evidence, as well as an understanding of the concept of chain of custody.

11.4 Authenticating Documents and Self-Authentication

Self-Authenitication
A document that "speaks for itself" in tems of its authenticity. Neither a witness nor other extrinsic evidence is needed to lay the foundation for its admission.

We have mentioned that the use of documentary evidence can sometimes replace testimony in chain of custody situations. In fact, the use of documentary evidence is important in a substantial number of varying situations. The next question, then, is how do we authenticate documents?

We already know that by handwriting identification, a witness can authenticate a handwritten or signed document so long as the witness can provide testimony as to how the witness knows what the writer's handwriting or signature looks like (either through personal knowledge, or scientific expertise). This is one way of authenticating a document.

There are a substantial number of other ways to authenticate documents, which vary with the type of document involved. You will be relieved to know that certain documents are self-authenticating and require no extrinsic evidence to establish authenticity. FRE 902. Such documents include:

FRE 902, P. 287

- Domestic public documents either signed under seal or certified under seal, FRE 902(1) and (2);
- Foreign public documents that, on their face, are attested in an official capacity (aren't you relieved to know you won't have to fly in that French notary to authenticate that French deed?), FRE 902(3);
- Certified copies of public records including birth or death certificates and certified court records, FRE 902(4);
- Official publications, FRE 902(5);
- Newspapers and periodicals, FRE 902(6);
- Trade inscriptions, FRE 902(7);
- Notarized documents, FRE 902(8);
- Commercial paper, FRE 902(9);
- Certified domestic business records accompanied by a written declaration of its custodian or other qualified person, FRE 902(11); and
- Certified foreign business records accompanied by a written declaration of its custodian or other qualified person, FRE 902(12).

Consider the following example.

In a hearing to determine child support levels, the custodial parent, Bertha, offered evidence to prove that the assets of the noncustodial parent, Gil, were greater than Gil admitted. Bertha introduced evidence of Gil's stock holdings and then moved to introduce the stock prices during the week of the hearing date to establish their value. Bertha proffered copies of the *Wall Street Journal* with its stock quotes. (Remember, even though market reports in commercial publications are hearsay, they are admissible as excepted from the hearsay rule pursuant to FRE 803(17).) The newspaper is admissible if it purports to be the *Wall Street Journal*, without the requirement that extrinsic testimony authenticate it as such. FRE 902(6).

FRE 803(17), P. 283

FRE 902(6), P. 288

11.5 Authenticating Business Records

FRE 803(6), P. 281

We know that business records are admissible under the business records exception to the hearsay rule. FRE 803(6). We also learned when we studied FRE 803(6) in Section 10.8 that the party offering the business record now has several methods by which to authenticate or lay the foundation for the record. To show that the business record is what it purports to be, the proponent may use the traditional method of calling a witness to testify accordingly or the proponent now may dispense with a witness by obtaining a certified business record under the new rules, FRE 902(11) and FRE 902(12).

The traditional way to authenticate a business record and of course the one with which courts and lawyers are most familiar is through the testimony of the custodian of the record. The paralegal will want to be familiar with FRE 803(6) in order to efficiently interview the witness. The custodian or other qualified person must be able to establish that the record was compiled by a person with knowledge of what was recorded or from information transmitted by a person with knowledge. The witness must establish that the record was kept in the ordinary course of the regularly conducted business activity. This foundational requirement protects against documents being prepared in anticipation of being used in the litigation (not that anyone would do such a thing).

As you can see, the custodian or other qualified person is not required to have personal knowledge of the contents of the business record but only that the business record is indeed a business record made by or transmitted by a person with knowledge. The following questions exemplify the type of interview questions to ask a witness who will authenticate a record.

- Do you recognize this record, and if so, how do you recognize it?
- What is the extent of your responsibilities as the custodian or keeper of the records of the business organization?
- How long have you had the care of the records?
- What did you do to locate this record?
- Is this record the type of record regularly prepared for the business? How do you know?
- When, how, and by whom was this record prepared? Would that person have knowledge of the contents of the record, and if so, how?
- Are you personally familiar with the contents of this record?
- Did anyone tell you anything about this record? How would that person have knowledge of the record?
- Is there anyone else who would be able to explain the contents of this record?

The new and more efficient authentication method for either a domestic business record or a foreign business record is by self-authentication. FRE 902(11) and FRE 902(12), effective December 1, 2000. The record must still qualify as a business record. The custodian or other qualified person must still be able to declare that the record comports with the criteria delineated by the business record exception. Instead of testifying, however, the custodian of the record certifies the declaration in writing and attaches it to the original business record or its copy. The proponent of the business record must provide timely written notice to the adverse party to allow inspection and opportunity to challenge the record. The record and the certification may be admitted without further foundation.

The paralegal may not need to interview the custodian in the same manner as described above, but should insure that the certification contains the requisite elements. A certification should track the language in FRE 902(11) and FRE 902(12) and might follow the format below.

I, the undersigned, _____ , knowing that I am subject to criminal penalty under the laws of the United States/foreign country for an intentionally false declaration, declare that I am employed by XYZ Company as a custodian of the records and by reason of my position am authorized and qualified to make this declaration.

I further declare that the documents attached are the original records or true copies of records that were:

1. made at or near the time of the occurrence of the matters set forth by, or from information transmitted by, a person with knowledge of those matters;
2. were kept in the course of the regularly conducted activity; and
3. were made by the regularly conducted activity as a regular practice.

The originals or copies of the records are kept in the country of the United States/foreign country.

Date of execution: _____
Place of execution: _____
Signature: _____

A business record introduced as evidence in this way has obvious benefits both in terms of saving time and expense.

Another frequently used and expeditious method to admit a business record is a stipulation prepared by the parties if there is no genuine dispute about the record's authenticity. If you have documents that are not self-authenticating and that do not require interpretive testimony, you should consider suggesting the use of a stipulation.

Once the business record is authenticated and admitted as evidence, the custodian of the record or more likely another witness will be needed to explain or to interpret the contents of the record.

Consider the following case in which the defendant challenged the use of the new rule, FRE 902(11).

United States v. Kinging

315 F.3d 803 (7th Cir. 2003)

Edward Kinging appeals his conviction under 18 U.S.C. §228(a)(3), better known as the Deadbeat Parents Punishment Act ("DPPA"), for willful failure to pay court-ordered child support. . . . Kinging claims that the district court's admission of certain business records into evidence without foundation testimony by the record custodian, as permitted by Rules 803(6) and 902(11) of the Federal Rules of Evidence, violated his Sixth Amendment right to confront witnesses. For the reasons stated below, we reject Kinging's constitutional arguments and affirm his conviction.

*   *   *

Edward Kinging ("Kinging") and Pamela Edwards (now Kerce) married in 1977 in Lake County, Illinois, and together had three sons, Christopher, Craig, and Cory Kinging. After Kinging and Pamela divorced in 1989, Pamela gained full custody of their sons and Kinging was ordered by the court to pay child support until the boys reached adulthood.

*   *   *

Kinging fell behind in his child support payments as early as 1991 and sporadically made payments through 1998. At the time of his arrest in July 2001, Kinging owed $78,574.37 in past due child support obligations.

*   *   *

Before trial, the government filed a motion *in limine* regarding its intent to offer various business records as evidence pursuant to Fed. R. Evid. 803(6). As amended in 2000, Rule 803(6) permits introduction of business records without foundation testimony from the record custodian so long as the records are authenticated according to Fed. R. Evid. 902(11). At trial, the government offered these business records accompanied by written certifications in compliance with Rule 902(11). The district court ruled some of the proffered documents inadmissible under amended Rule 803(6) because they lacked the inherent reliability required under the hearsay exception, but admitted five W-2 wage statements over Kinging's objection.

*   *   *

Kinging asks this court to find the 2000 amendment to Fed. R. Evid. 803(6) unconstitutional because it violates his rights as a criminal defendant under the Confrontation Clause. . . . Kinging contends that Rule 803(6) violates his right to confront witnesses against him because the amended rule does not require the government to prove either the reliability of business records through foundation testimony or the unavailability of the foundation witness. Kinging also claims that the amendment does not derive from a firmly rooted hearsay exception. In response the government argues that the amended rule is constitutional on its face for two reasons. First, the amendment to Rule 803(6) derives from a firmly rooted hearsay exception for business records. And second, the amendment makes the rule for admissibility of domestic business records the same as for foreign business records, which has repeatedly withstood Confrontation Clause challenges. Kinging's facial challenge to the constitutionality of amended Fed. R. Evid. 803(6) is an issue of first impression in this and other courts of appeal.

*   *   *

Despite the novelty of the question, we are not entirely without guidance on this issue. Amended Rule 803(6), and related authentication Rules 902(11)-(12), attempt to place domestic business records on par with foreign business records, whose rule for admissibility is codified at 18 U.S.C. §3505. Both Rule 803(6) and §3505 permit admission of pre-certified business records into evidence without confrontation of the record keeper by the opposing party, in this case a criminal defendant. Rule 803(6) was amended to avoid the expense and inconvenience of producing time-consuming foundation witness testimony in situations where the authenticity of the business records could be confirmed by written declaration pursuant to Rules 902(11)-(12).

*   *   *

Before it was amended, Rule 803(6) was considered a firmly rooted hearsay exception for certain business records that had adequate indicia of reliability. In fact, the foreign business records exception, §3505, derived specifically from an earlier version of Rule 803(6) and has itself withstood Confrontation Clause attacks in several circuits. (Citations omitted) Given this history, we see no reason to conclude that Rule 803(6) is any less firmly rooted as a hearsay exception now that it permits admission of pre-certified domestic business records without foundation testimony. Thus, we hold that amended Rule 803(6) does not on its face violate a criminal defendant's rights under the Confrontation Clause.

Even though the defendant did not appreciate the efficient and less expensive way in which the government was permitted to introduce his W-2 wage statements, the case demonstrates one way in which the new rule FRE 902(11) has been implemented. The case also provides background for the concept of pre-certified business records. As the appellate court discussed, the practice has withstood challenges with respect to admitting pre-certified foreign business records in criminal cases pursuant to the cited federal statute. Also keep in mind that because business records must be just that—records about the business—and not records generated for purposes of litigation, the W-2 wage statements would survive the *Crawford* analysis because the "primary purpose" of the W-2 statements was to document the wages rather than to establish facts potentially relevant to a later criminal prosecution.

11.6   Ancient Documents

As is now evident, the presence of a hearsay exception is not sufficient by itself to admit a document. The proponent of the document must provide some evidence supporting the document's authenticity, even though the document falls under a hearsay exception. It is safe to assume that if there is a hearsay exception that would allow the document to be admitted, there is some procedure or a list of criteria for the document's authentication.

One hearsay exception that poses interesting problems in terms of authentication is the exception relating to ancient documents (over 20 years old), when such documents are not self-authenticating.

FRE 803(16), P. 283

FRE 803(16). We know that an ancient document is admissible. However, in order to authenticate this type of document, evidence must be presented that the document (a) is in such condition as to create no suspicion concerning its authenticity, (b) was in a place where, if authentic, it would have been likely to be, and (c) has been

FRE 901(b)(8), P. 287

in existence 20 years or more at the time it is offered. FRE 901(b)(8). This can sometimes be difficult to show, but the standards applied by the courts for admissibility are not insurmountable.

The following case illustrates the method by which an ancient document was properly authenticated.

United States v. Liudas Kairys

782 F.2d 1374 (7th Cir. 1986)

[The government instituted proceedings to denaturalize (take away the citizenship of) defendant Kairys on the basis that his citizenship had been obtained illegally. Evidence showed that although Kairys denied it on his application for entry into the United States, Kairys had been a Nazi camp guard, which made him ineligible for entry and citizenship. A document purporting to be the defendant's Nazi SS personnel card was held admissible to prove his identity as an SS guard. Kairys argued that the evidence used against him was not properly authenticated.]

Kairys's argument focuses on the accuracy and admissibility of a Personalbogen, which is a German Waffen Schutzstaffel (SS) identity card. The government relied in part on the Personalbogen to establish its version of the defendant's identity. The district court admitted the Personalbogen under the Federal Rule of Evidence 901(b)(8). The defendant argues that the admission of the document was error, claiming that it is a forgery fraught with inaccuracies, erasures, inconsistencies, and unexplained problems. The government counters that the defendant failed to produce any substantive evidence that the document was anything other than what it was purported to be— the defendant's Nazi SS personnel card.

A. ADMISSIBILITY

Federal Rule of Evidence 901(b)(8) governs the admissibility of ancient documents. The Rule states that a document is admissible if it "(A) is in such condition as to create no suspicion concerning its authenticity, (B) was in a place where it, if authentic, would likely be, and (C) has been in existence 20 years or more at the time it is offered." The question of whether evidence is suspicious and therefore inadmissible is a matter of the trial court's discretion.

Although the Rule requires that the document be free of suspicion, that suspicion goes not to the content of the document, but rather to whether the document is what it purports to be. As Rule 901(a) states: "The requirement of authentication . . . as a condition precedent to admissibility is satisfied by evidence sufficient to support a finding that the matter in question is what its proponent claims." In other words, the issue of admissibility is whether the document is a Personalbogen from the German SS records located in the Soviet Union archives and is over 20 years old. Whether the contents of the document correctly identify the defendant goes to its weight and is a matter for the trier-of-fact; it is not relevant to the threshold determination of its admissibility.

The defendant does argue that a question was raised about whether the document was actually an original Personalbogen. First, the defendant raises general allegations that the Soviet Union routinely disseminates forged documents as part of propaganda campaigns. Next the defendant contends that the thumbprint ink was "unusual" and that it could have been placed on the document by mechanical means. But government witnesses testified that the only likely way for the print to appear on the Personalbogen was from the defendant's pressing his thumb to the paper. Additionally, the defendant notes that the government failed to establish the proper chain of custody from Treblinka to the Soviet archives. However, it is not necessary to show a chain of custody for ancient documents. Rule 901(b)(8) merely requires that the document be found in a place where, if authentic, it would likely be. All that is left, then, is the vague allegation that the Soviet Union regularly releases forged documents. That is not sufficient to make the document suspicious for purposes of admissibility.

There was sufficient evidence in the record that the document was a German SS Personalbogen. It matched other authenticated Personalbogens in form, 600 F. Supp. at 1261; it was found in the Soviet Union archives, the depository for German SS documents, id.; and its paper fiber was consistent with that of documents more than 20 years old, id. at 1260. Its admission was not error.

As the above case illustrates, the fact that the authenticity of a document is vigorously disputed does not make it inadmissible. As long as the proponent of the document offers sufficient preliminary evidence that the document is authentic, the trier-of-fact is given the opportunity to come to its own conclusions about whether or not the document is what the proponent says it is. In the *Kairys* case, the trial court found that the evidence showed that the document matched others of its type, was found where others of its type were kept, and was on paper consistent with being more than 20 years old. That was a sufficient foundation of authenticity for admissibility.

11.7 Computer and Other Technologically Generated Records

Intangible
Incapable of being touched, i.e., documents stored on soft media such as a computer disk.

Today, we have records that are **intangible.** Records are compiled, created, and kept in "soft" media as opposed to hard copy. Computer disks and videotapes hold data instead of books and journals. These high-tech records are often important evidence, but they carry with them a burden of requiring special types of authentication. The more highly technical the record, the more diligent the court will be to assure that the trier-of-fact is not being misled. The authentication required by the court for such evidence is called "process or system" evidence. FRE 901(b)(9). Process evidence may be required for evidence ranging from computerized business records, to computerized electrocardiograms. The process evidence must provide proof that a particular process or system is reliable and accurate.

FRE 901(b)(9), P. 287

Consider the following hypothetical.

A warranted tape recording is made of a conversation between two individuals. The recording device is hidden, and neither individual knows he is being recorded. Because of the limitations of the hidden recording device, the tape is barely audible and extremely noisy. An engineer takes the tape, feeds it into a computer, "digitizes" the sounds (converts the sounds to numerical values), and then reconstructs the conversation by eliminating the noise, and enhancing the volume of those sounds that are part of the conversation. The evidence in its new form is a compact disk recording on which the taped conversation is now clearly audible. The content of the recording can be authenticated, that is, a witness who was listening at the time of the tape recording can testify that the recording is an accurate replication of the conversation it depicts; however, this alone is not sufficient. The proponent must also present evidence about the process used in making the compact disk, to show that the process itself produced an accurate result.

Today, the courtroom can be a high-tech forum. Computer records can be projected directly from a computer to a large screen for the jury to view. In some jurisdictions, the jurors each have individual monitors from which they can better observe the exhibits. The proffering party presents the computer data directly to the trier-of-fact who sees the information on the screen, rather than in a secondary form such as a printout. The rules of evidence safeguard the integrity of this type of evidence by requiring not only that the information in the computer be properly authenticated, but that the computer operator who has orchestrated the presentation of the data to the jury is a knowledgeable person, who has handled the data in a manner that insures that no changes or deletions have been made.

Many of us have videocameras at home, complete with tape recordings of family picnics and birthday parties. Although they are familiar pieces of equipment, videocameras are highly technical devices. Before admitting a videotape, the court may well require that the video photographer who operated the equipment provide evidence as to his or her qualifications, the authenticity and accuracy of the video recording, and the absence of changes or deletions since the time the recording was made.

Even an ordinary photograph is not self-authenticating, but all that is usually required is the testimony of witness that the photograph is an accurate reflection of the real scene. Sometimes, however, photographs taken by highly technical cameras will require process authentication. The following is a case in which the use of photographs required special authentication. The security cameras that took the photographs were self-activating, and no individual could testify as to whether the photographs were accurate replications of the crime scene.

United States v. Taylor and Hicks

530 F.2d 639 (5th Cir. 1976)

Appellants James Crawford Hicks and Freddie Lee Taylor were convicted by a jury . . . for armed robbery of a federally insured state bank. Briefly stated, the facts surrounding the robbery and their arrests are as follows: at approximately 9 a.m. on February 10, 1975, the Havana State Bank in Havana, Florida, was robbed of about $6,700 at gun point by two men wearing masks. The robbers took the money, ordered everyone present into the bank vault, and locked them inside. A bank camera, tripped after the bank personnel were locked in the vault, took pictures of the robbers.

*   *   *

Hicks . . . argues that the district court erred in admitting into evidence contact prints made from the film taken by the bank camera after the tellers and a bank official, Henry Slappey, were locked in the bank vault. Appellant contends that the government failed to lay the proper foundation for admission of these photographs since none of the eyewitnesses to the robbery testified that the pictures accurately represented the bank interior and the events that transpired.

In the case before us it was, of course, impossible for any of the tellers to testify that the film accurately depicted the events as witnessed by them, since the camera was activated only after the bank personnel were locked in the vault. The only testimony offered as foundation for the introduction of the photographs was by government witnesses who were not present during the actual robbery. These witnesses, however, testified as to the manner in which the film was installed in the camera, how the camera was activated, the fact that the film was removed immediately after the robbery, the chain of its possession, and the fact that it was property developed and contact prints made from it. Under the circumstances of this case, we find that such testimony furnished sufficient authentication for the admission of the contact prints into evidence. Admission of this type of photographic evidence is a matter largely within the discretion of the court and it is clear that the district court did not abuse its discretion here.

*   *   *

In the above case, the use of evidence that described the process by which the photographs were taken served to authenticate that the photographs were taken of the perpetrators. No individual could have testified with personal knowledge that the cameras activated during the incident. The process evidence, however, showed that this is what occurred.

For any evidence that is processed through modern technology, it is wise to give special attention to the potential need for process or system evidence.

11.8   State Statutes and Acts of Congress

FRE 902(10), P. 289

There are various statutory schemes in both the federal and state systems that allow for certain documents to be self-authenticating even though they are not specifically enumerated in the Rules of Evidence. Under the Federal Rules of Evidence, Congress has the right to provide that documents generated within a statutory scheme are self-authenticating. FRE 902(10). For example, the signature on a federal tax return is considered to be genuine without signature identification, pursuant to the Internal Revenue Code.

Likewise, states may have statutes allowing certain types of documents to be self-authenticating. When researching the admission of documentary evidence, it is important to look at the relevant procedural and substantive statutes to see if there are authentication provisions outside the Rules of Evidence.

11.9   Best Evidence Rule—Original, Duplicate, and Unavailable Documents

FRE 1002, P. 290

The "best evidence rule" requires that the proponent of the evidence use the best evidence available. The tricky part of this rule is determining what the best evidence is, and what happens when the best evidence isn't available.

The best evidence rule is distinct from the hearsay and authentication rules. It is another rule to consider when gathering evidence.

The best evidence of a written document is the original written document itself. FRE 1002. A document is "original" even if it is a duplicate, as long as it was treated as an original at the time of execution.

Jim and Dean wrote a contract and made a photocopy. They each signed both the original and the photocopy. Each document counts as an "original."

Many times an original document is not available. In states that do not follow the Federal Rules of Evidence, a special showing may be required to prove the unavailability of an original before a nonoriginal

FRE 1003, P. 290

FRE 1005, P. 291

FRE 1007, P. 291

duplicate is admitted. Under the Federal Rules, any duplicate is admissible without a showing that the original is unavailable, unless there are problems with authenticity. FRE 1003. Therefore, under the Federal Rules, any photocopy of a document is ordinarily not precluded by the best evidence rule. When the photocopy is a certified copy of a public record, it is treated as an original. FRE 1005.

When the contents of a record, writing, or recording are described in an opposing party's deposition, written admission, or other testimony, the original writing need not be produced. FRE 1007. Introducing the party-opponent's description is considered "best evidence" for these situations. The original writing may or may not be unavailable for this rule to apply.

Rachel was deposed by Attorney Isaac, during which deposition Rachel admitted, "I wrote Joseph a letter, telling him to get lost." The actual letter to Joseph is not required to prove its contents, since Rachel already admitted the contents of the letter in her deposition.

Except as provided in the preceding paragraph, the best evidence of a writing is the language in the writing itself. The expression used in the law is "the document speaks for itself." The parties are not allowed to testify as to the content of a letter, contract, or other written document, if the document itself is available. (However, the parties may be allowed to explain what is said in the document.) The following hypothetical is illustrative.

Marie believed that her life was in danger and, in her affidavit, asked that a restraining order be issued against Donnie. In her affidavit, Marie said that she had gotten a threatening letter in the mail from Donnie. She went on to describe the contents of the letter. Testimony of the letter's contents is inadmissible under the best evidence rule. The letter must be submitted if it is available, so that it may "speak for itself."

If a document is unavailable (i.e., destroyed, unobtainable through the judicial process, or lost), then the proponent of the evidence has an "excuse" not to produce the best evidence. After laying a foundation to establish the excuse, the proponent can introduce evidence that isn't the "best." The proponent can, in such circumstances, have a witness testify as to the contents of the unavailable document. A proponent cannot, however, create an "excuse." If the writing is unavailable because of the conduct of the proponent (i.e., if the proponent tore up the document, or didn't take proper legal steps to subpoena it to court), the best evidence rule will bar introduction of "second best" testimony of its contents.

11.10   Summaries of Documents

FRE 1006, P. 291

When the contents of a set of documents are so voluminous that they cannot be examined conveniently in court, their contents may be presented in a chart, summary, or other abbreviated representation. FRE 1006. This allows the admission into evidence of a documentary equivalent of demonstrative or illustrative evidence, which, instead of depicting real evidence, depicts other documentary evidence.

The Federal Rule merely requires that the volume of documents be "inconvenient" to review in court, not impossible. Therefore, even a relatively small number of documents (e.g., 20), can be summarized in a chart if the documents are extremely cumbersome to review, and charts can present the data more clearly. Summaries admitted under FRE 1006 are evidence. In this respect they are distinguishable from other types of demonstrative devices that are used to instruct the trier-of-fact. A chart can always be used to summarize or emphasize points to a jury. Under such circumstances, the chart is not admitted into evidence—it is just used to clarify evidence that is being otherwise introduced. Conversely, FRE 1006 allows summary information to be introduced as evidence. The underlying (voluminous) documents are never admitted or seen by the trier-of-fact (although they have to have been made available to the other side for review). Some states do not allow summary evidence to be admitted.

Summaries offered as evidence pursuant to FRE 1006 should not be confused with business record summaries that are not made in preparation for litigation, but are made in the ordinary course of business. Business record summaries prepared in the ordinary course of business are not subject to the restrictions of Rule 1006.

FRE 1006, P. 291

FRE 1006 can be a powerful tool to present evidence to the jury in a manner that clearly presents your case. Evidence created under this provision is scrupulously examined by the court when challenges are raised claiming inaccuracy or misleading presentation.

11.11   In Summary

- Before evidence can be admitted, a preliminary showing must be made as to its authenticity. The evidence may be: (1) relevant, (2) nonhearsay or hearsay subject to an exception, and (3) admissible in terms of its probative value versus its prejudicial effect; but it must be authenticated before it can be admitted.
- Authenticating a document requires testimony, certification, or a stipulation. Generally, a witness must testify to lay sufficient foundation for the document's admissibility. A document which is a public record or a business record, however, may be authenticated by obtaining a certification that states the document is authentic;

the public record or business record is then self-authenticating and a witness is not required to establish foundation. The parties may also prepare and submit a stipulation that the document is authentic. Once the document is admitted, the trier-of-fact decides what value, if any, to give the document.

■ Any evidence submitted must be the best evidence available. If the evidence is a document, the document must be admitted, and not merely talked about in testimony. Photocopies are generally acceptable in the federal system, in lieu of originals.

■ If a document is unavailable through no fault of the proponent, "second best" evidence is admissible in the form of testimony or other descriptive evidence.

End of Chapter Review Questions

1. What does "authenticating a document" mean?
2. What is a chain of custody? When is evidence of chain of custody relevant?
3. What is self-authentication?
4. What is an ancient document?
5. Other than by stipulation, what are the ways to establish foundation for a business record under the hearsay exception in FRE 803(6) and for a public record under the hearsay exception in FRE 803(8)? What must be shown for each method?
6. What must be done to authenticate an intangible or high-tech record?
7. What is the "best evidence rule"?
8. What is summary evidence, and when is it admissible?

Applications

Consider the following hypothetical situation.

Bambi married Melvin on July 20, 1993. On September 15 of that same year, Bambi filed for divorce and asked for $10,000 per month for spousal maintenance. To prove Mel's ability to pay, Bambi produced a list of bonds owned by Mel, which list provided both present and maturity values for each bond. This listing was prepared in the ordinary course of business by Prudential Securities, who prepares such lists monthly for its customers.

1. How might this list be authenticated?

Consider the following hypothetical situation.

Melvin testified that Bambi only married him for his money. (The court showed no signs of being shocked by this news.) Melvin further testified that Bambi was not really divorced from her previous husband and was consequently not entitled to spousal support from him. To prove Bambi's marital status, Mel introduced a certified copy of a court record purporting to dismiss a divorce action between Bambi and her previous spouse.

2. How might this court record be authenticated?
3. Mel and Bambi had entered into a premarital agreement. Mel can't find his copy, but he remembers what the agreement said. Is Mel permitted to testify as to the contents of the premarital agreement? How might such testimony be made admissible?

Constitutional Constraints on the Admissibility of Evidence

12.1 Introduction

This chapter will provide the student with a general understanding of the effect of the Fourth, Fifth, and Sixth Amendments on the admissibility of evidence and other related issues.

The Fourth Amendment of the Constitution has presented the legal system and legal scholars with an unending and ever changing area of study. It is likely that the paralegal student will study or has studied the Fourth Amendment in a criminal procedure or constitutional law course. An in-depth study of the Fourth Amendment would reveal the continuing scrutiny and debate regarding the meaning of the Fourth Amendment's language and its application to real-life factual situations. The Rules of Evidence are silent, however, regarding the admissibility of evidence obtained by a search. Consequently, our purpose here is to discuss ways in which the Constitution affects the admissibility or inadmissibility of items seized pursuant to a search warrant.

The Fifth Amendment prohibits the police from forcing a statement from a suspect that then is used to incriminate the accused in a criminal trial. The right conferred is called the "right against compelled self-incrimination." Police interrogation techniques eventually caused the Supreme Court to prescribe procedural safeguards for custodial interrogation that, if not followed, may render any statement, incriminating or otherwise, inadmissible at the criminal trial.

The Sixth Amendment of the Constitution conveys certain trial rights to the accused in criminal trials. We will consider the right to confront one's accusers.

12.2   An Overview of the Fourth Amendment

The Fourth Amendment protects the individual's privacy rights from governmental overreaching. The amendment states:

> The right of the people to be secure in their persons, houses, papers, and effects, against unreasonable searches and seizures shall not be violated, and no Warrants shall issue, but upon **probable cause,** supported by Oath or affirmation, and particularly describing the place to be searched, and the persons or things to be seized.

Probable Cause
Reasonable grounds for belief.

The student may better understand the rationale for the Fourth Amendment in light of its historical background. The amendment was largely in response to the colonists' experience with the search and seizure practices employed by English officials. Local colony officials in America, under the authority of a "writ of assistance" or a legal document from the King of England, were able to arbitrarily enter and search the colonists' homes for smuggled goods. In England, the King's general warrants enabled officials to forcibly enter and search homes for evidence of **seditious publications**. The Fourth Amendment was drafted in memory of the unreasonable, intrusive searches and seizures experienced by the colonists in the privacy of their homes.

Seditious Publications
Literature intended to cause political opposition to the government.

The Fourth Amendment protects the individual from unreasonable police intrusion. The amendment is intended to guarantee all individuals in America, whether here legally or illegally, the right to be free from unreasonable searches and seizures of their person and the places in which they have a reasonable privacy expectation. The limitation gives way when the government has probable cause to believe that criminal evidence will be discovered on the person or in the place to be searched.

It is important to remember that the Fourth Amendment does not apply to a private individual's conduct, unless the individual is acting as an agent of the government. Consider the following example.

A snoopy neighbor is looking around Billy's property without Billy's permission when she discovers marijuana plants hidden behind a trellis wall. She calls the police and informs them about the plants. The police get a warrant based on the neighbor's tip, seize the plants, and arrest Billy. Although the snoopy neighbor may have been guilty of various torts such as trespass or invasion of privacy, her conduct did not raise to the level of unconstitutionality because she is not the government, nor was she acting on behalf of the government when she snooped. Therefore, evidence of the marijuana plants in Billy's backyard will not be excludable on Fourth Amendment grounds.

In general, the Fourth Amendment requires that the police request a search warrant from an impartial judge by presenting an affidavit that sets forth the basis for the officer's belief that criminal evidence will be discovered in the place to be searched. This procedure is the constitutional safeguard against arbitrary privacy intrusions. Under the example above, the informant's (snoopy neighbor's) tip that marijuana was growing in Billy's backyard provided sufficient evidence for the issuance of a search warrant.

Courts have also approved numerous types of warrantless searches over the years. So, although the warrant procedure was originally believed to be a condition precedent to a search and seizure, police may now search without a warrant in certain situations considered reasonable in light of the circumstances.

12.3 The Fourth Amendment's Search and Seizure Requirement

The Fourth Amendment contains numerous concepts and constraints. In general, it can be separated into two parts for analysis. One part of the amendment proscribes unreasonable searches and seizures. This portion of the Fourth Amendment is commonly called the "reasonableness clause" or the "reasonableness requirement." The reasonableness clause sets forth who and what is protected and the nature of the protection. The "people" in the United States are protected. "[T]heir persons, houses, papers, and effects" are protected. The nature of the protection is "to be secure . . . against unreasonable searches and seizures."

The second part of the Fourth Amendment, referred to as the "warrant clause" sets forth the proper grounds and the proper form for the warrant. The proper grounds are "upon probable cause" and "supported by Oath or affirmation." The proper form for the warrant itself is to "particularly describ[e] the place to be searched, and the persons or things to be seized." This aspect of the warrant clause is referred to as the "particularity requirement."

As we stated in the introduction to this chapter, the meaning of the language in the Fourth Amendment has been the subject of intense debate. Scholars have wrestled with whether the "reasonableness" language refers to the search and seizure clause or to the warrant clause. Historically, the general rule has been that "a warrantless search is per se unreasonable." Under the general rule, even if the police conduct a search based on probable cause, the search is unreasonable and violative of the Fourth Amendment if the police have failed to obtain a warrant from a judge. In recent years, however, the Supreme Court has moved away from that approach. The focus now is whether the police action was reasonable in the specific circumstances. The courts must determine whether the societal interests outweigh the individual's privacy interests; if so, then the warrantless search may be considered reasonable. To be sure, Fourth Amendment issues will continue to be raised particularly in light of the Supreme Court's changing attitude toward governmental interference with a person's private life.

For our purposes, it is sufficient to remember that

1. The search and seizure, with or without a warrant, must be reasonable;
2. The search and seizure must be based on probable cause; and
3. If a warrant was obtained from a judge, the warrant must particularly describe what is to be searched and who and what is to be seized.

12.4 Exceptions to the Search Warrant Requirement

By now, we have encountered many exceptions in our discussions of the Rules of Evidence. Let's call the exceptions that allow the admissibility of evidence from warrantless search the "Ya, but" exceptions. Consider the following situation.

Officer Cool, in the heat of the moment, chased a crook into the crook's house. He didn't even knock, let alone stop to get a search warrant from a judge. Afterwards, the judge suppressed the evidence that Officer Cool had found in the crook's hand in the house and told Officer Cool that he should have gotten a warrant before entering the house. Officer Cool replied: "'Ya, but' the crook was going to flush the stuff that I saw him steal down the toilet if I didn't get it right then."

Under current law, Officer Cool's conduct would be considered reasonable in light of the circumstances. Over the years, police officers have used various "Ya, but" arguments in exceptional search and seizure situations where stopping to first obtain a warrant from a judge would produce undesirable societal results. Accordingly, the Supreme Court has allowed warrantless searches where it would be neither reasonable nor in the interests of justice to force the police to stop the investigation to obtain a warrant. So, although all searches must be reasonable to be constitutional, not all searches must be based on a search warrant. Some of the approved "Ya, but" exceptions follow below:

- Searches incident to a lawful arrest of the detainee and the detainee's immediate surroundings in order to secure safety of the officers and other people nearby;
- Searches of moving vehicles where police have probable cause to believe that the vehicle contains evidence of a crime;
- Searches of impounded vehicles for inventory purposes to insure police and public safety and to protect against lost property or claims of lost property;
- Searches of areas in plain view when police have a lawful right to be in the area, such as areas observed during a "protective sweep" pursuant to a lawful search; the protective sweep enables the police to secure the premises for safety reasons;
- Searches of abandoned property;
- Searches without probable cause when the police have reasonable suspicion that a crime is occurring such as when the police "stop-and-frisk" or "pat-down" for weapons to insure officer safety;
- Searches without probable cause at the international borders;
- Searches of the occupants at a place when a search warrant is executed;
- Searches under exigent circumstances such as threatened destruction of evidence, escape of a suspect, and hot pursuit of a fleeing suspect;
- Searches of person or place pursuant to consent;
- Searches in places in which there is no reasonable expectation of privacy, such as in a prison.

12.5   The Fifth Amendment and the Right against Compelled Self-Incrimination

Self-Incrimination
Information such as statements and documents provided by an individual that could implicate or inculpate that individual in criminal conducts.

Inculpate
To impute guilt.

Accused
Person who is the defendant in a criminal case.

Coerced Confession
A confession obtained through physical force or unconscionable conduct on the part of the police.

The Fifth Amendment provides that "[n]o person . . . shall be compelled in any criminal case to be a witness against himself." The right conferred by the Fifth Amendment is commonly called the "right against **self-incrimination**." The right actually prohibits compelled or forced confessions, so it may be better for us to refer to the Fifth Amendment protection as the "right against compelled self-incrimination." The Supreme Court declared this privilege a fundamental right and applied it to the states through the Fourteenth Amendment's due process clause.

The privilege against self-incrimination is different from the privileges that will be discussed in Chapter 13. Those privileges involve the inadmissibility of communications that have occurred during specific types of relationships such as the marital relationship or the attorney-client relationship. If a common law privilege applies, neither party to the relationship can be compelled to repeat any communication that has occurred within the privacy of that relationship. As we will discuss in Chapter 13, the public has an interest in encouraging a person to seek out and to trust in those relationships.

On the other hand, the privilege against compelled self-incrimination is a personal right. The Constitution's founders intended to insure that the government could not force **inculpatory** statements from a person and then use those statements against him at a criminal trial. Thus, the Fifth Amendment provides a personal guarantee that a person shall not be compelled to be a "witness against himself" in any criminal case.

For self-incriminating statements to be admissible, the government must show that the statements were made voluntarily and that the **accused** was advised of his rights not to self-incriminate. Just as with the Fourth Amendment, the proscription against **coerced confessions** applies to governmental conduct in obtaining the confession, not to the conduct of private individuals. An entire body of law has evolved interpreting this part of the Fifth Amendment and prohibiting the use of statements obtained in violation of the privilege.

The privilege encompasses testimonial or communicative evidence. A person's physical characteristics are not considered testimonial in nature and are not constitutionally protected. The government may legally require a suspect to provide samples or exemplars, such as handwriting, fingerprints, hair, and blood. The police may take scrapings from underneath a suspect's fingernails and swab the hands for evidence. The scientific examination of such exemplars could result in either inculpatory or exculpatory evidence that would be admissible.

There are endless ways in which nontestimonial evidence could become relevant and such exemplars necessary. Consider the following.

A ransom note is found at the scene of a kidnapping. The prime suspect who is in custody is asked for a handwriting sample, which she gives under protest. The handwriting exemplar is admissible, and compelling the accused to provide it did not violate her Fifth Amendment rights. This is because the evidence is not testimonial in nature and not covered under the Fifth Amendment.

12.6   The Miranda Warnings

We are all very familiar with the following words:

You have the right to remain silent. Anything you say can and will be used against you in a court of law. You have the right to the presence of an attorney during questioning. If you cannot afford an attorney, one will be appointed for you.

Indeed, anyone who watches television or goes to the movies has heard these words many times. Commonly called the Miranda warnings, their purpose has caused confusion and debate. More than one accused has probably complained that his constitutional rights had been violated because the police had failed to read the Miranda warning at the time of arrest. At least one of these individuals was told by a judge, "Son, you have been watching too much TV!"

Historically, police efforts in securing confessions evolved from physical to psychological coercion. The courts became frustrated with the imprecise judicial analysis for voluntariness that provided little, if any, guidance for the police. To insure a meaningful application of the Fifth Amendment right against compelled self-incrimination, the Supreme Court in *Miranda v. Arizona*, 384 U.S. 436 (1966), implemented a prophylactic rule to guard against coerced confessions. This safeguard was once viewed as a constitutional necessity in all circumstances. Today, however, failure to properly "Mirandize" a suspect is not considered a constitutional violation but rather a procedural impediment. Although the procedural impediment of having failed to properly advise a suspect of his or her Miranda rights may cause a confession to be excluded from evidence, it does not render the statements inadmissible for all purposes. Statements taken from the suspect in violation of his or her Miranda rights may be used in specific situations, such as for impeachment, which will be discussed in Section 12.8.

The reason that many people become confused about Miranda violations is because they fail to understand at what point in an investigation the police are required to advise the suspect. The famous case mentioned above, *Miranda v. Arizona*, compels the police to inform anyone in custody of their constitutional rights prior to any interrogation. The key words are "custody" and "interrogation." It is not a procedural defect if a person is questioned while not in custody, nor is there a defect if a person is in custody but not questioned. Be mindful, then, that the Miranda warnings are required prior to **custodial interrogation**.

Custodial Interrogation
Questioning initiated by law enforcement after a suspect has been taken into custody or otherwise deprived of his freedom of action in any significant way.

The general rule is that a confession or a statement will not be admissible against a suspect who has given a confession or a statement during custodial interrogation absent the Miranda warnings. Similarly, if a suspect does not understand the rights or does not waive the rights, the subsequent confession or statement during the custodial interrogation will not be admissible. Because the police continually confront different circumstances, the courts are also continually making determinations whether the Miranda rule has been properly applied. As always, the paralegal should explore the most recent legal decisions in this area because the Supreme Court's philosophical approach toward criminal procedure changes with the personalities of the Court.

The following situations are circumstances in which a suspect need not be advised of her constitutional rights prior to interrogation.

- **Public safety exception:** Miranda warnings are not required in a situation that places the officer or the public in danger.
- **Undercover interrogation exception:** Miranda warnings are not required when the suspect does not know that the other person is a police officer or other governmental agent, such as when a suspect is talking to an undercover agent.
- **Routine booking question exception:** Miranda warnings are not required for routine questions for booking such as biographical information about the suspect.

12.7   The Sixth Amendment's Confrontation Clause

The Sixth Amendment of the Constitution provides, in part, that "In all criminal prosecutions, the accused shall enjoy the right . . . to be confronted with the witnesses against him. . . ." This language in the Sixth Amendment is referred to as the "confrontation clause." Generally, the confrontation clause affords the accused the right to be physically present at the trial, to hear and otherwise observe the witnesses' testimony against him, and to question or confront the witnesses about their testimony.

This brief discussion of the confrontation clause has hopefully conjured up another "Ya, but" rule that has compelled the student to say "Ya, but" what about the hearsay exceptions that permit statements made out of court to be admitted at the trial against the accused. Recall that in Chapter 10 we talked about the potential conflict between the Sixth Amendment guarantee, the recent *Crawford* analysis, and the hearsay rules. Keep in mind that the Sixth Amendment preceded the codification of the evidentiary rules; hence, the language of the Sixth Amendment is silent regarding hearsay issues. However, the hearsay rules were drafted to conform to court interpretation of the confrontation clause.

Consider the following example.

In a prosecution for fraud against Mrs. Lint, Prosecutor Starry calls Mr. Lint to testify about a set of books that he has kept in which several of Mrs. Lint's transactions were recorded. The set of books is in the custody of Mr. Lint's secretary. Mr. Lint has refused to testify, asserting the marital privilege (see section 13.5). Prosecutor Starry offers the set of books as evidence under the business records hearsay exception, through the testimony of the custodian-secretary. Mrs. Lint's defense counsel argues a violation of the Sixth Amendment confrontation clause since Mr. Lint's refusal to testify renders Mrs. Lint unable to "confront" him about the entries in the book. Mrs. Lint loses this argument.

In the above example, the out-of-court statement (the set of books and the entries in it) is a business record. The hearsay rules create an exception for the admissibility of business records because they are considered inherently reliable. It is true that if admitted against Mrs. Lint, the evidence would appear to violate the confrontation clause since Mrs. Lint cannot directly confront Mr. Lint about the entries in the books. However, use of the business records exception has been upheld as constitutional, even in criminal proceedings. Generally, if hearsay meets sufficient standards of reliability, its admission will not be found to violate the Sixth Amendment. The types of hearsay excepted in the Federal Rules of Evidence are generally held to be sufficiently reliable to meet constitutional standards. In her own defense, Mrs. Lint may, of course, impeach the accuracy of the entries in the books.

12.8   The Exclusionary Rule— The Cure for Constitutional Violations

A problem facing the courts in the first half of this century (and earlier) was that police officers had an incentive to break the law and violate the constitutional rights of citizens to garner the evidence necessary to obtain convictions. The problem with the zealous good intentions of the police was that innocent people could be subjected to groundless searches without recourse, and the police had no incentive to discontinue their conduct. The right against unlawful search and seizure so carefully crafted in the Constitution was perceived by some to be merely advisory because it had no "teeth."

The "cure" for the problem established in the courts is commonly called "the exclusionary rule." The exclusionary rule applies to violations of Fourth, Fifth, and Sixth Amendment rights and holds that evidence taken in violation of those rights is generally inadmissible. The exclusionary rule is not a personal right guaranteed to the aggrieved person, but rather a judicial cure crafted primarily to deter government officials from exceeding their constitutional authority. The consequence of impermissive overreaching by law enforcement is the exclusion of evidence obtained in violation of constitutional constraints. The incentive of law enforcement to violate constitutional rights to garner evidence is thereby removed, in somewhat dramatic fashion.

The Fourth Amendment exclusionary rule was first established in the federal courts and then applied to the states in the well-known case of *Mapp v. Ohio*, 367 U.S. 643 (1961). The facts underlying the Mapp decision and some of the Court's comments are presented below to provide some additional insight into the rationale for the exclusionary rule.

Mapp v. Ohio

367 U.S. 643 (1961)

*　　*　　*

[Facts]

On May 23, 1957, three Cleveland police officers arrived at appellant's residence in that city pursuant to information that "a person (was) hiding out in the home, who was wanted for questioning in connection with a recent bombing, and that there was a large amount of policy paraphernalia being hidden in the home." Miss Mapp and her daughter by a former marriage lived on the top floor of the two-family dwelling. Upon their arrival at that house, the officers knocked on the door and demanded entrance, but appellant, after telephoning her attorney, refused to admit them without a search warrant. They advised their headquarters of the situation and undertook a surveillance of the house.

The officers again sought entrance some three hours later when four or more additional officers arrived on the scene. When Miss Mapp did not come to the door immediately, at least one of the several doors to the house was forcibly opened and the policemen gained admittance. Meanwhile Miss Mapp's attorney arrived, but the officers, having secured their own entry, and continuing in their defiance of the law, would permit him neither to see Miss Mapp nor to enter the house. It appears that Miss Mapp was halfway down the stairs from the upper floor to the front door when the officers, in this highhanded manner, broke into the hall. She demanded to see the search warrant. A paper, claimed to be a warrant, was held up by one of the officers. She grabbed the "warrant" and placed it in her bosom. A struggle ensued in which the officers recovered the piece of paper and as a result of which they handcuffed appellant because she had been "belligerent" in resisting their official rescue of the "warrant" from her person. Running roughshod over appellant, a policeman "grabbed" her, "twisted (her) hand," and she "yelled (and) pleaded with him" because "it was hurting." Appellant, in handcuffs, was then forcibly taken upstairs to her bedroom where the officers looked into a photo album and through personal papers belonging to the appellant. The search spread to the rest of the second floor including the child's bedroom, the living room, the kitchen, and a dinette. The basement of the building and a trunk found therein were also searched. The obscene materials for possession of which she was ultimately convicted were discovered in the course of that widespread search.

At the trial no search warrant was produced by the prosecution, nor was the failure to produce one explained or accounted for. At best, "There is, in the record, considerable doubt as to whether there was any warrant for the search of defendant's home."

*   *   *

Since the Fourth Amendment's right of privacy has been declared enforceable against the States through the Due Process Clause of the Fourteenth, it is enforceable against them by the same sanction of exclusion as is used against the Federal Government.

*   *   *

"However much in a particular case insistence upon such rules may appear as a technicality that inures to the benefit of a guilty person, the history of the criminal law proves that tolerance of shortcut methods in law enforcement impairs its enduring effectiveness. . . ."

There are those who say, as did Justice (then Judge) Cardozo, that under our constitutional exclusionary doctrine "(t)he criminal is to go free because the constable has blundered." In some cases this will undoubtedly be the result. But as was said in Elkins, "there is another consideration—the imperative of judicial integrity." The criminal goes free, if he must, but it is the law that sets him free. Nothing can destroy a government more quickly than its failure to observe its own laws, or worse, its disregard of the charter of its own existence. As Mr. Justice Brandeis . . . said . . . , "Our government is the potent, the omnipresent teacher. For good or for ill, it teaches the whole people by its example. If the government becomes a lawbreaker, it breeds contempt for law; it invites every man to become a law unto himself; it invites anarchy."

[The court went on to reason that "the purpose of the exclusionary rule is to deter—to compel respect for the constitutional guaranty in the only effectively available way—by removing the incentive to disregard it," citing *Elkins v. United States*, 364 U.S. at 217.]

The Court found the facts of the *Mapp* case so offensive that it took dramatic steps to insure that no individual would be subjected to such treatment by the police. Cases like the *Mapp* case cause the court to review whether or not the rights guaranteed to us as citizens under the Constitution are real or theoretical, and to fashion remedies to insure that the constitutional rights are real.

A more recent case has taken a kinder approach towards law enforcement misconduct. The misconduct was minimal, however, and was not the reason the evidence was seized. In *Hudson v. Michigan*, 126 S. Ct. 2159 (2006), the United States Supreme Court refused to suppress the seized evidence for which the police had a search warrant but where the police entered by an unconstitutional knock-and-announce violation. The police arrived at the home to execute the warrant, knocked on the door but waited only a few seconds before entering the unlocked door. The Court's reasoning encompassed the concepts that suppression should be the last remedy, that the evidence would have been lawfully seized due to the warrant, and that suppression would have minimal police deterrence balanced against the societal interests. The case may be a foreshadowing, or perhaps it is simply a reminder that the cure for a constitutional violation is not always exclusion of the evidence.

Although much of the case law regarding the exclusionary rule relates to search and seizure situations, as we stated above, the rule also applies to the Fifth and Sixth Amendments. The student should be careful to distinguish a confession obtained in violation of the Fifth Amendment, which is usually a coerced or involuntary confession, and statements obtained in violation of *Miranda*. An accused's coerced confession is inadmissible for any purpose at a criminal proceeding. The coerced confession may not be used even to impeach the accused because the coerced confession is not considered reliable. If a person is physically beaten into confession, it is at least as likely that the confession is given to stop the beating, as that it is the truth.

Miranda violations create less of a problem regarding the reliability of the statements made by the accused. Ordinarily, any statements resulting from *Miranda* violations are not admissible against the accused unless he testifies inconsistently with the custodial statement. If the accused does testify in a manner inconsistent with statements made during a custodial interrogation, even though the defendant hadn't been properly "Mirandized" prior to making the statements, they may be used for impeachment purposes. The distinction emanates from current thinking that *Miranda* violations are not constitutional violations but rather violations of a prophylactic procedural rule. Consequently, by testifying, the accused potentially opens the door for the prosecutor to use a confession or statement otherwise excludable under the *Miranda* rules. The following case illustrates.

Harris v. New York

401 U.S. 222 (1971)

We granted the writ in this case to consider petitioner's claim that a statement made by him to police under circumstances rendering it inadmissible to establish the prosecution's case in chief under *Miranda v. Arizona* may not be used to impeach his credibility.

The State of New York charged petitioner in a two-count indictment with twice selling heroin to an undercover police officer. At a subsequent jury trial the officer was the State's chief witness, and he testified as to details of the two sales. A second officer verified collateral details of the sales, and a third offered testimony about the chemical analysis of the heroin.

Petitioner took the stand in his own defense. He admitted knowing the undercover police officer but denied a sale on January 4, 1966. He admitted making a sale of contents of a glassine bag to the officer on January 6 but claimed it was baking powder and part of a scheme to defraud the purchaser.

On cross-examination petitioner was asked *seriatim* whether he had made specified statements to the police immediately following his arrest on January 7—statements that partially contradicted petitioner's direct testimony at trial. In response to the cross-examination, petitioner testified that he could not remember virtually any of the questions or answers recited by the prosecutor. At the request of petitioner's counsel the written statement from which the prosecutor had read questions and answers in his impeaching process was placed in the record for possible use on appeal; the statement was not shown to the jury.

The trial judge instructed the jury that the statements attributed to petitioner by the prosecution could be considered only in passing on petitioner's credibility and not as evidence of guilt. In closing summations both counsels argued the substance of the impeaching statements. The jury then found petitioner guilty on the second count of the indictment. The New York Court of Appeals affirmed.

At trial the prosecution made no effort in its case in chief to use the statements allegedly made by petitioner, conceding they were inadmissible under *Miranda v. Arizona*. The transcript of the interrogation used in the impeachment, but not given to the jury, shows that no warning of a right to appointed counsel was given before questions were put to petitioner when he was taken into custody. Petitioner makes no claim that the statements made to the police were coerced or involuntary.

Some comments in the *Miranda* opinion can indeed be read as indicating a bar to use of an uncounseled statement for any purpose, but discussion of that issue was not at all necessary to the Court's holding and cannot be regarded as controlling. *Miranda* barred the prosecution from making its case with statements of an accused made while in custody prior to having or effectively waiving counsel. It does not follow from *Miranda* that evidence inadmissible against an accused in the prosecution's case in chief is barred for all purposes, provided of course that the trustworthiness of the evidence satisfies legal standards.

Every criminal defendant is privileged to testify in his own defense, or to refuse to do so. But that privilege cannot be construed to include the right to commit perjury. Having voluntarily taken the stand, petitioner was under an obligation to speak truthfully and accurately, and the prosecution here did no more than utilize the traditional truth-testing devices of the adversary process. Had inconsistent statements been made by the accused to some third person, it could hardly be contended that the conflict could not be laid before the jury by way of cross-examination and impeachment.

The shield provided by *Miranda* cannot be perverted into a license to use perjury by way of a defense, free from the risk of confrontation with prior inconsistent utterances. We hold, therefore, that petitioner's credibility was appropriately impeached by use of his earlier conflicting statements.

[AFFIRMED in a 5-4 decision. Dissents were filed by Justices Black, Brennan, Douglas, and Marshall.]

The court in *Harris* gave a limiting instruction that told the jurors to use the suspect's statements for determining only his credibility and not as evidence of his guilt. In such situations, technically, the statements are admissible only for impeachment purposes; however, it is reasonable to believe that a jury hearing a confession for impeachment purposes will consider that confession for its truthfulness as well. The courts are therefore very careful to assess whether the confession is inadmissible because of a technical noncompliance with *Miranda* or whether the confession was coerced. As we stated above, when the confession appears to be coerced or unlawfully forced, it will not be admissible even for impeachment purposes.

The exclusionary rule and its exceptions are complex and controversial. We have provided only a brief overview here. The student would be wise to review the law in further depth when approaching evidence seized pursuant to a search, seizure, or arrest.

We have studied several constitutional and constitutionally based rights in this chapter that are subject to the exclusionary rule: the right against unreasonable search and seizures, the right against compelled self-incrimination, and the rights pursuant to the *Miranda* warning. Other constitutionally protected areas of which the student should be aware and that are subject to the exclusionary rule include uncounseled or suggestive lineups and electronic eavesdropping, commonly referred to as "wiretaps."

12.9   Fruit of the Poisonous Tree

The exclusionary rule encompasses all evidence that is the "fruit" of an illegal search or arrest. This is called the "fruit of the poisonous tree" doctrine. It extends not only to evidence first found through the illegal governmental activity but also to the evidence obtained by exploiting the original illegality. The rationale is that if the tree is poisonous, the fruit will be poisonous also. Consider this example.

The police search Lonika's house without either a warrant or probable cause. They seize a diary in which she identifies a friend to whom she confessed about lying to the police. The police then interview the "friend," who tells all. Here, the diary is the direct result of the poisonous tree or the illegal search. The friend's statements resulted from the exploitation of the original police misconduct. The statements are the fruit of the poisonous tree. Both the diary and the friend's statements would be inadmissible at a criminal proceeding against Lonika.

Tainted
Made legally "impure" and inadmissible as a consequence of a preceding unlawful act.

In the above example, the police were not acting illegally by interviewing the friend. Nevertheless, the friend's statements are considered "**tainted**" by the original illegal search and seizure. Thus, the fruit of the poisonous tree doctrine provides that the government will be unable to use any evidence directly or indirectly obtained from a violation of the Constitution.

As the student might expect, the "Ya, but" rule also applies to various aspects of the fruit of the poisonous tree doctrine. In fact, the courts have found several ways to remove the "taint" and allow exceptions to the exclusionary rule over the years.

- **Good faith exception:** evidence obtained by police reasonably relying in good faith on a defective or otherwise illegal warrant or arrest.
- **Inevitable discovery doctrine:** evidence that would have been discovered despite the police misconduct. For example, after

the defendant's illegally obtained confession, the police discover the victim's body, which a search party would have found anyway.

- **Attenuation doctrine:** unlawfully obtained evidence that is so far removed, or "attenuated," from the constitutional violation that the "taint" has dissipated, such as where defendant, who was unlawfully arrested then released, returned voluntarily days later to confess.

- **Independent source doctrine:** evidence obtained from a source independent of the illegal conduct. For example, police illegally enter a house and see evidence, but then discover the same evidence pursuant to lawful search warrant based on information unrelated to the initial entry.

12.10   In Summary

- The Fourth Amendment protects citizens from unreasonable intrusions into their homes by police or other government agents.

- The general rule is that for searches and seizures to be "reasonable" pursuant to the Fourth Amendment, a warrant describing what is to be searched and seized must be issued prior to the search. The many exceptions to this general rule developed over time in response to situations where it was either necessary or at least justifiable in public policy terms to conducting the search prior to obtaining a warrant. (The rule: You should have gotten a warrant. The defense: "Ya, but there were exigent circumstances, or Ya, but my life was in danger, or Ya, but . . .")

- The privilege against compelled self-incrimination protects suspects from being coerced into confessions and provides procedurally for suspects to be advised of their *Miranda* rights.

- Most hearsay exceptions do not violate the Sixth Amendment's right of confrontation as long as the hearsay is sufficiently reliable to meet constitutional standards; a hearsay statement may be inadmissible if its primary purpose was "testimonial" as we discussed in Chapter 10.

- Evidence that is taken in violation of the constitutional rights of a suspect will be deemed inadmissible under the exclusionary rule.

- Evidence that is found after an illegal search or an unlawfully garnered confession as a result of leads from the unconstitutional conduct will generally be inadmissible as "fruit of the poisonous tree."

- There are many "Ya, but" exceptions to the "fruit of the poisonous tree" doctrine. (The rule: The evidence should be excluded because an illegal search led the police to the evidence. The defense: "Ya, but we would have inevitably found the evidence anyway, or Ya, but we found it through an independent source, or Ya, but . . .")

End of Chapter Review Questions

1. What is the standard that must be met for the court to issue a search warrant?
2. If a private citizen trespasses on property without any authority and finds evidence of unlawful activity, is the evidence admissible?
3. Name three situations in which a search made without a warrant will be held constitutional.
4. What is the difference between a coerced confession and a confession made without proper Miranda warnings?
5. What is the exclusionary rule?
6. What is the "fruit of the poisonous tree" doctrine?
7. What is the right of confrontation?
8. Explain in what way the *Crawford* case alters previously approved hearsay exceptions.

Applications

Consider the following hypothetical situation.

After three days of being held in isolation and being interrogated for long periods of time, Jonathan confessed to the murder of two teenage girls in a park near his home. Jonathan had been advised of his *Miranda* rights and had asked to speak with an attorney; however, the interrogation continued after his request for an attorney went unanswered.

1. Is Jonathan's confession admissible in the prosecution's case in chief?
2. Is the confession admissible for impeachment purposes?

Consider the following hypothetical situation.

Swifty rented a truck in San Diego to drive to Ohio. He put the leasing agreement with his signature on it in the glove box of the truck so that he would not lose it. After his long drive to Ohio, Swifty wanted some sleep, so he got a motel room. He parked the truck in the motel parking lot. When Swifty woke up, he observed that police dogs were sniffing out his cocaine cargo, so he snuck away unobserved.

In the course of their subsequent search of the impounded truck, the police found the leasing agreement that Swifty had placed in his glove box. The police used the name on the leasing agreement to track down Swifty. He denied any knowledge of the cocaine cargo in the truck, claiming he had returned the truck prior to the time the police found it at the motel and that he was never at the motel where the truck was found. Several days later, the police thought to inquire at the motel for any documentation that would indicate that Swifty had stayed at the motel. The manager still had records with Swifty's name and signature on the check-in card. The police again visited Swifty and in their fervor forgot to advise him of his Fifth Amendment rights. They asked him to give them a sample of his signature. He did so. They then asked him if the signature on the motel check-in card was his. He admitted it was.

3. Assuming there was no search warrant, was the search of Swifty's glove compartment legal?
4. Was the writing sample that Swifty gave to the police lawfully obtained, even though Swifty had not been "Mirandized"?
5. Was the admission by Swifty that it was his signature on the motel check-in card admissible, even though he had not been "Mirandized" when he made that admission?

Common Law Privileges

13.1   Introduction to Common Law Privileges

Privilege
The legal right and/or obligation to refuse to testify on certain matters.

The laws regarding legal common law **privileges** are constantly evolving. The U.S. Supreme Court has noted that the Federal Rules of Evidence

> acknowledge the authority of the federal courts to continue the evolutionary development of testimonial privileges in federal criminal trials "governed by the principles of the common law as they may be interpreted in the light of reason and experience. Fed. Rule Evid. 501." *Trammel v. United States*, 445 U.S. 40, 47 (1980).

FRE 501, P. 270

Unfortunately, the common law evolution referred to in the *Trammel* case cited causes the application of legal privilege doctrines to be inconsistent between federal jurisdictions. In addition, FRE 501 provides that in diversity cases, it is state law that governs privilege, and such law is not consistent between the states. Those privileges constitutionally based, such as the privilege against self-incrimination and the privilege against unreasonable search and seizure (discussed in the previous chapter), are the only ones that are applied with relative uniformity.

FRE 501, P. 270

Privileges are often the source of controversy because they can be used to cause important evidence to be suppressed. A privilege allows evidence that might help prove guilt to be kept out of court.

On the other hand, privacy is deeply respected in a democracy. Privileges withstand public censure because most people, at some time in their lives, want to feel that they can communicate openly and freely without fear of exposure, to someone with whom they have a confidential relationship. They also want the government to have to exercise restraint when invading their privacy and their property, and to refrain from so doing without good reason. As a result, our legal system allows privileges, but constantly weighs, evaluates, and remodels them to attempt to ensure that their benefit is not overshadowed by their burden.

To sum up then, there is a complex, inconsistent body of federal law, a fractious, diverse body of state law, and a notable amount of constitutional law from which privileges can be asserted.

This chapter will concentrate on presenting a general overview of existing and evolving common law privileges.

13.2 The Politics of the Attorney-Client Privilege

Perhaps the most controversial and complex privilege in the law is the attorney-client privilege. Although most states have statutes specifying the existence of the attorney-client privilege, all states define this privilege in varying ways through case law. This privilege has its origins in the British common law, and throughout its history it has been accompanied by public scorn. It is argued by some that the privilege only serves to allow guilty people to get good legal advice. The majority, however, see the privilege as providing positive social outcomes. Many people consult with attorneys to find out what the law is and how to do the "right" thing. This "counseling" aspect of providing legal advice would be seriously impaired if people believed that by asking for the advice, they might be getting themselves into trouble.

The attorney-client privilege has been under intense public scrutiny and often vitriolic debate in light of numerous political scandals. Most paralegal students are too young to remember the fireworks surrounding President Richard Nixon's attempt to exert an executive privilege to withhold secret Oval Office tape recordings. He lost the effort which inevitably led to his presidential resignation. President Clinton was the first president since Richard Nixon to exert a privilege. During the "Monica Lewinsky" scandal, President Clinton invoked both executive privilege and attorney-client privilege to block disclosure of information about his sexual relationship with the White House intern, Monica Lewinsky. A federal judge ultimately ruled that Clinton could not use his executive privilege to prevent the special prosecutor from questioning the White House senior aides about conversations concerning Monica Lewinsky. The federal judge concluded that the need to investigate obstruction of justice charges outweighed Clinton's confidentiality interests of the White House discussions. The federal judge also rejected Clinton's assertion of attorney-client privilege reasoning that he could not use government-funded White House attorneys to assist his defense in the criminal investigation.

Mrs. Clinton had her own attorney-client issues. She spoke with White House counsel regarding several Whitewater matters (with her private attorney present), and the Office of Independent Counsel subpoenaed the records of those conversations. Mrs. Clinton attempted to quash the subpoena claiming that the records were protected under the attorney-client privilege. The D.C. Circuit Court of Appeals decided that there was no privilege between government attorneys and private citizens. Communications are not "confidential" and therefore not privileged if they are made in the presence of a third party who is not covered under the privilege. Because the court determined that communications made in the presence of government counsel by private party Mrs. Clinton were not confidential as a matter of law, the appellate court compelled the production of the records. The United States Supreme Court denied certiorari, and the law stands.

Another interesting issue considered by the Supreme Court was whether certain notes taken by the attorney of former White House counsel Vince Foster were privileged. The notes were taken during a conference between Foster and his attorney shortly before Foster committed suicide. Had he lived, the attorney-client privilege could have been asserted by Foster with regard to the notes in controversy; however the Office of Independent Counsel argued that there should be no continuing privilege after death and wanted the documents produced. The Court granted certiorari and decided that the attorney-client privilege does not end at death. Foster's confidential communications to his lawyer just prior to his death remain confidential.

More recently, commentators speculated whether the attorney-client privilege would be asserted by any top government officials regarding the firing of eight United States Attorneys. There was much public wrath regarding Monica Goodling, former counsel to the Attorney General Albert Gonzales, being granted immunity to testify before congressional hearings about her involvement in the alleged effort by the White House to place politically and ideologically loyal appointees throughout the Justice Department.

As you have probably discerned, the politics of evidentiary privileges are argued for other than strictly legal reasons. Most of the arguments used against the Clintons (especially in the public forum by Republican opponents of the President) were arguments that were once vigorously opposed by the Republican party when the Democrats used them to compel then President Richard Nixon to make disclosures. It is fascinating to watch the politics but, more importantly, to watch the trends to see how the privilege is shaping up. Each time there is an exclusion or exception made at the Supreme Court level, even when the person who is asserting the privilege is the President of the United States, the decision may cause the law to be altered for everyone.

13.3 Communications That Fall Outside the Attorney-Client Privilege

Confidential Communications
Communications made in confidence with the expectation of nondisclosure.

There are many instances where the attorney may be forced to testify against a client because the privilege doesn't apply. Paralegals are considered representatives of the lawyer, and they are consequently subject to the attorney-client privilege. If **confidential communications** are made to a paralegal in his or her capacity as the attorney's representative, then those communications are privileged. Although it is critical for the paralegal to understand the importance of preserving the privilege when protected confidential communications are made to him or her, it is also important for the paralegal to know when communications are not covered under the privilege.

Communications made in the presence of others who are not a part of the legal team are not considered confidential, and the privilege consequently does not apply. Consider the following example.

A troubled client is waiting to be seen in the waiting room. The paralegal comes out to the waiting room, where several other clients are present. The troubled client begins to speak loudly to the paralegal about problems in his pending case. This communication is not confidential because persons other than those to whom the privilege applies are able to hear the client's comments. Under such circumstances, the paralegal should caution the client that what he says may be subject to disclosure. If asked about statements

made by the client under these circumstances, the paralegal would most likely have to disclose the communications.

In the early common law, eavesdroppers who overheard confidential communications could testify about them, even if the client did not know of their presence. In other words, if the client started talking, thinking he was alone with the lawyer or the lawyer's representative, an eavesdropper could force the privilege to be lost. Under modern law, eavesdroppers do not cause the privilege to be waived, and if the client is unaware that his communication is being observed, he can assert the privilege and preclude the disclosure of the information that was supposed to be confidential.

Ordinarily, only actual communications are covered under the privilege. If an attorney or paralegal observes conduct, this is not protected. For example, assume that an attorney observes a client committing a crime. The perpetrator cannot use the attorney-client privilege to prevent the attorney from testifying, nor can the attorney refuse to testify because of the privilege.

A client's identity is usually not protected in an adversarial proceeding. If an attorney or a paralegal is called by the opposing party and asked whether that office represents the other party, it is ordinarily perceived to be the right of that opposing party to be informed by whom their opponent is being represented. However, there are times when an attorney is called on to represent a client in secret, and under such circumstances, the identity of the client may be subject to the attorney-client privilege. This is rare, but consider the following hypothetical.

Bellows owed a substantial amount of income tax he obtained unlawfully. (Yes, you can be held liable for failure to pay taxes on monies that you weren't supposed to earn.) Not wanting to cheat on his taxes, Bellows had his attorney file an anonymous tax return in his behalf. If the Internal Revenue Service (IRS) audits Bellows, he will be able to show that he paid taxes on all of his ill-gotten gains. However, the IRS will not be able to gain Bellows' identity through the attorney who filed the return in his behalf, unless Bellows wants that attorney to tell (i.e., in the event of an audit).

This type of confidence has been held to be privileged by the courts, even though a client's identity is not ordinarily privileged.

Corporations have a well-established attorney-client privilege under modern law. It applies to communications between corporate employees and counsel made at the direction of corporate superiors in order to secure legal advice. The problem is that although the communications are privileged for the corporation, the individual who is giving the evidence does not control the privilege. That means that the corporation can, at any time, waive the privilege, and the confidential communication can be disclosed, even over the objection of the employee who gave the evidence. If an employee is personally at risk for civil or criminal liability, he or she has no protection under the attorney-client privilege that exists between the corporation and its counsel. That protection is only for the corporation to assert and may not be raised by the individual employee who gives the evidence. Often, the lines between personal liability and corporate liability are blurred. It is important, therefore, to identify who the client is (the corporation, the individual, or both) to assure that the client confidences are maintained.

As one might deduce after learning that a corporation may waive its attorney-client privilege and release confidential information, any individual holding the privilege may waive the confidentiality of a communication. If confidentiality is waived, an attorney may testify. In fact, usually the attorney does not have the right to refuse to testify once the client has waived confidentiality.

13.4   The Crime-Fraud Exception to the Attorney-Client Privilege

The most difficult exception to the attorney-client privilege is the crime-fraud exception. The rule simply provides that a client may not protect communications with his or her attorney made in furtherance of a crime or fraud. If the client asks for help in committing a crime, the attorney is not privileged to refuse to testify as to what the client asked. Similarly, the attorney is not able in any way to assist the client in concealing evidence. Consider the following hypothetical.

A young man, with help of counsel, pleads guilty to a reduced misdemeanor possession of narcotics charge as part of a plea bargain. After entering his guilty plea, the young man was sentenced to one year in jail, suspended, subject to two years of supervised probation, during which time he was ordered as a condition of probation to refrain from all illegal drug use and to take drug tests as demanded by his probation officer. Shortly after his probation period began, he called his attorney's office in something of a panic. He made the following statements to his attorney's legal assistant:

"My probation officer just called and told me I have to go in for a test tomorrow. Could you get me out of it, just for a few days? Make up something like I'm sick, or have an appointment. If I have to test tomorrow, I'm gonna come up dirty."

The legal assistant spent a great deal of time trying to reach her boss, who cut her off before she could finish her sentence. He told her to tell the client that the office could not help him. He recognized that the client may have inadvertently turned the legal assistant into a witness against him.

The above problem is troublesome because neither an attorney nor a paralegal ever wants to be in a position of having to testify against a client.

The following case speaks to the crime-fraud exception. Although the specific facts on which the case was based were not presented in the opinion, the court found that the government showed that there was reasonable cause to believe that the attorney's services were used by the defendants to further illegal activity. The attorney was compelled to testify against her client.

In re Grand Jury Proceedings

867 F.2d 539 (9th Cir. 1988)

Appellant John Doe is a target of a grand jury investigation. Mary Roe, an attorney, represented Doe in certain proceedings in the United States District Court for the Northern District of California. The grand jury subpoenaed Roe. Doe moved to quash the subpoena on the ground that the attorney-client privilege and work product doctrine prevented disclosure of the information the grand jury sought from attorney Roe. The government opposed the motion. It contended the crime-fraud exception applied. In support of this contention, it submitted material which the district court reviewed in camera. The district court rejected Doe's request to examine this material, and ordered Roe to testify except as to her "opinion fact product" or her "mental impressions." Doe appeals. We affirm.

THE CRIME-FRAUD EXCEPTION

The purpose of the attorney-client privilege is to encourage clients to communicate freely and completely with their attorney. But all reasons for the privilege are eviscerated when a client consults an attorney for legal assistance to carry out a contemplated or ongoing crime. To defeat the attorney-client privilege, a prima facie case of the existence of the crime-fraud exception must be established. In this circuit, we require that the prima facie showing be made from evidence independent of the communications between the client and the attorney. In the present case, the government made the required independent showing by the material which the district court

In Camera
Judicial review of records in
private or in chambers.

reviewed **in camera** (emphasis added). The district court noted in its
order that, based upon its review of this material, there was reasonable
cause to believe that, beginning in the spring of 1987 and continuing
through April of 1988, there was an ongoing conspiracy by [Doe] and
others to commit a crime, and that the witness-attorney's [Roe's]
legal services were utilized by [Doe] and others in furtherance of
the ongoing unlawful scheme. We have also examined this material,
and agree with the district court that the government has made a
prima facie case for the crime-fraud exception.

The District Court's Order

While the district court concluded that the materials it reviewed
established a prima facie case that Doe and others were engaged in
criminal activity, and that Doe had employed Roe in furtherance of
that activity, it determined that the government had failed to make a
prima facie showing that Roe knowingly participated in any criminal
activity. Based upon this distinction, the district court required Roe
to testify concerning "fact work product," but upheld her refusal to
testify to "opinion work product" or "mental impressions" formu-
lated in the course of her representation. The district court ordered
that (1) Roe "must obey the subpoena and appear before the grand
jury and answer all unprivileged questions and all questions otherwise
privileged that are no longer privileged by virtue of the crime/fraud
exception"; (2) that Roe must answer all "questions not calling for
disclosure of confidential communications, including those with or
witnessed by third parties not encompassed by the [attorney-client]
privilege"; (3) that Roe must answer "questions, whether or not
related to confidential communications, concerning [her] representation of [Doe] in the ... matter [then] pending" before the
United States District Court for the Northern District of California;
and (4) that Roe had the right not to disclose "opinion work product"
as distinguished from "fact work product" in connection with her
representation of Doe. We hold that the district court did not abuse
its discretion in entering this order.
AFFIRMED.

In the preceding case, the court seemed circumspect and rational
with regard to compelling the attorney to testify regarding matters
that would otherwise have been privileged. Although the attorney had
to testify about confidential communications, she was not forced to
reveal the legal opinions she provided to the defendants, nor did she
have to share her personal impressions since the government had not
presented evidence that she was a knowing participant in the crime
scheme.

There are, however, potentially troublesome aspects to the crime-fraud exception that need to be explored in the courts in the coming years. According to various political analysts, the law regarding the crime-fraud exception appears to be one that may encourage prosecutorial indiscretion. Recently, the Office of independent Counsel investigating President Clinton has charged several attorneys with crimes related to client conduct. Adversaries argue that it is possible for a prosecutor to charge attorneys with crimes in order to penetrate through the attorney-client privilege. Since the courts are fairly strict about the evidence needed to allow the attorney-client privilege to be breached, an indictment against the attorney could provide an easier way to pressure that attorney to testify against the client. An attorney is allowed to breach the privilege if necessary to do so in his or her own defense.

On the other hand, there are those who would correctly point out that grand jury indictments are not the "rubber stamps" they are inaccurately reputed to be, and it is no small burden to get an indictment. Furthermore, the legal privileges of an indicted individual would be greater than those of a reluctant witness should that individual refuse to capitulate to prosecutorial pressures. Both sides to the argument seem to have merit.

13.5   Spousal Privilege

Most communications between husbands and wives are privileged. In some places, only the spouse called to testify can espouse the privilege. So, for example, if a wife does not wish to testify against her husband, she can refuse to do so.

In other jurisdictions, either spouse can assert the privilege. In such places, the spouse who wants to testify can be compelled to be silent. So, for example, if a husband does wish to testify against his wife, he can be prevented by him from doing so. (These are known as the "sit down and shut up" jurisdictions.)

In some states, the privilege ends when the marriage ends. In others, the privilege continues on. Finally, in some states only "confidential communications" between spouses are protected, so if third parties are present or if the communication is made in such a manner that others could overhear, then the disclosure is not confidential.

The most interesting aspect to the spousal privilege is that it has changed dramatically over the past three decades. Whereas the general rule at the beginning of this century prohibited spouses from testifying against each other under any circumstances, the end of the century finds a significantly altered privilege in the majority of jurisdictions. The following case is the landmark U.S. Supreme Court case dealing with the spousal privilege as it applies in the federal court system.

Trammel v. United States

440 U.S. 934 (1979)

We granted certiorari to consider whether an accused may invoke the privilege against adverse spousal testimony so as to exclude the voluntary testimony of his wife. This calls for a re-examination of *Hawkins v. United States* [the landmark precedent that had affirmed the privilege].

On March 10, 1976, petitioner Otis Trammel was indicted with two others . . . for importing heroin into the United States from Thailand and the Philippine Islands. . . . The indictment also named six unindicted co-conspirators, including petitioner's wife Elizabeth Ann Trammel. According to the indictment, petitioner and his wife flew from the Philippines to California in August 1975, carrying with them a quantity of heroin. Freeman and Roberts assisted them in its distribution. Elizabeth Trammel then traveled to Thailand where she purchased another supply of the drug. On November 3, 1975, with four ounces of heroin on her person, she boarded a plane for the United States. During a routine customs search in Hawaii, she was searched, the heroin was discovered, and she was arrested. After discussions with Drug Enforcement Administration agents, she agreed to cooperate with the Government.

Prior to trial on this indictment, petitioner moved to sever his case from that of Roberts and Freeman. He advised the court that the Government intended to call his wife as an adverse witness and asserted his claim to a privilege to prevent her from testifying against him. At a hearing on the motion, Mrs. Trammel was called as a Government witness under a grant of use immunity. She testified that she and petitioner were married in May 1975 and that they remained married. She explained that her cooperation with the government was based on assurances that she would be given lenient treatment. She then described, in considerable detail, her role and that of her husband in the heroin distribution conspiracy.

After hearing this testimony, the District Court ruled that Mrs. Trammel could testify in support of the Government's case to any act she observed during the marriage and to any communication "made in the presence of a third person"; however, confidential communications between petitioner and his wife were held to be privileged and inadmissible. At trial, Elizabeth Trammel testified within the limits of the court's pretrial ruling; her testimony, as the Government concedes, constituted virtually its entire case against petitioner. He was found guilty. . . .

*   *   *

Hawkins ... left the federal privilege for adverse spousal testimony [to be] "a rule which bars the testimony of one spouse against the other unless both consent." However, in so doing, the Court made clear that its decision was not meant to "foreclose whatever changes in the rule may eventually be dictated by 'reason and experience.'"

*   *   *

Our consideration of the foundations for the privilege and its history satisfy us that "reason and experience" no longer justify so sweeping a rule as that found acceptable by the Court in *Hawkins*. Accordingly, we conclude that the existing rule should be modified so that the witness-spouse alone has a privilege to refuse to testify adversely; the witness may be neither compelled to testify nor foreclosed from testifying. This modification—vesting the privilege in the witness-spouse—furthers the important public interest in marital harmony without unduly burdening legitimate law enforcement needs. Here, petitioner's spouse chose to testify against him. That she did so after immunity and assurances of lenient treatment does not render her testimony involuntary. ... Accordingly, the District Court and the Court of Appeals were correct in rejecting petitioner's claim of privilege, and the judgment of the Court of Appeals is AFFIRMED.

The *Trammel* case overturned a precedent and applied a new rule retroactively to Trammel, who was convicted on the basis of testimony that would have been excluded under the old rule. The courts show marginal loyalty to privileges that appear to perpetuate injustice, and, as dramatically demonstrated in the *Trammel* case, the courts can change the extent of a privilege or eliminate it altogether without warning.

13.6   The Physician-Patient Privilege

The physician-patient privilege is probably one of the most difficult to pin down. When a patient consults with a doctor for diagnosis or treatment, generally the communications between them are thought to be confidential. Nonetheless, many states do not acknowledge a legal privilege protecting the confidence of physician-patient communications. Even in those states where the privilege is allowed, **peripheral statements** made to the physician, even if made "in confidence," are not privileged. For example, if the patient makes a statement about having just escaped from prison, the privilege would not preclude the physician from testifying as to that statement.

Peripheral Statements
Statements made not directly covered under the privilege.

Some jurisdictions require that any time a medical provider treats a bullet wound, the provider must report the wound to the authorities. Conversations about the origin of the bullet wound are not privileged, nor are details of the nature of the wound itself.

13.7 Religious Communication Privilege

A narrow privilege for communications between clergy and followers exists in most states. The most prevalent privilege exists with regard to confessions made to Catholic priests for absolution. At common law, this was referred to as the "priest-penitent privilege." Catholic confession is still the most protected of the religious communications. A conversation between a minister and a parishioner made in a counseling setting is not as well protected. This is because some jurisdictions apply the privilege only where the communication is made as a result of a religious law or mandate and not simply as a personal quest for support.

13.8 Counselors, Therapists, and Social Workers and Chiropractors, Nurses, and Dentists

A privilege for the communications between counselors and therapists and their patients is widely acknowledged. Some states also have statutes protecting communications between people and their social workers, chiropractors, nurses, and even dentists.

13.9 Military Secrets

State and military secrets are protected by privilege for purposes of national security. When Richard Nixon was president, the U.S. Supreme Court recognized a privilege for presidential communications made in confidence as being in the best interests of the national security. *U.S. v. Nixon*, 418 U.S. 683 (1974).

When there is a national security issue, the court may review material "in camera" to determine whether the privilege applies (in camera means in private). When looking at material in camera the judge reviews the material privately in chambers. The party requesting the disclosure does not get to see the material unless the court determines that the privilege does not apply. The government is thereby prevented from abusing the privilege to keep discoverable material from the opposing party while the national security is not impaired.

13.10   Privileges on the Horizon

A privilege that is not fully recognized but has gained a great deal of press in recent years is the "reporter-informant privilege." Many times reporters refuse to identify their confidential sources and end up in jail for contempt of court. Some state statutes (and some courts) have tried to carve out a limited privilege, so that reporters have at least some right to maintain their source's confidences. However, if the state has a compelling need for the identity of the informant and there is no other way for the state to get the information, the privilege will not apply. It is unlikely that a full privilege will ever be granted to reporters because of the potential for abuse.

FRE 502, P. 271

Watch for a new rule limiting the waiver of attorney-client privilege and wavier of work product. In April 2007, the Advisory Committee on Evidence Rules approved proposed FRE 502. It will be considered for final approval at the end of 2007. The intent of the rule is to ease the risk of forfeiting the attorney-client privilege or work-product protection in the discovery process so that every single document produced need not be scrutinized. The proposed rule would be beneficial particularly in complex cases involving thousands of pages of documents where an inadvertent disclosure of privileged or protected information could constitute a waiver of the attorney-client privilege or waiver of work product.

13.11   In Summary

- Privileges evolved in the common law and are often inconsistent between jurisdictions.
- The attorney-client privilege, under which paralegals are governed, generally allows the client to reveal information to counsel without fear of public disclosure; however, the privilege has exceptions.
- The crime-fraud exception to the attorney-client privilege is the largest exception, and under this exception attorneys (and paralegals) may be forced to disclose confidential information if the client was using the attorney's advice to further a course of criminal conduct, or if the attorney was involved in illegal activity with the client, or if the attorney observed illegal activity. Communications are not privileged when a client asks his or her attorney to help conceal evidence.
- The spousal privilege may vary from state to state, but in federal court, only the testifying spouse may exert the privilege, under the *Trammel* case.

- Depending on the jurisdiction, available legal privileges may include physician-patient privilege; spousal privilege; religious communication privilege; privilege between an individual and counselor, therapist, social worker, chiropractor, nurse, or dentist; and other privileges currently evolving.
- The government has a military secret privilege to protect it from being forced to disclose national security information.

End of Chapter Review Questions

1. What is a privilege?
2. What is the attorney-client privilege?
3. What is the crime-fraud exception?
4. What is the spousal privilege, and who holds the privilege in federal court today?
5. How do states treat the physician-patient privilege?
6. Does the military have to answer subpoenas for documents related to an ongoing investigation?
7. Can a client waive the attorney-client privilege?

Applications

Consider the following hypothetical situation.

Mr. Smith told the second Mrs. Smith that he murdered the first Mrs. Smith. The second Mrs. Smith left Mr. Smith, but never filed for divorce. Mr. Smith was later tried for murdering the first Mrs. Smith.

1. At Mr. Smith's trial for murdering the first Mrs. Smith, is testimony of his confession to the second Mrs. Smith admissible?
2. If the second Mrs. Smith does not wish to testify, but her testimony is crucial to gaining a conviction, can she be compelled to do so?

Consider the following hypothetical situation.

Jonathan came to a prescheduled appointment with his attorney, who was representing him on a burglary charge. When Jonathan was sure that he was alone with his attorney, he removed a package from his jacket, which he claimed contained a gun that he used to kill the man with whom he had committed the burglary. He asked his attorney to hide the gun for him or to tell him what to do with it.

3. Is the attorney compelled to testify about Jonathan's confession regarding the murder?
4. May the attorney advise Jonathan regarding how to deal with the gun?

Federal Rules of Evidence for United States Courts and Magistrates

Article I.   General Provisions

Rule 101.   Scope

These rules govern proceedings in the courts of the United States and before United States bankruptcy judges and United States magistrates, to the extent and with the exceptions stated in rule 1101.

Rule 102.   Purpose and Construction

These rules shall be construed to secure fairness in administration, elimination of unjustifiable expense and delay, and promotion of growth and development of the law of evidence to the end that the truth may be ascertained and proceedings jusdy determined.

Rule 103.   Rulings on Evidence

(a) **Effect of erroneous ruling.** Error may not be predicated upon a ruling which admits or excludes evidence unless a substantial right of the party is affected, and

(1) **Objection.** In case the ruling is one admitting evidence, a timely objection or motion to strike appears of record,

stating the specific ground of objection, if the specific ground was not apparent from the context; or

(2) Offer of proof. In case the ruling is one excluding evidence, the substance of the evidence was made known to the court by offer or was apparent from the context within which questions were asked.

Once the court makes a definitive ruling on the record admitting or excluding evidence, either at or before trial, a party need not renew an objection or offer of proof to preserve a claim of error for appeal.

(b) Record of offer and ruling. The court may add any other or further statement which shows the character of the evidence, the form in which it was offered, the objection made, and the ruling thereon. It may direct the making of an offer in question and answer form.

(c) Hearing of jury. In jury cases, proceedings shall be conducted, to the extent practicable, so as to prevent inadmissible evidence from being suggested to the jury by any means, such as making statements or offers of proof or asking questions in the hearing of the jury.

(d) Plain error. Nothing in this rule precludes taking notice of plain errors affecting substantial rights although they were not brought to the attention of the court.

Rule 104.   Preliminary Questions

(a) Questions of admissibitity generally. Preliminary questions concerning the qualification of a person to be a witness, the existence of a privilege, or the admissibility of evidence shall be determined by the court, subject to the provisions of subdivision (b). In making its determination it is not bound by the rules of evidence except those with respect to privileges.

(b) Relevancy conditioned on fact. When the relevancy of evidence depends upon the fulfillment of a condition of fact, the court shall admit it upon, or subject to, the introduction of evidence sufficient to support a finding of the fulfillment of the condition.

(c) Hearing of jury. Hearings on the admissibility of confessions shall in all cases be conducted out of the hearing of the jury. Hearings on other preliminary matters shall be so conducted when the interests of justice require, or when an accused is a witness and so requests.

(d) Testimony by accused. The accused does not, by testifying upon a preliminary matter, become subject to cross-examination as to other issues in the case.

(e) Weight and credibility. This rule does not limit the right of a party to introduce before the jury evidence relevant to weight or credibility.

Rule 105.   Limited Admissibility

When evidence which is admissible as to one party or for one purpose but not admissible as to another party or for another purpose is admitted, the court, upon request, shall restrict the evidence to its proper scope and instruct the jury accordingly.

Rule 106.   Remainder of or Related Writings or Recorded Statements

When a writing or recorded statement or part thereof is introduced by a party, an adverse party may require the introduction at that time of any other part or any other writing or recorded statement which ought in fairness to be considered contemporaneously with it.

Article II.   Judicial Notice

Rule 201.   Judicial Notice of Adjudicative Facts

(a) Scope of rule. This rule governs only judicial notice of adjudicative facts.

(b) Kinds of facts. A judicially noticed fact must be one not subject to reasonable dispute in that it is either (1) generally known within the territorial jurisdiction of the trial court or (2) capable of accurate and ready determination by resort to sources whose accuracy cannot reasonably be questioned.

(c) When discretionary. A court may take judicial notice, whether requested or not.

(d) When mandatory. A court shall take judicial notice if requested by a party and supplied with the necessary information.

(e) Opportunity to be heard. A party is entitled upon timely request to an opportunity to be heard as to the propriety of taking judicial notice and the tenor of the matter noticed. In the absence of prior notification, the request may be made after judicial notice has been taken.

(f) Time of taking notice. Judicial notice may be taken at any stage of the proceeding.

(g) Instructing jury. In a civil action or proceeding, the court shall instruct the jury to accept as conclusive any fact judicially noticed.

In a criminal case, the court shall instruct the jury that it may, but is not required to, accept as conclusive any feet judicially noticed.

Article III.   Presumptions in Civil Actions and Proceedings

Rule 301.   Presumptions in General in Civil Actions and Proceedings

In all civil actions and proceedings not otherwise provided for by Act of Congress or by these rules, a presumption imposes on the party against whom it is directed the burden of going forward with evidence to rebut or meet the presumption, but does not shift to such party the burden of proof in the sense of the risk of nonpersuasion, which remains throughout the trial upon the party on whom it was originally cast.

Rule 302.   Applicability of State Law in Civil Actions and Proceedings

In civil actions and proceedings, the effect of a presumption respecting a fact which is an element of a daim or defense as to which State law supplies the rule of decision is determined in accordance with State law.

Article IV.   Relevancy and Its Limits

Rule 401.   Definition of "Relevant Evidence"

"Relevant evidence" means evidence having any tendency to make the existence of any feet that is of consequence to the determination of the action more probable or less probable than it would be without the evidence.

Rule 402.   Relevant Evidence Generally Admissible; Irrelevant Evidence Inadmissible

All relevant evidence is admissible, except as otherwise provided by the Constitution of the United States, by Act of Congress, by these rules, or by other rules prescribed by the Supreme Court pursuant to statutory authority. Evidence which is not relevant is not admissible.

Rule 403.   Exclusion of Relevant Evidence on Grounds of Prejudice, Confusion, or Waste of Time

Although relevant, evidence may be excluded if its probative value is substantially outweighed by the danger of unfair prejudice, confusion of the issues, or misleading the jury, or by considerations of undue delay, waste of time, or needless presentation of cumulative evidence.

Rule 404.   Character Evidence Mot Admissible to Prove Conduct; Exceptions; Other Crimes

(a) Character evidence generally. Evidence of a person's character or a trait of character is not admissible for the purpose of proving action in conformity therewith on a particular occasion, except:

> **(1) Character of accused.** In a criminal case, evidence of a pertinent trait of character offered by an accused, or by the prosecution to rebut the same, or if evidence of a trait of character of the alleged victim of the crime is offered by an accused and admitted under Rule 404(a)(2), evidence of the same trait of character of the accused offered by the prosecution;
>
> **(2) Character of alleged victim.** In a criminal case, and subject to the limitation imposed by Rule 412, evidence of a pertinent trait of character of the alleged victim of the crime offered by an accused, or by the prosecution to rebut the same, or evidence of a character trait of peacefulness of the alleged victim offered by the prosecution in a homicide case to rebut evidence that the alleged victim was the first aggressor;
>
> **(3) Character of witness.** Evidence of the character of a witness, as provided in Rules 607, 608, and 609.

(b) Other crimes, wrongs, or acts. Evidence of other crimes, wrongs, or acts is not admissible to prove the character of a person in order to show action in conformity therewith. It may, however, be admissible for other purposes, such as proof of motive, opportunity, intent, preparation, plan, knowledge, identity, or absence of mistake or accident, provided that upon request by the accused, the prosecution in a criminal case shall provide reasonable notice in advance of trial, or during trial if the court excuses pretrial notice on good cause shown, of the general nature of any such evidence it intends to introduce at trial.

Rule 405.   Methods off Proving Character

(a) Reputation or opinion. In all cases in which evidence of character or a trait of character of a person is admissible, proof may be made by testimony as to reputation or by testimony in the form of an opinion. On cross-examination, inquiry is allowable into relevant specific instances of conduct.

(b) Specific instances of conduct. In cases in which character or a trait of character of a person is an essential element of a charge, claim, or defense, proof may also be made of specific instances of that person's conduct.

Rule 406.   Habit; Routine Practice

Evidence of the habit of a person or of the routine practice of an organization, whether corroborated or not and regardless of the presence of eyewitnesses, is relevant to prove that the conduct of the person or organization on a particular occasion was in conformity with the habit or routine practice.

Rule 407.   Subsequent Remedial Measures

When, after an injury or harm allegedly caused by an event, measures are taken that, if taken previously, would have made the injury or harm less likely to occur, evidence of the subsequent measures is not admissible to prove negligence, culpable conduct, a defect in a product, a defect in a product's design, or a need for a warning or instruction. This rule does not require the exclusion of evidence of subsequent measures when offered for another purpose, such as proving ownership, control, or feasibility of precautionary measures, if controverted, or impeachment.

Rule 408.   Compromise and Offers to Compromise

(a) **Prohibited Uses.** Evidence of the following is not admissible on behalf of any party, when offered to prove liability for, invalidity of, or amount of a claim that was disputed as to validity or amount, or to impeach through a prior inconsistent statement or contradiction:

> (1) furnishing or offering or promising to furnish—or accepting or offering or promising to accept—a valuable consideration in compromising or attempting to compromise the claim; and
>
> (2) conduct or statements made in compromise negotiation regarding the claim, except when offered in a criminal case and the negotiations related to a claim by a public office or agency in the exercise of regulatory, investigative, or enforcement authority.

(b) **Permitted uses.** This rule does not require exclusion if the evidence is offered for purposes not prohibited by subdivision (a). Examples of permissible purposes include proving a witness's bias or prejudice; negating a contention of undue delay; and proving an effort to obstruct a criminal investigation or prosecution.

Rule 409.   Payment of Medical and Similar Expenses

Evidence of furnishing or offering or promising to pay medical, hospital, or similar expenses occasioned by an injury is not admissible to prove liability for the injury.

Rule 410.   Inadmissibility of Pleas, Plea Discussions, and Related Statements

Except as otherwise provided in this rule, evidence of the following is not, in any civil or criminal proceeding, admissible against the defendant who made the plea or was a participant in the plea discussions:

    (1) a plea of guilty which was later withdrawn;

    (2) a plea of *nolo contendere;*

    (3) any statement made in the course of any proceedings under rule 11 of the Federal Rules of Criminal Procedure or comparable state procedure regarding either of the foregoing pleas; or

    (4) any statement made in the course of plea discussions with an attorney for the prosecuting authority which do not result in a plea of guilty or which result in a plea of guilty later withdrawn.

However, such a statement is admissible (i) in any proceeding wherein another statement made in the course of the same plea or plea discussions has been introduced and the statement ought in fairness be considered contemporaneously with it, or (ii) in a criminal proceeding for perjury or raise statement if the statement was made by the defendant under oath, on the record, and in the presence of counsel.

Rule 411.   Liability Insurance

Evidence that a person was or was not insured against liability is not admissible upon the issue whether the person acted negligently or otherwise wrongfully. This rule does not require the exclusion of evidence of insurance against liability when offered for another purpose, such as proof of agency, ownership, or control, or bias or prejudice of a witness.

Rule 412.   Sex Offense Cases: Relevance of Alleged Victim's Past Sexual Behavior or Alleged Sexual Predisposition

    (a) Evidence generally inadmissible. The following evidence is not admissible in any civil or criminal proceeding involving alleged sexual misconduct except as provided in subdivisions (b) and (c):

   (1) evidence offered to prove that any alleged victim engaged in other sexual behavior;

   (2) evidence offered to prove any alleged victim's sexual predisposition.

(b) Exceptions.

   (1) In a criminal case, the following evidence is admissible, if otherwise admissible under these rules:

   (A) evidence of specific instances of sexual behavior by the alleged victim offered to prove that a person other than the accused was the source of semen, injury, or other physical evidence;

   (B) evidence of specific instances of sexual behavior by the alleged victim with respect to the person accused of the sexual misconduct offered by the accused to prove consent or by the prosecution; and

   (C) evidence the exclusion of which would violate the constitutional rights of the defendant.

   (2) In a civil case, evidence offered to prove the sexual behavior or sexual predisposition of any alleged victim is admissible if it is otherwise admissible under these rules and its probative value substantially outweighs the danger of harm to any victim and of unfair prejudice to any party. Evidence of an alleged victim's reputation is admissible only if it has been placed in controversy by the alleged victim.

(c) Procedure to determine admissibility.

   (1) A party intending to offer evidence under subdivision (b) must:

   (A) file a written motion at least 14 days before trial specifically describing the evidence and stating the purpose for which it is offered unless the court, for good cause, requires a different time for filing or permits filing during trial; and

   (B) serve the motion on all parties and notify the alleged victim or, when appropriate, the alleged victim's guardian or representative.

   (2) Before admitting evidence under this rule the court must conduct a hearing in camera and afford the victim and parties a right to attend and be heard. The motion, related papers, and the record of the hearing must be sealed and remain under seal unless the court orders otherwise.

Rule 413.   Evidence of Similar Crimes in Sexual Assault Cases

(a) In a criminal case in which the defendant is accused of an offense of sexual assault, evidence of the defendant s commission of another offense or offenses of sexual assault is admissible, and may be considered for its bearing on any matter to which it is relevant.

(b) In a case in which the Government intends to offer evidence under this rule, the attorney for the Government shall disclose the evidence to the defendant, including statements of witnesses or a summary of the substance of any testimony that is expected to be offered, at least fifteen days before the scheduled date of trial or at such later time as the court may allow for good cause.

(c) This rule shall not be construed to limit the admission or consideration of evidence under any other rule.

(d) For purposes of this rule and Rule 415, "offense of sexual assault" means a crime under Federal law or the law of a State (as defined in Section 513 of tide 18, United States Code) that involved—

    (1) any conduct proscribed by chapter 109A of title 18, United States Code;

    (2) contact, without consent, between any part of the defendant's body or an object and the genitals or anus of another person;

    (3) contact, without consent, between the genitals or anus of the defendant and any part of another person's body;

    (4) deriving sexual pleasure or gratification from the infliction of death, bodily injury, or physical pain on another person; or

    (5) an attempt or conspiracy to engage in conduct described in paragraphs (l)-(4).

Rule 414.   Evidence of Similar Crimes in Child Molestation Cases

(a) In a criminal case in which the defendant is accused of an offense of child molestation, evidence of the defendant's commission of another offense or offenses of child molestation is admissible, and may be considered for its bearing on any matter to which it is relevant.

(b) In a case in which the Government intends to offer evidence under this rule, the attorney for the Government shall disclose the evidence to the defendant, including statements of witnesses or a summary of the substance of any testimony that is expected to be offered, at least fifteen days before the scheduled date of trial or at such later time as the court may allow for good cause.

(c) This rule shall not be construed to limit the admission or consideration of evidence under any other rule.

(d) For purposes of this rule and Rule 415, "child" means a person below the age of fourteen, and "offense of child molestation" means a crime under Federal law or the law of a State (as defined in section 513 of tide 18, United States Code) that involved

  (1) any conduct proscribed by chapter 109A of title 18, United States Code, that was committed in relation to a child:

  (2) any conduct proscribed by chapter 110 of title 18, United States Code,

  (3) contact between any part of the defendants body or an object and the genitals or anus of a child;

  (4) contact between the genitals or anus of the defendant and any part of the body of a child;

  (5) deriving sexual pleasure or gratification from the infliction of death, bodily injury, or physical pain on a child; or

  (6) an attempt or conspiracy to engage in conduct described in paragraphs (l)-(5).

Rule 415.   Evidence of Similar Acts in Civil Cases Concerning Sexual Assault or Child Molestation

(a) In a civil case in which a claim for damages or other relief is predicated on a party's alleged commission of conduct constituting an offense of sexual assault or child molestation, evidence of that party's commission of another offense or offenses of sexual assault or child molestation is admissible and may be considered as provided in Rule 413 and Rule 4l4 of these rules.

(b) A party who intends to offer evidence under this Rule shall disclose the evidence to the party against whom it will be offered, including statements of witnesses or a summary of the substance of any testimony that is expected to be offered, at least fifteen days before the scheduled date of trial, or at such later time as the court may allow for good cause.

(c) This rule shall not be construed to limit the admission or consideration of evidence under any other rule.

Article V.   Privileges

Rule 501.   General Rule

Except as otherwise required by the Constitution of the United States or provided by Act of Congress or in rules prescribed by the Supreme Court pursuant to statutory authority, the privilege of a witness, person, government, State, or political subdivision thereof shall be governed by the principles of the common law as they may be interpreted by the courts of the United States in the light of reason and experience. However, in civil actions and proceedings, with respect to an element of a claim or defense as to which State law supplies the rule of decision, the privilege of a witness, person, government, State, or political subdivision thereof shall be determined in accordance with State law.

Rule 502.   Attorney-Client Privilege and Work Product; Limitations on Waiver (Proposed)

The following provisions apply, in the circumstances set out, to disclosure of a communication or information covered by the attorney-client privilege or work-product protection.

(a) **Disclosure made in a federal proceeding or to a federal office or agency; scope of waiver.** When the disclosure is made in a federal proceeding or to a federal office or agency and waives the attorney client privilege or work production, the waiver extends to an undisclosed communication or information in a federal or stated proceeding only if:

(1) the waiver is intentional;

(2) the disclosed and undisclosed communications or information concern the same subject matter; and

(3) they ought in fairness to be considered together.

(b) **Inadvertent disclosure.** When made in a federal proceeding or a federal officer or agency, the disclosure does not operate as a waiver in a federal or state proceeding if:

(1) the disclosure in inadvertent;

(2) the holder of the privilege or protection took reasonable steps to prevent disclosure; and

(3) the holder promptly took reasonable steps to rectify the error, including (if applicable) following Fed. R. Civ. P. 26(b)(5)(B).

(c) **Disclosure made in a state proceeding,** When the disclosure is made in a state proceeding and is not the of a state-court order, the disclosure does not operate as a waiver in a federal proceeding if the disclosure:

(1) would not be a waiver under this rule if it had been made in a federal proceeding; or

(2) is not a waiver under the law of the state where the disclosure occurred.

(d) **Controlling effect of court order.** A federal court may order that the privilege or protection is not waived by disclosure connected with the litigation pending before the court. The order binds all personas and entities in all federal or state proceedings, whether or not they were parties to the litigation.

(e) Controlling effect of party agreement. An agreement of the effect of disclosure is binding on the parties to the agreement, but not on other parties unless it is incorporated into a court order.

(f) Controlling effect of this rule. Notwithstanding Rules 101 and 1101, this rule applies to state proceedings in the circumstances set out in the rule. And notwithstanding Rule 501, this rule applies even if state law provides the rule of decision.

(g) Definitions. In this rule:

(1) "attorney-client privilege" means the protection that applicable law provides for confidential attorney-client communications; and

(2) "work-product protection; means the protection that applicable law provides for tangible material (or its intangible equivalent) prepared in anticipation of litigation for trial.

Article VI.   Witnesses

Rule 601.   General Rule of Competency

Every person is competent to be a witness except as otherwise provided in these rules. However, in civil actions and proceedings, with respect to an element of a claim or defense as to which State law supplies the rule of decision the competency of a witness shall be determined in accordance with State law.

Rule 602.   Lack of Personal Knowledge

A witness may not testify to a matter unless evidence is introduced sufficient to support a finding that the witness has personal knowledge of the matter. Evidence to prove personal knowledge may, but need not, consist of the witness' own testimony. This rule is subject to the provisions of rule 703, relating to opinion testimony by expert witnesses.

Rule 603.   Oath or Affirmation

Before testifying, every witness shall be required to declare that the witness will testify truthfully, by oath or affirmation administered in a form calculated to awaken the witness' conscience and impress the witness" mind with the duty to do so.

Rule 604.   Interpreters

An interpreter is subject to the provisions of these rules relating to qualification as an expert and the administration of an oath or affirmation to make a true translation.

Rule 605.   Competency of Judge as Witness

The judge presiding at the trial may not testify in that trial as a witness. No objection need be made in order to preserve the point.

Rule 606.   Competency of Juror as Witness

(a) **At the trial.** A member of the jury may not testify as a witness before that jury in the trial of the case in which the juror is sitting. If the juror is called so to testify, the opposing party shall be afforded an opportunity to object out of the presence of the jury.

(b) **Inquiry into validity of verdict or indictment.** Upon an inquiry into the validity of a verdict or indictment, a juror may not testify as to any matter or statement occurring during the course of the jury's deliberations or to the effect of anything upon that or any, other juror's mind or emotions as influencing the juror to assent to or dissent from the verdict or indictment or concerning the juror's mental processes in connection therewith. But a juror may testify about (1) whether extraneous prejudicial information was improperly brought to the jury's attention, (2) whether any outside influence was improperly brought to bear upon any juror, or (3) whether there was a mistake in entering the verdict onto the verdict form. A juror's affidavit or evidence of any statement by the juror may not be received on a matter about which the juror would be precluded from testifying.

Rule 607.   Who May Impeach

The credibility of a witness may be attacked by any party, including the party calling the witness.

Rule 608.   Evidence of Character and Conduct of Witness

(a) **Opinion and reputation evidence of character.** The credibility of a witness may be attacked or supported by evidence in the form of opinion or reputation, but subject to these limitations: (1) the evidence may refer only to character for truthfulness or untruthfulness, and (2) evidence of truthful character is admissible only after the character of the witness for truthfulness has been attacked by opinion or reputation evidence or otherwise.

(b) Specific instance of conduct. Specific instances of the conduct of a witness, for the purpose of attacking or supporting the witness' credibility, other than conviction of crime as provided in rule 609, may not be proved by extrinsic evidence. They may, however, in the discretion of the court, if probative of truthfulness or untruthfulness, be inquired into on cross-examination of the witness (1) concerning the witness' character for truthfulness or untruthfulness, or (2) concerning the character for truthfulness or untruthfulness of another witness as to which character the witness being cross-examined has testified.

The giving of testimony, whether by an accused or by any other witness, does not operate as a waiver of the accused's or the witness' privilege against self-incrimination when examined with respect to matters which relate only to credibility.

Rule 609. Impeachment by Evidence of Conviction of Crime

(a) General rule. For the purpose of attacking the character for truthfulness of a witness,

(1) evidence that a witness other than an accused has been convicted of a crime shall be admitted, subject to rule 403, if the crime was punishable by death or imprisonment in excess of one year under the law under which the witness was convicted, and evidence that an accused has been convicted of such a crime shall be admitted if the court determines that the probative value of admitting this evidence outweighs its prejudicial effect to the accused; and

(2) evidence that any witness has been convicted of a crime shall be admitted, regardless of the punishments, if it readily can be determined that establishing the elements of the crime required proof or admission of an act of dishonesty or false statement by the witness.

(b) Time limit. Evidence of a conviction under this rule is not admissible if a period of more than ten years has elapsed since the date of the conviction or of the release of the witness from the confinement imposed for that conviction, whichever is the later date, unless the court determines, in the interests of justice, that the probative value of the conviction supported by specific facts and circumstances substantially outweighs its prejudicial effect. However, evidence of a conviction more than 10 years old as calculated herein, is not admissible unless the proponent gives to the adverse party sufficient advance written notice of intent to use such evidence to provide the adverse party with a fair opportunity to contest the use of such evidence.

(c) Effect of pardon, annulment, or certificate of rehabilitation. Evidence of a conviction is not admissible under this rule if (1) the conviction has been the subject of a pardon, annulment, certificate of rehabilitation, or other equivalent procedure based on a finding of the rehabilitation of the person convicted, and that person has not been convicted of a subsequent crime that was punishable by death or imprisonment in excess of one year, or (2) the conviction has been the subject of a pardon, annulment, or other equivalent procedure based on a finding of innocence.

(d) Juvenile adjudications. Evidence of juvenile adjudications is generally not admissible under this rule. The court may, however, in a criminal case allow evidence of a juvenile adjudication of a witness other than the accused if conviction of the offense would be admissible to attack the credibility of an adult and the court is satisfied that admission in evidence is necessary for a fair determination of the issue of guilt or innocence.

(e) Pendency of appeal. The pendency of an appeal therefrom does not render evidence of a conviction inadmissible. Evidence of the pendency of an appeal is admissible.

Rule 610.   Religious Beliefs or Opinions

Evidence of the beliefs or opinions of a witness on matters of religion is not admissible for the purpose of showing that by reason of their nature the witness' credibility is impaired or enhanced.

Rule 611.   Mode and Order of Interrogation and Presentation

(a) Control by court. The court shall exercise reasonable control over the mode and order of interrogating witnesses and presenting evidence so as to (1) make the interrogation and presentation effective for the ascertainment of the truth, (2) avoid needless consumption of time, and (3) protect witnesses from harassment or undue embarrassment.

(b) Scope of cross-examination. Cross-examination should be limited to the subject matter of the direct examination and matters affecting the credibility of the witness. The court may, in the exercise of discretion, permit inquiry into additional matters as if on direct examination.

(c) Leading questions. Leading questions should not be used on the direct examination of a witness except as may be necessary to develop the witness' testimony. Ordinarily leading questions should be permitted on cross-examination. When a party calls a hostile witness, an adverse party, or a witness identified with an adverse party, interrogation may be by leading questions.

Rule 612. Writing Used to Refresh Memory

Except as otherwise provided in criminal proceedings by section 3500 of title 18, United States Code, if a witness uses a writing to refresh memory for the purpose of testifying, either—

(1) while testifying, or

(2) before testifying, if the court in its discretion determines it is necessary in the interests of justice,

an adverse party is entitled to have the writing produced at the hearing, to inspect it, to cross-examine the witness thereon, and to introduce in evidence those portions which relate to the testimony of the witness. If it is claimed that the writing contains matters not related to the subject matter of the testimony the court shall examine the writing in camera, excise any portions not so related, and order delivery of the remainder to the party entitled thereto. Any portion withheld over objections shall be preserved and made available to the appellate court in the event of an appeal. If a writing is not produced or delivered pursuant to order under this rule, the court shall make any order justice requires, except that in criminal cases when the prosecution elects not to comply, the order shall be one striking the testimony or, if the court in its discretion determines that the interests of justice so require, declaring a mistrial.

Rule 613. Prior Statements of Witnesses

(a) **Examining witness concerning prior statement.** In examining a witness concerning a prior statement made by the witness, whether written or not, the statement need not be shown nor its contents disclosed to the witness at that time, but on request the same shall be shown or disclosed to opposing counsel.

(b) **Extrinsic evidence of prior inconsistent statement of witness.** Extrinsic evidence of a prior inconsistent statement by a witness is not admissible unless the witness is afforded an opportunity to explain or deny the same and the opposite party is afforded an opportunity to interrogate the witness thereon, or the interests of justice otherwise require. This provision does not apply to admissions of a party-opponent as defined in rule 801(d)(2).

Rule 614. Calling and Interrogation of Witnesses by Court

(a) **Calling by court.** The court may, on its own motion or at the suggestion of a party, call witnesses, and all parties are entitled to cross-examine witnesses thus called.

(b) **Interrogation by court.** The court may interrogate witnesses whether called by itself or by a party.

(c) Objections. Objections to the calling of witnesses by the court or to interrogation by it may be made at the time or at the next available opportunity when the jury is not present.

Rule 615. Exclusion of Witnesses

At the request of a party the court shall order witnesses excluded so that they cannot hear the testimony of other witnesses, and it may make the order of its own motion. This rule does not authorize exclusion of (1) a party who is a natural person, or (2) an officer or employee of a party which is not a natural person designated as its representative by its attorneyj or (3) a person whose presence is shown by a party to be essential to the presentation of the party's cause.

Article VII. Opinions and Expert Testimony

Rule 701. Opinion Testimony by Lay Witnesses

If the witness is not testifying as an expert, the witness' testimony in the form of opinions or inferences is limited to those opinions or inferences which are (a) rationally based on the perception of the witness, (b) helpful to a clear understanding of the witness' testimony or the determination of a fact in issue, and (c) not based on scientific, technical, or other specialized knowledge within the scope of Rule 702.

Rule 702. Testimony by Experts

If scientific, technical, or other specialized knowledge will assist the trier-of-fact to understand the evidence or to determine a fact in issue, a witness qualified as an expert by knowledge, skill, experience, training, or education, may testify thereto in the form of an opinion or otherwise, if (1) the testimony is based upon sufficient facts or data, (2) the testimony is the product of reliable principles and methods, and (3) the witness has applied the principles and methods reliably to the facts of the case.

Rule 703. Bases of Opinion Testimony by Experts

The facts or data in the particular case upon which an expert bases an opinion or inference may be those perceived by or made known to the expert at or before the hearing. If of a type reasonably relied upon by experts in the particular field in forming opinions or inferences upon the subject, the facts or data need not be admissible in evidence in order for the opinion or inference to be admitted. Facts or data that are otherwise inadmissible shall not be disclosed to the jury by the proponent of the opinion or inference unless the court determines that their probative value in assisting the jury to evaluate the expert's opinion substantially outweighs their prejudicial effect.

Rule 704.   Opinion on Ultimate Issue

(a) Except as provided in subdivision (b), testimony in the form of an opinion or inference otherwise admissible is not objectionable because it embraces an ultimate issue to be decided by the trier-of-fact.

(b) No expert witness testifying with respect to the mental state or condition of a defendant in a criminal case may state an opinion or inference as to whether the defendant did or did not have the mental state or condition constituting an element of the crime charged or of a defense thereto. Such ultimate issues are matters for the trier-of-fact alone.

Rule 705.   Disclosure of Facts or Data Underlying Expert Opinion

The expert may testify in terms of opinion or inference and give reasons therefor without first testifying to the underlying facts or data, unless the court requires otherwise. The expert may in any event be required to disclose the underlying facts or data on cross-examination.

Rule 706.   Court Appointed Experts

(a) **Appointment.** The court may on its own motion or on the motion of any party enter an order to show cause why expert witnesses should not be appointed, and may request the parties to submit nominations. The court may appoint any expert witnesses agreed upon by the parties, and may appoint expert witnesses of its own selection. An expert witness shall not be appointed by the court unless the witness consents to act. A witness so appointed shall be informed of the witness' duties by the court in writing, a copy of which shall be filed with the clerk, or at a conference in which the parties shall have opportunity to participate. A witness so appointed shall advise the parties of the witness' findings, if any; the witness' deposition may be taken by any party; and the witness may be called to testify by the court or any party. The witness shall be subject to cross-examination by each party, including a party calling the witness.

(b) Compensation. Expert witnesses so appointed are entitled to reasonable compensation in whatever sum the court may allow. The compensation thus fixed is payable from funds which may be provided by law in criminal cases and civil actions and proceedings involving just compensation under the Fifth Amendment. In other civil actions and proceedings the compensation shall be paid by the parties in such proportion and at such time as the court directs, and thereafter charged in like manner as other costs.

(c) Disclosure of appointment. In the exercise of its discretion, the court may authorize disclosure to the jury of the fact that the court appointed the expert witness.

(d) Parties' experts of own selection. Nothing in this rule limits the parties in calling expert witnesses of their own selection.

Article VIII.   Hearsay

Rule 801.   Definitions

The following definitions apply under this article:

(a) Statement. A "statement" is (1) an oral or written assertion or (2) nonverbal conduct of a person, if it is intended by the person as an assertion.

(b) Declarant. A "declarant" is a person who makes a statement.

(c) Hearsay. "Hearsay" is a statement, other than one made by the declarant while testifying at the trial or hearing, offered in evidence to prove the truth of the matter asserted.

(d) Statements which are not hearsay. A statement is not hearsay if—

    (1) Prior statement by witness. The declarant testifies at the trial or hearing and is subject to cross-examination concerning the statement, and the statement is (A) inconsistent with the declarants testimony, and was given under oath subject to the penalty of perjury at a trial, hearing, or other proceeding, or in a deposition, or (B) consistent with the declarants testimony and is offered to rebut an express or implied charge against the declarant of recent fabrication or improper influence or motive, or (C) one of identification of a person made after perceiving the person; or

    (2) Admission by a party-opponent. The statement is offered against a party and is (A) the party's own statement in either an individual or representative capacity, or (B) a statement of which the party has manifested an adoption or belief in its truth, or (C) a statement by a person authorized by the party to make a statement concerning the subject, or (D) a statement by the party's agent or servant concerning a matter within the scope of the agency or employment made during the existence of the relationship, or (E) a statement by a co-conspirator of a party during the course and in furtherance of the conspiracy. The contents of the statement shall be considered but are not alone sufficient to establish the declarant's authority under subdivision (C), the agency or employment relationship and scope thereof under subdivision (D), or the existence of the conspiracy and the participation therein of the declarant and the party against whom the statement is offered under subdivision (E).

Rule 802.   Hearsay Rule

Hearsay is not admissible except as provided by these rules or by other rules prescribed by the Supreme Court pursuant to statutory authority or by Act of Congress.

Rule 803.   Hearsay Exceptions; Availability of Declarant Immaterial

The following are not excluded by the hearsay rule, even though the declarant is available as a witness:

(1) **Present sense impression.** A statement describing or explaining an event or condition made while the declarant was perceiving the event or condition, or immediately thereafter.

(2) **Excited utterance.** A statement relating to a startling event or condition made while the declarant was under the stress of excitement caused by the event or condition.

(3) **Then existing mental, emotional, or physical condition.** A statement of the declarants then existing state of mind, emotion, sensation, or physical condition (such as intent, plan, motive, design, mental feeling, pain, and bodily health), but not including a statement of memory or belief to prove the fact remembered or believed unless it relates to the execution, revocation, identification, or terms of declarant's will.

(4) **Statements for purposes of medical diagnosis or treatment.** Statements made for purposes of medical diagnosis or treatment and describing medical history, or past or present symptoms, pain, or sensations, or the inception or general character of the cause or external source thereof insofar as reasonably pertinent to diagnosis or treatment.

(5) Recorded recollection. A memorandum or record concerning a matter about which a witness once had knowledge but now has insufficient recollection to enable the witness to testify fully and accurately, shown to have been made or adopted by the witness when the matter was fresh in the witness' memory and to reflect that knowledge correctly. If admitted, the memorandum or record may be read into evidence but may not itself be received as an exhibit unless offered by an adverse party.

(6) Records of regularly conducted activity. A memorandum, report, record, or data compilation, in any form, of acts, events, conditions, opinions, or diagnoses, made at or near the time by, or from information transmitted by, a person with knowledge, if kept in the course of a regularly conducted business activity, and if it was the regular practice of that business activity to make the memorandum, report, record, or data compilation, all as shown by the testimony of the custodian or other qualified witness, or by certification that complies with Rule 902(11), Rule 902(12), or a statute permitting certification, unless the source of information or the method or circumstances of preparation indicate lack of trustworthiness. The term "business" as used in this paragraph includes business, institution, association, profession, occupation, and calling of every kind, whether or not conducted for profit.

(7) Absence of entry in records kept in accordance with the provisions of paragraph (6). Evidence that a matter is not included in the memoranda, reports, records, or data compilations, in any form, kept in accordance with the provisions of paragraph (6), to prove the nonoccurrence or nonexistence of the matter, if the matter was of a kind of which a memorandum, report, record, or data compilation was regularly made and preserved, unless the sources of information or other circumstances indicate lack of trustworthiness.

(8) Public records and reports. Records, reports, statements, or data compilations, in any form, of public offices or agencies, setting forth (A) the activities of the office or agency, or (B) matters observed pursuant to duty imposed by law as to which matters there was a duty to report, excluding, however, in criminal cases matters observed by police officers and other law enforcement personnel, or (C) in civil actions and proceedings and against the Government in criminal cases, factual findings resulting from an investigation made pursuant to authority granted by law, unless the sources of information or other circumstances indicate lack of truthworthiness.

(9) Records of vital statistics. Records or data compilations, in any form, of births, fetal deaths, deaths, or marriages, if the report thereof was made to a public office pursuant to requirements of law.

(10) Absence of public record or entry. To prove the absence of a record, report, statement, or data compilation, in any form, or the nonoccurrence or nonexistence of a matter of which a record, report, statement, or data compilation, in any form, was regularly made and preserved by a public office or agency, evidence in the form of a certification in accordance with rule 902, or testimony, that diligent search failed to disclose the record, report, statement, or data compilation, or entry.

(11) Records of religious organizations. Statement of births, marriages, divorces, deaths, legitimacy, ancestry, relationship by blood or marriage, or other similar facts of personal or family history, contained in a regularly kept record of a religious organization.

(12) Marriage, baptismal, and similar certificates. Statements of fact contained in a certificate that the maker performed a marriage or other ceremony or administered a sacrament, made by a clergyman, public official, or other person authorized by the rules or practices of a religious organization or by law to perform the act certified, and purporting to have been issued at the time of the act or within a reasonable time thereafter.

(13) Family records. Statements of fact concerning personal or family history contained in family Bibles, genealogies, charts, engravings on rings, inscriptions on family portraits, engravings on urns, crypts, or tombstones, or the like.

(14) Records of documents affecting an interest in property. The record of a document purporting to establish or affect an interest in property, as proof of the content of the original recorded document and its execution and delivery by each person by whom it purports to have been executed, if the record is a record of a public office and an applicable statute authorizes the recording of documents of that kind in that office.

(15) Statements in documents affecting an interest in property. A statement contained in a document purporting to establish or affect an interest in property if the matter stated was relevant to the purpose of the document, unless dealings with the property since the document was made have been inconsistent with the truth of the statement or the purport of the document.

(16) Statements in ancient documents. Statements in a document in existence twenty years or more the authenticity of which is established.

(17) Market reports, commercial publications. Market quotations, tabulations, lists, directories, or other published compilations, generally used and relied upon by the public or by persons in particular occupations.

(18) Learned treatises. To the extent called to the attention of an expert witness upon cross-examination or relied upon by the expert witness in direct examination, statements contained in published treatises, periodicals, or pamphlets on a subject of history, medicine, or other science or art, established as a reliable authority by the testimony or admission of the witness or by other expert testimony or by judicial notice. If admitted, the statements may be read into evidence but may not be received as exhibits.

(19) Reputation concerning personal or family history. Reputation among members of a persons family by blood, adoption, or marriage, or among a persons associates, or in the community, concerning a persons birth, adoption, marriage, divorce, death, legitimacy, relationship by blood, adoption, or marriage, ancestry, or other similar fact of personal or family history.

(20) Reputation concerning boundaries or general history. Reputation in a community, arising before the controversy, as to boundaries of or customs affecting lands in the community, and reputation as to events of general history important to the community or State or nation in which located.

(21) Reputation as to character. Reputation of a person's character among associates or in the community.

(22) Judgment of previous conviction. Evidence of a final judgment, entered after a trial or upon a plea of guilty (but not upon a plea of nolo contendere), adjudging a person guilty of a crime punishable by death or imprisonment in excess of one year, to prove any fact essential to sustain the judgment, but not including, when offered by the Government in a criminal prosecution for purposes other than impeachment, judgments against persons other than the accused. The pendency of an appeal may be shown but does not affect admissibility.

(23) Judgment as to personal, family, or general history, or boundaries. Judgments as proof of matters of personal, family or general history, or boundaries, essential to the judgment, if the same would be provable by evidence of reputation.

Rule 804.   Hearsay Exceptions; Declarant Unavailable

(a) **Definition of unavailability.** "Unavailability as a witness" includes situations in which the declarant—

(1) is exempted by ruling of the court on the ground of privilege from testifying concerning the subject matter of the declarant's statement; or

(2) persists in refusing to testify concerning the subject matter of the declarants statement despite an order of the court to do so; or

(3) testifies to a lack of memory of the subject matter of the declarant's statement; or

(4) is unable to be present or to testify at the hearing because of death or then existing physical or mental illness or infirmity; or

(5) is absent from the hearing and the proponent of a statement has been unable to procure the declarants attendance (or in the case of a hearsay exception under subdivision (b)(2), (3), or (4), the declarant's attendance or testimony) by process or other reasonable means.

A declarant is not unavailable as a witness if exemption, refusal, claim of lack of memory, inability, or absence is due to the procurement or wrongdoing of the proponent of a statement for the purpose of preventing the witness from attending or testifying.

(b) **Hearsay exceptions.** The following are not excluded by the hearsay rule if the declarant is unavailable as a witness:

(1) **Former testimony.** Testimony given as a witness at another hearing of the same or a different proceeding, or in a deposition taken in compliance with law in the course of the same or another proceeding, if the party against whom the testimony is now offered, or, in a civil action or proceeding, a predecessor in interest, had an opportunity and similar motive to develop the testimony by direct, cross, or redirect examination.

(2) **Statement under belief of impending death.** In a prosecution for homicide or in a civil action or proceeding, a statement made by a declarant while believing that the declarant's death was imminent, concerning the cause or circumstances of what the declarant believed to be impending death.

(3) **Statement against interest.** A statement which was at the time of its making so far contrary to the declarant's pecuniary or proprietary interest, or so far tended to subject the declarant to civil or criminal liability, or to render invalid a claim by the declarant against another, that a reasonable person in the declarant's position would not have made

the statement unless believing it to be true. A statement tending to expose the declarant to criminal liability and offered to exculpate the accused is not admissible unless corroborating circumstances clearly indicate the trustworthiness of the statement.

(4) **Statement of personal or family history.** (A) A statement concerning the declarant's own birth, adoption, marriage, divorce, legitimacy, relationship by blood, adoption, or marriage, ancestry, or other similar fact of personal or family history, even though declarant had no means of acquiring personal knowledge of the matter stated; or (B) a statement concerning the foregoing matters, and death also, of another person, if the declarant was related to the other by blood, adoption, or marriage or was so intimately associated with the other's family as to be likely to have accurate information concerning the matter declared.

(5) **Transferred to Rule 807.**

(6) **Forfeiture by wrongdoing.** A statement offered against a party that has engaged or acquiesced in wrongdoing that was intended to, and did, procure the unavailability of the declarant as a witness.

Rule 805.   Hearsay within Hearsay

Hearsay included within hearsay is not excluded under the hearsay rule if each part of the combined statements conforms with an exception to the hearsay rule provided in these rules.

Rule 806.   Attacking and Supporting Credibility of Declarant

When a hearsay statement, or a statement defined in Rule 801(d)(2), (C), (D), or (E), has been admitted in evidence, the credibility of the declarant may be attacked, and if attacked may be supported, by any evidence which would be admissible for those purposes if declarant had testified as a witness. Evidence of a statement or conduct by the declarant at any time, inconsistent with the declarant's hearsay statement, is not subject to any requirement that the declarant may have been afforded an opportunity to deny or explain. If the party against whom a hearsay statement has been admitted calls the declarant as a witness, the party is entitled to examine the declarant on the statement as if under cross-examination.

Rule 807.   Residual Exception

A statement not specifically covered by Rule 803 or 804 but having equivalent circumstantial guarantees of trustworthiness is not excluded by the hearsay rule, if the court determines that (A) the statement is offered as evidence of a material fact; (B) the statement is more probative on the point for which it is offered than any other evidence which the proponent can procure through reasonable efforts; and (C) the general purposes of these rules and the interests of justice will best be served by admission of the statement into evidence. However, a statement may not be admitted under this exception unless the proponent of it makes known to the adverse party sufficiently in advance of the trial or hearing to provide the adverse party with a fair opportunity to prepare to meet it, the proponent's intention to offer the statement and the particulars of it including the name and address of the declarant.

Article IX.   Authentication and Identification

Rule 901.   Requirement of Authentication or Identification

(a) **General provision.** The requirement of authentication or identification as a condition precedent to admissibility is satisfied by evidence sufficient to support a finding that the matter in question is what its proponent claims.

(b) **Illustrations.** By way of illustration only, and not by way of limitation, the following are examples of authentication or identification conforming with the requirements of this rule:

(1) **Testimony of witness with knowledge.** Testimony that a matter is what it is claimed to be.

(2) **Nonexpert opinion on handwriting.** Nonexpert opinion as to the genuineness of handwriting, based upon familiarity not acquired for purposes of the litigation.

(3) **Comparison by trier or expert witness.** Comparison by the trier-of-fact or by expert witnesses with specimens which have been authenticated.

(4) **Distinctive characteristics and the like.** Appearance, contents, substance, internal patterns, or other distinctive characteristics, taken in conjunction with circumstances.

(5) **Voice identification.** Identification of a voice, whether heard firsthand or through mechanical or electronic transmission or recording, by opinion based upon hearing the voice at any time under circumstances connecting it with the alleged speaker.

(6) **Telephone conversations.** Telephone conversations, by evidence that a call was made to the number assigned at the time by the telephone company to a particular person or business, if (A) in the case of a person, circumstances, including self-identification, show the person answering to be the one called, or (B) in the case of a business, the call was made to a place of business and the conversation related to business reasonably transacted over the telephone.

(7) **Public records or reports.** Evidence that a writing authorized by law to be recorded or filed and in feet recorded or filed in a public office, or a purported public record, report, statement, or data compilation, in any form, is from the public office where items of this nature are kept.

(8) **Ancient documents or data compilation.** Evidence that a document or data compilation, in any form, (A) is in such condition as to create no suspicion concerning its authenticity, (B) was in a place where it, if authentic, would likely be, and (C) has been in existence 20 years or more at the time it is offered.

(9) **Process or system.** Evidence describing a process or system used to produce a result and showing that the process or system produces an accurate result.

(10) **Methods provided by statute or rule.** Any method of authentication or identification provided by Act of Congress or by other rules prescribed by the Supreme Court pursuant to statutory authority.

Rule 902.   Self-Authentication

Extrinsic evidence of authenticity as a condition precedent to admissibility is not required with respect to the following:

(1) **Domestic public documents under seal.** A document bearing a seal purporting to be that of the United States, or of any State, district, Commonwealth, territory, or insular possession thereof, or the Panama Canal Zone, or the Trust Territory of the Pacific islands, or of a political subdivision, department, officer, or agency thereof, and a signature purporting to be an attestation or execution.

(2) **Domestic public documents not under seal.** A document purporting to bear the signature in the official capacity of an officer or employee of any entity included in paragraph (1) hereof, having no seal, if a public officer having a seal and having official duties in the district or political

subdivision of the officer or employee certifies under seal that the signer has the official capacity and that the signature is genuine.

(3) **Foreign public documents.** A document purporting to be executed or attested in an official capacity by a person authorized by the laws of a foreign country to make the execution or attestation, and accompanied by a final certification as to the genuineness of the signature and official position (A) of the executing or attesting person, or (B) of any foreign official whose certificate of genuineness of signature and official position relates to the execution or attestation or is in a chain of certificates of genuineness of signature and official position relating to the execution or attestation. A final certification may be made by a secretary of an embassy or legation, consul general, consul, vice consul, or consular agent of the United States, or a diplomatic or consular official of the foreign country assigned or accredited to the United States. If reasonable opportunity has been given to all parties to investigate the authenticity and accuracy of official documents, the court may, for good cause shown, order that they be treated as presumptively authentic without final certification or permit them to be evidenced by an attested summary with or without final certification.

(4) **Certified copies of public records.** A copy of an official record or report or entry therein, or of a document authorized by law to be recorded or filed and actually recorded or filed in a public office, including data compilations in any form, certified as correct by the custodian or other person authorized to make the certification, by certificate complying with paragraph (1), (2), or (3) of this rule or complying with any Act of Congress or rule prescribed by the Supreme Court pursuant to statutory authority.

(5) **Official publications.** Books, pamphlets, or other publications purporting to be issued by public authority.

(6) **Newspapers and periodicals.** Printed materials purporting to be newspapers or periodicals.

(7) **Trade inscriptions and the like.** Inscriptions, signs, tags, or labels purporting to have been affixed in the course of business and indicating ownership, control, or origin.

(8) **Acknowledged documents.** Documents accompanied by a certificate of acknowledgment executed in the manner provided by law by a notary public or other officer authorized by law to take acknowledgments.

(9) **Commercial paper and related documents.** Commercial paper, signatures thereon, and documents relating thereto to the extent provided by general commercial law.

(10) Presumptions under Acts of Congress. Any signature, document, or other matter declared by Act of Congress to be presumptively or prima facie genuine or authentic.

(11) Certified domestic records of regularly conducted activity. The original or a duplicate of a domestic record of regularly conducted activity that would be admissible under Rule 803(6) if accompanied by a written declaration of its custodian or other qualified person, in a manner complying with any Act of Congress or rule prescribed by the Supreme Court pursuant to statutory authority, certifying that the record—

   (A) was made at or near the time of the occurrence of the matter set forth by, or from information transmitted by, a person with knowledge of those matters;

   (B) was kept in the course of the regularly conducted activity; and

   (C) was made by the regularly conducted activity as a regular practice.

A party intending to offer a record into evidence under this paragraph must provide written notice of that intention to all adverse parties, and must make the record and declaration available for inspection sufficiently in advance of their offer into evidence to provide an adverse party with a fair opportunity to challenge them.

(12) Certified foreign records of regularly conducted activity. In a civil case, the original or a duplicate of a foreign record of regularly conducted activity that would be admissible under Rule 803(6) if accompanied by a written declaration by its custodian or other qualified person certifying that the record—

   (A) was made at or near the time of the occurrence of the matters set forth by, or from information transmitted by, a person with knowledge of those matters;

   (B) was kept in the course of the regularly conducted activity; and

   (C) was made by the regularly conducted activity as a regular practice.

The declaration must be signed in a manner that, if falsely made, would subject the maker to criminal penalty under the laws of the country where the declaration is signed. A party intending to offer a record into evidence under this paragraph must provide written notice of that intention to all adverse parties, and must make the record and declaration available for inspection sufficiently in advance of their offer into evidence to provide an adverse party with a fair opportunity to challenge them.

Rule 903.   Subscribing Witness' Testimony Unnecessary

The testimony of a subscribing witness is not necessary to authenticate a writing unless required by the laws of the jurisdiction whose laws govern the validity of the writing.

Article X.   Contents of Writings, Recordings, and Photographs

Rule 1001.   Definitions

For purposes of this article the following definitions are applicable:
(1) **Writings and recordings.** "Writings" and "recordings" consist of letters, words, or numbers, or their equivalent, set down by handwriting, typewriting, printing, photostating, photographing, magnetic impulse, mechanical or electronic recording, or other form of data compilation.
(2) **Photographs.** "Photographs" include still photographs, X-ray films, video tapes, and motion pictures.
(3) **Original.** An "original" of a writing or recording is the writing or recording itself or any counterpart intended to have the same effect by a person executing or issuing it. An "original" of a photograph includes the negative or any print therefrom. If data are stored in a computer or similar device, any printout or other output readable by sight, shown to reflect the data accurately, is an "original."
(4) **Duplicate.** A "duplicate" is a counterpart produced by the same impression as the original, or from the same matrix, or by means of photography, including enlargements and miniatures, or by mechanical or electronic re-recording, or by chemical reproduction, or by other equivalent technique which accurately reproduces the original.

Rule 1002.   Requirement of Original

To prove the content of a writing, recording, or photograph, the original writing, recording, or photograph is required, except as otherwise provided in these rules or by Act of Congress.

Rule 1003.   Admissibility of Duplicates

A duplicate is admissible to the same extent as an original unless (1) a genuine question is raised as to the authenticity of the original or (2) in the circumstances it would be unfair to admit the duplicate in lieu of the original.

Rule 1004. Admissibility of Other Evidence of Contents

The original is not required, and other evidence of the contents of a writing, recording, or photograph is admissible if—

    (1) Originals lost or destroyed. All originals are lost or have been destroyed, unless the proponent lost or destroyed them in bad faith; or

    (2) Original not obtainable. No original can be obtained by any available judicial process or procedure; or

    (3) Original in possession of opponent. At a time when an original was under the control of the party against whom offered, that party was put on notice, by the pleadings or otherwise, that the contents would be a subject of proof at the hearing, and that party does not produce the original at the hearing; or

    (4) Collateral matters. The writing, recording, or photograph is not closely related to a controlling issue.

Rule 1005. Public Records

The contents of an official record, or of a document authorized to be recorded or filed and actually recorded or filed, including data compilations in any form, if otherwise admissible, may be proved by copy, certified as correct in accordance with rule 902 or testified to be correct by a witness who has compared it with the original. If a copy which complies with the foregoing cannot be obtained by the exercise of reasonable diligence, then other evidence of the contents may be given.

Rule 1006. Summaries

The contents of voluminous writings, recordings, or photographs which cannot conveniently be examined in court may be presented in the form of a chart, summary, or calculation. The originals, or duplicates, shall be made available for examination or copying, or both, by other parties at [a] reasonable time and place. The court may order that they be produced in court.

Rule 1007. Testimony or Written Admission of Party

Contents of writings, recordings, or photographs may be proved by the testimony or deposition of the party against whom offered or by that party's written admission, without accounting for the nonproduction of the original.

Rule 1008. Functions of Court and Jury

When the admissibility of other evidence of contents of writings, recordings, or photographs under these rules depends upon the fulfillment of a condition of fact, the question whether the condition has been fulfilled is ordinarily for the court to determine in accordance with the provisions of Rule 104. However, when an issue is raised (a) whether the asserted writing ever existed, or (b) whether another writing, recording, or photograph produced at the trial is the original, or (c) whether other evidence of contents correctly reflects the contents, the issue is for the trier-of-fact to determine as in the case of other issues of fact.

Article XI. Miscellaneous Rules

Rule 1101. Applicability of Rules

(a) **Courts and magistrates.** These rules apply to the United States district courts, the District Court of Guam, the District Court of the Virgin islands, the District Court for the Northern Mariana islands, the United States courts of appeals, the United Srates Claims Court, and to United States bankruptcy judges and United States magistrate judges, in the actions, cases, and proceedings and to the extent hereinafter set forth. The terms "judge" and "court" in these rules include United States bankruptcy judges and United States magistrate judges.

(b) **Proceedings generally.** These rules apply generally to civil actions and proceedings, including admiralty and maritime cases, to criminal cases and proceedings, to contempt proceedings except those in which the court may act summarily, and to proceedings and cases under title 11, United States Code.

(c) **Rule of privilege.** The rule with respect to privileges applies at all stages of all actions, cases, and proceedings.

(d) **Rules inapplicable.** The rules (other than with respect to privileges) do not apply in the following situations:

(1) **Preliminary questions of fact.** The determination of questions of fact preliminary to admissibility of evidence when the issue is to be determined by the court under Rule 104.

(2) **Grand jury.** Proceedings before grand juries.

(3) **Miscellaneous proceedings.** Proceedings for extradition or rendition; preliminary examinations in criminal cases; sentencing, or granting or revoking probation; issuance of warrants for arrest, criminal summonses, and search warrants; and proceedings with respect to release on bail or otherwise.

(e) Rules applicable in part. In the following proceedings these rules apply to the extent that matters of evidence are not provided for in the statutes which govern procedure therein or in other rules prescribed by the Supreme Court pursuant to statutory authority: the trial of misdemeanor and other petty offenses by United States magistrates; review of agency actions when the facts are subject to trial de novo under section 706(2)(F) of title 5, United States Code; review of orders of the Secretary of Agriculture under section 2 of the Act entitled "An Act to authorize association of producers of agricultural products" approved February 18, 1922 (7 U.S.C. 292), and under sections 6 and 7(c) of the Perishable Agricultural Commodities Act, 1930 (7 U.S.C. 499f, 499g(c)); naturalization and revocation of naturalization under sections 310-318 of the Immigration and Nationality Act (8 U.S.C. 1421-1429); prize proceedings in admiralty under sections 7651-7681 of title 10, United States Code; review of orders of the Secretary of the Interior under section 2 of the Act entitled "An Act authorizing associations of producers of aquatic products" approved June 25, 1934 (15 U.S.C. 522); review of orders of petroleum control boards under section 5 of the Act entitled "An Act to regulate interstate and foreign commerce in petroleum and its products by prohibiting the shipment in such commerce of petroleum and its products produced in violation of State law, and for other purposes," approved February 22, 1935 (15 U.S.C. 715d); actions for fines, penalties, or forfeitures under part V of title IV of the Tariff Act of 1930 (19 U.S.C. 1581-1624), or under the Anti-Smuggling Act (19 U.S.C. 1701-1711); criminal libel for condemnation, exclusion of imports, or other proceedings under the Federal Food, Drug, and Cosmetic Act (21 U.S.C. 301-392); disputes between seamen under sections 4079, 4080, and 4081 of the Revised Statutes (22 U.S.C. 256-258); habeas corpus under sections 2241-2254 of title 28, United States Code; motions to vacate, set aside or correct sentence under section 2255 of title 28, United States Code; actions for penalties for refusal to transport destitute seamen under section 4578 of the Revised Statutes (46 U.S.C. 679); actions against the United States under the Act entitled "An Act authorizing suits against the United States in admiralty for damage caused by and salvage service rendered to public vessels belonging to the United States, and for other purposes," approved March 3,1925 (46 U.S.C. 781-790), as implemented by section 7730 of title 10, United States Code.

Glossary

Accused   Person who is the defendant in a criminal case.

Admissible   Evidence allowed to be considered by the trier-of-fact.

Adversary system   A system of justice where the parties work in opposition to each other, and each party tries to win a favorable result for itself.

Advisory Committee   Committee that proposed the Federal Rules of Evidence.

Advisory Notes   Comments accompanying the FRE proposals.

Affirmation   A witness's solemn promise to tell the truth before testifying. It does not require the witness to swear before God as does an oath.

Ancient documents   Documents 20 or more years old.

Authenticity   The genuineness of a piece of evidence.

Case-in-chief   The presentation of evidence by the party who has the burden of proof after which the party rests its case.

Cautionary instruction   An instruction given by the judge warning the jurors to exercise caution in evaluating a certain type of testimony such as the testimony of a confidential informant.

Chain of custody   A chronology of the custody of the evidence to show it was not tampered with between the time of seizure and the time of analysis or presentation in court.

Circumstantial evidence   Evidence based on inferences and not on personal knowledge or observation.

Closing argument   The argument to the jury that each party makes at the end of the case to persuade the jurors in the party's favor.

Coerced confession   A confession obtained through threats, physical force, or otherwise unconscionable conduct on the part of the police.

Collateral evidence   Evidence that is tangential and only marginally probative.

Collateral issues   Questions or issues which are not directly related to the matter.

Competent witness   A witness who is determined by the court to be qualified to give testimony.

Compromise   A settlement based on concessions made by each side.

Conclusive   Evidence that is irrefutable or allows only a single inference to be drawn.

Confidential communications   Communications made in confidence with the expectation of nondisclosure.

Contempt of court   A judge's ruling that a person has disobeyed a court order.

Corroborating evidence   Other evidence supporting the same point.

Credible evidence   Evidence that is worthy of belief; trustworthy evidence.

Cross-examination   The first questioning of a witness by the adversary to test the truth of the witness's testimony or to further develop it. The questions typically suggest an answer and are called *leading questions*.

Cumulative evidence   Evidence repetitive of other evidence.

Custodial interrogation   Questioning initiated by law enforcement after a suspect has been taken into custody.

Demonstrative exhibits Exhibits that illustrate or demonstrate something, but are not the "real" thing.

Direct evidence Evidence based on personal knowledge or observation.

Direct examination The first questioning of a witness by the party calling the witness. The questions generally do not suggest an answer.

Discovery The process by which parties in a lawsuit obtain information and evidence from others, including their opponents.

Discredit To cause the witness or exhibit to be doubted or found not to be believable.

Discretionary provision A rule that is not absolute and gives the court latitude to decide.

Distinguishable Capable of being differentiated or separately identified.

Diversity jurisdiction Federal subject matter jurisdiction based on litigants' being domiciled in different states from each other.

Documentary evidence Evidence in the form of a writing or other documents.

Dying declaration Statement made by a declarant who is either dying, or thinks he is dying.

Elements Specific components that must be proven for a cause of action to be proved.

Enjoin To cause an action to stop through a court-ordered injunction.

Essential element An integral part of the cause of action.

Excited utterance Statements made during or shortly after an occurrence while the declarant is agitated or excited.

Excluded evidence Evidence that the court has ruled inadmissible.

Exhibits Physical items that are admitted as evidence and shown to the trier-of-fact.

Expert opinion The opinion of an expert with specialized knowledge that may assist the trier-of-fact in understanding evidence or determining an issue.

Expurgated Cleared out or removed.

Extrinsic evidence Evidence that comes from sources not legitimately before the trier-of-fact.

Extrinsic offense An offense not charged or directly at issue in the current proceeding.

Forensic evidence Scientific evidence in which the sciences are applied to matters in the law.

Habit One's regular, nearly automatic response to a repeated situation.

Hearsay An out-of-court statement offered to prove the truth contained in the statement.

Hearsay within hearsay Out-of-court statements that contain other out-of-court statements.

Hung jury When the jurors are unable to reach a verdict.

Identification Evidence that the offer of proof is what it purports to be.

Immaterial evidence Evidence that is not related in a way to resolve an issue in the case.

Impeachment Attacking a witness's credibility.

In camera Judicial review of records in private or in chambers.

Incompetent witness A witness determined by the judge to be unqualified to testify.

Inculpate To impute guilt.

Inference A conclusion derived from implied as well as direct information.

Intangible Incapable of being touched, i.e., documents stored on soft media such as a computer disk.

Interested parties   Parties who have an interest in the outcome of the case.

Judgment   Written record of the final court decision in a legal proceeding.

Judicial discretion   The judge's latitude of choice.

Judicial notice   Facts the court accepts as true without evidentiary proof because they are common knowledge and generally indisputable.

Jury instruction   The court's instruction to the jury on the law which governs the type of case.

Lay opinion   An opinion of an ordinary person applying no particular expertise in offering testimony.

Laying a foundation   Providing sufficient preliminary evidence to identify, authenticate, and properly connect evidence to the issues in the case.

Leading questions   Questions which suggest an answer such as "Isn't it true you hid the weapon?"

Limited admissibility   Evidence admitted for a restricted purpose.

Limiting instruction   An instruction given by the judge to the jury to restrict their use of a specific item of evidence.

Litigants   The parties in the litigation.

Material evidence   Evidence that affects the outcome of the case.

Memoranda   Legal essays that provide the court with facts, law, and argument in support of the proponent's position.

Mitigate   Reduce or lessen.

Modus operandi   The mode of operation, or repetitious conduct of a criminal in the course of committing similar crimes.

Motion in limine   Motion made usually before trial on the admissibility or excludability of specific evidence.

Negotiation   Discussion and exchange of information between parties to reach a settlement.

No contest plea   A plea that leads to a conviction, without an admission of guilt.

Nolo contendere   A plea of nolo contendere is the same as a plea of no contest.

Nonverbal assertion   Gestures, such as a nod of the head meaning "yes," constitute nonverbal assertions.

Oath   A solemn promise a witness makes before testifying to be truthful which is accompanied by a swearing to God.

Objection   The statement a lawyer makes in court to the judge to protest the admissibility of evidence or an improper procedure.

Open ended question   A question that does not suggest an answer or put words in the witness's month.

Opening statement   The opening statement occurs after jury selection and before the introduction of evidence. Each party tells the jury what evidence to expect.

Opinion testimony   Testimony based on the witness's belief rather than on direct knowledge of the facts of the case.

Peripheral statements   Statements that are not directly covered under the privilege.

Personal bias   A witness's beliefs or prejudices that might influence the witness's perception of the facts.

Pertinent character traits   Character traits related to or relevant to the charges at issue.

Plea bargain   A negotiated agreement between the prosecution and the defendant in which charges or penalties are typically reduced in exchange for a guilty or no contest plea.

Precautionary measure   A design change that could have prevented an accident from occurring.

Present sense impression   Statement made about an experience during the experience.

Prior inconsistent statement   Statement made previously that either contradicts or departs from the current testimony.

Privilege   The legal right and/or obligation to refuse to testify on certain matters.

Probable cause   Reasonable grounds for belief.

Probative   Tending to prove or disprove a fact or issue in the case.

Proffered   Evidence tendered or offered.

Proponent   The party who proffers or presents the evidence; the party who argues in favor of something.

Prove up a denial   To introduce evidence to prove a fact that a witness has denied.

Public policy   The general principle that law should work for the public good.

Rebuttal evidence   Evidence given to explain or contradict testimony given by the opposing party.

Recorded recollection   A diary or other record of information recorded during the time that the person making the record had clear knowledge or recollection of the information.

Refresh a witness's recollection   To remind a witness of something that the witness once reported or knew to be true.

Rehabilitate   To establish a witness's credibility after it has been damaged.

Remedial measures   Measures taken to change a product after an accident to "remedy" or fix the problem.

Res gestae   An antiquated term referring to statements made in conjunction with gestures or events such that the words and the acts are intertwined. Such statements are now generally admissible under the hearsay exceptions such as present sense impression or excited utterance.

Seditious publications   Literature intended to cause political opposition to the government.

Self-authentication   A document that "speaks for itself" in terms of its authenticity. Neither a witness nor other extrinsic evidence is needed to lay the foundation for its admission.

Self-incrimination   Information such as statements and documents provided by an individual that could implicate or inculpate that individual in criminal conduct.

Settlement   Resolution of a dispute by the parties.

Stipulation   An agreement between the parties about some matter in the case.

Suppress   To keep out of court.

Tainted evidence   Made legally "impure" and inadmissible as a consequence of a preceding unlawful act.

Tangible   Something physically material, i.e., something you can touch.

Testamentary capacity   The legally required mental ability to make a will.

Testimony   The statements of a witness made under oath or affirmation in court, or in a deposition.

Trier-of-fact   Person who determines the facts in a legal proceeding—the jury in a jury trial and the judge in a bench trial. Also known as the factfinder.

Ultimate issue   A legal question that must be answered to resolve the case.

Unpublished opinion   A court opinion not selected for publication and therefore cannot be cited for precedential value.

Unsupported opinion   An opinion without a sound factual basis.

Verbal acts   Words that create a legal relationship or give legal context to an accompanying physical act.

Voir dire   The questioning of prospective jurors before the trial to determine their suitability as jurors.

Withdrawn plea   A plea that has been entered but then, for either technical or constitutional reasons, withdrawn with the court's permission.

Index

303